Frugal Value

Designing Business for a Crowded Planet

'Millstone silences the happy talk about business sustainability and brings the sustainability concept down to earth, literally. Brilliantly, she shows what sustainability truly requires for both individual businesses and for the economic system as a whole. Persuasively argued and well written, *Frugal Value* is a path-breaking synthesis that deserves an audience far beyond the business community.'

James Gustave Speth, former Dean, Yale School of Forestry and Environmental Studies, and author of *America the Possible: Manifesto for a New Economy*

'Ambitious, serious, and inspiring. At last someone's asking the right question. What will it really take to get business on a sustainable path? Millstone's unsparing critique of what passes today for "sustainable business" will provoke furious debate; her alternative lays out an agenda for business to become a real force for good. Required reading.'

Paul Gilding, Former Executive Director of Greenpeace International

'Corporate sustainability has made some progress over the last two decades, but nothing like enough. Carina Millstone's insightful book calls time on the "business case rationale" for companies trying to do the right thing, and urges instead a more radical "moral case", based on new design and operational principles.'

Jonathon Porritt, Founder Director, Forum for the Future

'A well-informed and forthright challenge to conventional wisdom. Love it or hate it, just read it! This is the spirited debate we need today.'

Ken Webster, Head of Innovation at the Ellen MacArthur Foundation

'A book that is unique and much needed ... The title will present a new concept, but it is an important one, which I hope will be accepted into common parlance.'

Professor Neva Goodwin, Co-Director of the Global Development and Environment Institute, Tufts University

'*Frugal Value* reminds us that sustainability – despite its widespread abuse as a concept over the past 30 years – remains non-negotiable. The Planet cannot be "traded off" for profit any more than oxygen can traded off for food. *Frugal Value* is a wake-up call to business leaders and sustainability practitioners alike: neither the "business case for sustainability" nor current "sustainable consumption and production" practices will get us anywhere near to the biodiverse and ecologically secure future we need to survive and thrive. Millstone calls attention to the elephant in the room – the current failure of so-called sustainable practices – and with skilful analysis, sketches out a more ambitious, transformational path: the imperative of redesigning our economic system and business models to achieve frugal value.'

Professor Wayne Visser, Cambridge Institute for Sustainability Leadership, and author of *Sustainable Frontiers*

'This tough-minded book isn't afraid to cast aside the cherished shibboleths of sustainable business. It asks the hard questions, and points the way forward with challenging answers.'

Professor Jem Bendell, Institute For Leadership And Sustainability (IFLAS), University of Cumbria

'Far from frugal, this book's recipe for achieving customer satisfaction is through massive reduction in resource use and wide social benefit rather than by sidestepping these issues. I can't recommend more that you read it.'

Sara Parkin, Founder Director of Forum for the Future and author of *The Positive Deviant*

FRUGAL VALUE

Designing Business for a Crowded Planet

CARINA MILLSTONE

Routledge
Taylor & Francis Group

LONDON AND NEW YORK

First published 2017
by Routledge
2 Park Square, Milton Park, Abingdon, Oxon OX14 4RN

and by Routledge
711 Third Avenue, New York, NY 10017

Routledge is an imprint of the Taylor & Francis Group, an informa business

British Library Cataloguing-in-Publication Data
A catalogue record for this book is available from the British Library

Library of Congress Cataloging-in-Publication Data
A catalog record for this book has been requested.

ISBN: 978-1-78353-388-6 (hbk)
ISBN: 978-1-78353-338-1 (pbk)
ISBN: 978-1-78353-339-8 (ebk)

Cover by Sadie Gornall-Jones.

To Isidore and Leopold

Contents

Acknowledgements

This book would not have been written without Irene Krarup, Neva Goodwin and the trustees of the V. Kann Rasmussen Foundation, who all understood from the very beginning what I sought to get at with this project. For their enthusiasm, confidence and generous support I am deeply grateful. Many academics, activists and students have provided feedback on this work at different stages of its elaboration. I would particularly like to thank André Reichel; John Blewitt; Sophie Dunkerley; Halina Brown and her students at Clark University; Ben Cattaneo; the teams at the New Economy Coalition and at the Institute for Policy Studies in Boston; the private sector team at Oxfam UK; the team at the International Institute for Environment and Development; the team and fellows of the Global Development and Environment Institute at Tufts University; Ian Roderick and the fellows of the Schumacher Institute; and the students of Forum for the Future. For enlightening conversations I would like to thank Tim Cooper, Howard Brown, Donnie Maclurcan, Gus Speth, Gar Alperovitz, Leslie Harroun, Katherine Trebeck and Emily Benson; and, for research, design and support in other ways, Kasia Hart, Sandra Moore, Allison Meierding, Claire Maxey and Daniel Millstone. Thank you to the team at Greenleaf Publishing, especially Rebecca Macklin and Victoria Halliday, for their guidance and patience. And, finally, thank you to Noah Millstone, for unwavering support and encouragement, fierce criticism and endless hours of lone parenting.

Introduction: the failure of sustainable business

This book is a challenge: a challenge to entrepreneurs, to business leaders, and to those who believe in sustainable business. For while there are already many books advocating "sustainable" business methods, the companies they describe cannot really be called sustainable. *Frugal Value* sets the record straight; it gets rid of the tinkering, the tokenism and the greenwash; and tries to re-imagine from the bottom up how companies could address the socio-environmental challenges of our time. What *does* business as a force for good look like *in our age*?

Businesses help deliver a high quality of life by providing many of us with goods and services at work and home. But business also comes at a high price. Many companies have inadvertently exacerbated or created some of the greatest challenges that we face today. All business activity requires resource use, and creates pollution and waste. Private-sector firms have helped bring the Planet to its knees, pushing us to the verge of environmental catastrophe, with staggering implications for human wellbeing, security and health. Recognising these dramatic, often accidental, effects, many companies have sought to become "responsible", better corporate "citizens", by adopting "sustainable" business practices. But good intentions have failed to stem the tide of pollution and waste.

In this introduction, I identify three key reasons for this failure: first, a failure to understand sustainability itself; second, a misguided over-reliance on creating business cases for sustainability; and, third, an overly narrow focus on technical interventions.

There is a great deal of confusion about what the terms "sustainable" and "sustainability" actually mean. They have somehow become words that are OK to abuse and misuse, and which "mean different things to different people"; nowadays, people often throw around the language of sustainability to describe anything from cosmetics to oil rigs. In fact, a commonly accepted definition of the term was coined almost 30 years ago by the United Nations (UN). The famous Brundtland Report of 1987 defined "sustainable" development as development that "seeks to meet the needs and aspirations of the present without compromising the ability to meet those of the future" (WCED, 1987: 39). By extension, the noun *sustainability* describes *conditions* or a *state* in which meeting present needs does not compromise meeting future needs. As detailed throughout the report, the meeting of need, today and in the future, rests on a sound ecological basis. The safeguarding of our planetary ecosystem is at the heart of sustainability. This was true 30 years ago, and remains true today. What has changed is the urgency of sustainability. When the report was written, the environmental crisis was just around the corner; today, we have turned that corner. The most obvious manifestation of this challenge is climate change; but human activities have also led to resource depletion, biodiversity loss, mass species extinctions, ocean acidification and freshwater scarcity. This new context has only intensified the need to protect the claims of future generations. And if the fractious UN managed to agree nearly 30 years ago on what sustainability was all about, we have no cause for confusion. Any claim to "sustainability" must be scrutinised carefully in light of these definitions.

If a "sustainable" product is not helping meet needs now, nor safeguarding our ability to meet future needs, "sustainability" is simply a PR stunt, or a lie. By remembering the meaning of sustainability, we can easily see how far this term is misused. Sometimes it means nothing: business-as-usual. Sometimes it refers to efforts to reduce the environmental and social impact of company activities. Good "corporate citizens" consider pollution prevention and abatement, health & safety measures, decent wages, and engagement with local communities as requirements, and not simply nice-to-haves. But, while these are steps in the right direction, they are not the same as safeguarding future ability to meet human need. The real question facing businesses that want to be sustainable is not "how do we reduce our environmental impact?" but "how do we ensure our products and processes do not affect the ability of future generations to meet their needs?" Asking this question yields answers that go beyond pollution minimisation. For example, rather than pursuing energy efficiency, thinking seriously about sustainability should lead companies towards shifting as far as possible toward renewable alternatives. And it should raise questions about what the business *actually does*: if it is using non-renewable resources for its value creation, how should it consider the opportunity cost of using these resources now, rather than leaving them for the use of future generations? In other words, how should it integrate the time dimension of sustainability, rather than simply considering environmental impact today? The time dimension of sustainability has been forgotten by many a sustainable business advocate (Bansal and DesJardine, 2014).

In the worst cases, "sustainable" business has come to mean the longevity of the firm *itself*, rather than the company's contribution to creating the conditions that would enable longevity in the meeting of need. But endurance is no indicator of contribution to sustainability. In fact, the opposite is likely to be true. There are plenty of long-lived firms out there, enduring corporate "persons", slowly making the Planet inhospitable for everyone else, including their executives and employees. Oil and gas companies are a case in point here: ExxonMobil, for example, has existed in one form or another for nearly 150 years, making an enormous contribution to planetary destruction.[1]

Creative, erroneous or self-serving interpretations of sustainability cloud what is at stake when we talk of "sustainable" business—and the stakes couldn't be higher. Companies must first understand what sustainability really means before they can clarify their *potential contribution* to it. This requires understanding the ecological context in which the firm's activities—and all economic activity—takes place. I describe this context and the challenges it poses in Part 1 of this book.

Even when sustainability has been more fully understood, it has often failed to reorient firms toward a less environmentally destructive path. Why? Paradoxically, advocates for sustainable business have often been part of the problem. Many well-meaning "sustainability practitioners" try very hard to speak the "language of business", which they think is essential in order to reach executives. Sustainability is then "sold" to business on the basis of a "business case"; companies, they argue, should embrace a sustainable agenda for the sake of "reputational risk management", or securing a "social licence to operate" or even for "brand positioning".[2] These arguments aim

---

1 One study suggests that Exxon Mobil is responsible for more than 3% of all historic global warming gas emissions; see Clark, 2013.
2 See, for example, Weybrecht, 2013 for some "business case" arguments in favour of corporate action for sustainability.

to demonstrate that environmental inaction could be costly, while positive steps could be lucrative. Alas, this is simply not the case. Crucially, the so-called "business case for sustainability" is the *exception* rather than the rule. Often, today, it makes more financial sense to conduct business "unsustainably"—barely scraping by on legal environmental compliance while avoiding changes to practice that often result in "unacceptable" cost increases. In fact, a survey conducted by the Massachusetts Institute of Technology (MIT) found that only one-third of companies that have developed a business case for sustainability reap any financial rewards for their efforts. In other words, for the remaining two-thirds of companies, a business case did not exist after all—even when they tried to formulate one (Kiron *et al.,* 2013). And these are companies that sought to develop a case; many more do not have such enthusiastic leadership. The absence of a business case raises some problematic questions. What now? What should a firm do when sustainability does not pay—that is, in the *majority of cases, most of the time*? (Incidentally, the fact that sustainability does not pay should be amply apparent from current private-sector practices: if it did, we would no doubt be living in a much different world, and not facing our difficult ecological predicament.) Usually, sustainability initiatives that go beyond environmental compliance are simply shelved, and companies either aim for regulatory compliance or for getting away with non-compliance, depending on where they are, the likelihood of getting policed, and whichever is cheapest.

The "business case" approach is problematic because it implies that sustainability makes sense, *because*, and *when*, it makes commercial sense. This leads to all sorts of methodologies, frameworks and "cost–benefit" analyses, all supposedly seeking to "balance" environment, society and financial returns. Sustainability is approached as a negotiation, a balancing act, and trade-off between different courses of action, each with their own economic, social and environmental benefits and disbenefits, and each with their own price tag. But "balancing the needs" of different "stakeholders" and managing trade-offs can never really happen when financial returns are prized above all other considerations. Very few projects are abandoned on environmental grounds if fortunes can be made.[3] More importantly, outside the office, there are no separate social, environmental and economic spheres. You can't really pick between the environment, society and the economy:

---

3 In my experience working as a corporate sustainability consultant for five years, no projects were abandoned on environmental grounds alone, regardless of the findings of the environmental impact assessment.

the socio-economic sphere is a sub-set of the environmental sphere. Sustainability must be about preserving the functioning and integrity of our ecological system all the time, and not only when this does not affect the "bottom line", or when the "numbers" tell us we can afford to keep a biodiversity habitat, but just this once.

Sustainability *cannot rest on a business case*. It needs to rest on something else: a *moral* case.[4] Those who consider themselves to be astute, effective businessmen may recoil from any talk of morality ("it's a dog-eat-dog world out there", they may respond), but it is nonetheless necessary. This is because sustainability itself is normative, based on the concepts of inter- and intra- generational equity. It rests on the ethical notion that we have a responsibility to others and the meeting of their needs, both those living today and those living in the future. This book therefore *does not assume and does not pretend* that there is necessarily a business case to make as to why companies may wish to adopt sustainable practices. It is simply not how I try to pique the interest of business practitioners. Whether a business case for sustainability exists or can be constructed depends on what a company actually does. When it exists, and sustainability pays, great. When it doesn't, the challenge is to find ways to change a company so that a case could be made. When that is not possible, only hard choices are left. But the inability to conjure up a business case for sustainability does not change the fact that designing businesses to contribute to sustainability is the *right* thing to do.

The final failure of "sustainable business" thinking comes from the widespread assumption that sustainability can be achieved simply by new production techniques, which would lead to "better", "eco" products and services. This process is known as "sustainable consumption and production" (SCP), defined, again, and not succinctly, by the UN, as "the use of services and related products, which respond to basic needs and bring a better quality of life while minimising the use of natural resources and toxic materials as well as the emissions of waste and pollutants over the life cycle of the service or product so as not to jeopardise the needs of future generations" (UNEP, 2010). Sustainability is thought to rest on developing products and services that have certain characteristics: minimal resource use, minimal toxic material conditions, minimal waste production. These characteristics, it is assumed, can be built through technical interventions in the

---

4 Thank you to Jonathon Porritt who first raised with me the moral case for sustainability during my studies at Forum for the Future.

production process, exclusively. Businesses, as the main provider of goods and services, therefore need to make technical improvements to the goods and services they offer, and all will be solved. And, while these technological improvements are necessary, and sustainable production and consumption as described by the UN is necessary for sustainability, technological interventions do not go far enough. What we also need to consider is how genuinely sustainable products and services might require considerable changes in the structure of business itself. For example, profit-seeking is likely to encourage a search for a manufacturing process with the lowest possible cost, not one that minimises wastes and pollution. In other words, what changes need to happen to business structure to make it an effective contributor to the transition to sustainability? And what should we do if there is something about the business form itself when it is ill suited to make this contribution? These questions, uncomfortable and thorny, are ignored by the "sustainable business" literature, despite warranting very close examination—since their answers risk challenging the discipline altogether.

Given these failures, can "sustainable business" be rescued from itself? While sustainability requires action by citizens and communities, governments, policymakers and civil society, it nonetheless remains of special concern and interest to business. It is the *distinctive* role that the private sector could play in sustainability that I explore in this book. *Frugal Value* is therefore addressed to those who are interested in shaping sustainable businesses; those who understand that business is at the core of our current crisis of unsustainability; and who believe that transforming business is a critical step in addressing our society's challenge. This book will interest business owners, executives and entrepreneurs that seek to make their company a force for good. Sustainability professionals within larger companies will hopefully find questions to reflect on. It is also addressed to the next generation of entrepreneurs and business leaders, especially those enrolled on business, social enterprise, sustainability or environmental management courses, and to their teachers. The general reader and environmentalist, curious about how goods and services could be provided without finishing off the Planet completely, may find some answers and further questions. *Frugal Value* is specifically addressed to those working or studying in richer countries, in the Global North: those countries consuming a large share of world resources, and where there is no chronic, abject poverty. (Numerous books have been written about business in the Global South. Challenges and priorities are different from those of richer countries, and beyond the scope of this book.)

Part 2 of this book is concerned with the products and services offered by businesses, while Part 3 describes the business activities and models that support their diffusion. Part 4 examines the operations and supply chains required to serve these models. Part 5 is concerned with the role of ownership, financing and legal form in creating companies with the products, activities and operations dealt with in earlier parts. Finally, Part 6 examines business itself—and the extent to which the business form, in its purpose and scope, can usefully contribute to the shift to sustainability.

Two final points.

In writing this book, I realised that the challenges presented by sustainability are rarely about generalities, and much more often about specific situations. For each issue considered in the different parts of this book, there is often a menu of possible interventions from which a business striving for sustainability could choose. I am therefore not trying to define new "models", "paradigms" or "toolkits" that would be applicable to all firms. This book is better understood as highlighting problems to consider, rather than providing set answers. The answer to any general question about sustainable business is often "it depends"—on context, on the nature of the value proposition, on local need. While general principles and approaches will be useful in the transition to sustainability, and these are outlined in the book, specific actions need to be formulated on a case-by-case basis.

Finally, as suggested in this book's subtitle, *Designing Business for a Crowded Planet*, what follows is about *design*. Our economic activity has hitherto taken shape around the availability of resources, the existence of markets and technological discoveries. Businesses have taken the shapes they have because they could. But design implies purpose, and purpose is what is required here: there are no reasons why resource availability, technological discoveries and market arrangements should automatically be aligned with the requirements of sustainability. As we'll see in Part 1, we do not have the same challenges today as we did in the early days of international trade and industrialisation. Companies need to be designed *specifically* to address the challenges of our time. Such companies I call *pioneering*, and this book is about them.

Part 1

The Crowded Planet

Books on sustainable business usually start in the same way. "All is not well on Planet Earth", they explain; we are in a deep and dangerous ecological mess. These opening chapters invariably feature football pitches or Olympic-sized swimming pools to help readers grapple with the scale of the environmental challenges, supported by pronouncements from prominent business leaders, politicians and celebrities.

Part 1 is my version of "All is not well on Planet Earth". But, rather than repeating crisis talk readily available elsewhere, this part instead addresses what I see as the main shortcoming of this chapter archetype: the failure to get to why pollution and wastes are created in the first place, and why they become such a problem. We explore this question in Chapter 1: What is it about the conditions we live in, what is it about the Planet, which means our activities have created such an ecological mess? Once we have identified the characteristics of our Planet and human activities on it, we can go about answering a further important question, far more accurately now that we have got to the *root causes* of unsustainability: what needs to happen to get out of this ecological mess? This is the question we explore in Chapter 2.

Part 1, then, is about the (very) big-picture context—the planetary scale—in which the global economy, and business activities of every single business that exists takes place. If we want to understand how individual companies are affected by, and affect, this bigger-picture context, we first need an *accurate* understanding of the conditions for sustainability, the current context of unsustainability, and what is required to get from the second to the first. So let's take a step back and have a closer look at Earth and its 7 billion Earthlings—a Crowded Planet.

1 The economy-in-Planet

A first, unsurprising fact: All economic activity takes place on Planet Earth. And yet most of us are pretty ignorant about our planetary host. This chapter goes back to basics. It is first about the Planet, and how it creates opportunities for, and constraints on, economic activity. It also defines the characteristics of a new, sustainable economy, congruent with its planetary host: the "*economy-in-Planet*".

The economic system is supported and constrained by its host planetary system

First and foremost, Planet Earth is a system. What is a system? Systems-thinking pioneer Donella H. Meadows defined a system as an "interconnected set of elements that is coherently organised in a way that achieves something" (Meadows, 2008). Like other systems, Planet Earth clearly has *different elements*: a biosphere, a lithosphere (or crust), an atmosphere, a hydrosphere. These elements are *interconnected*, for example through water cycles, the greenhouse effects and volcanic activity. Like other systems, the Planet can be understood as having *stocks*, *flows* and *feedback loops*. Its stocks are what we sometimes call resources: ores, metals, biomass (we return to these later); solar energy flows into the system from outside; and feedback loops that sometimes allow the system to achieve a certain stability (as with climate regulation) and sometimes create the potential for fundamental transformation (such as possible runaway climate change).[1] Over the past 10,000 years, these elements—stocks, flows and feedback loops—have together created stable, *self-regulating*, conditions perfect for the flourishing of human life.[2]

In addition, the Planet is a *closed* system; in other words, it exchanges energy with its surroundings, but not matter. The Planet receives solar energy, and releases heat into the surrounding atmosphere; but that's it. No significant materials are exchanged with space (other than a few rockets and stray asteroids). As a closed system, Earth is subject to the Second Law of Thermodynamics, also known as the entropy law, which states that available energy that we can use is continuously transformed into dissipated energy that we cannot use (Atkins, 2010). In better news, the inflow of solar energy the Planet receives from space can be used as energy before it dissipates back into space.

One final but crucial point about the planetary system: it's not getting any bigger. We cannot hope for an increase in the quantity of available materials and resources; the Planet, at its permanent, stable size, is all we've got.

These planetary characteristics are not quirky facts, but rather are crucial for understanding our economy. The Planet is after all where we conduct our business activity—as well as being where you and I, and everyone else, lives. The economy, then, is a *sub-system* of the planetary system: it takes place *within it.* And it relies entirely on its host system, the Planet, for its material basis, in a deep, irrevocable interrelationship.

---

1 According to Meadows, "stocks are the elements [. . .] you can see, feel, count or measure at any given time" (Meadows, 2008: 17). Stocks rise and fall, depending on *flows* into them: if inflows exceed outflows, stocks will rise, and vice versa. Stocks, therefore, are "the memory of the history of changing flows within the system" (Meadows, 2008: 17). *Feedback loops* are "a closed chain of causal connections from a stock, through a set of decisions or rules or physical laws or actions that are dependent on the level of the stock, and back again through a flow to change the stock" (Meadows, 2008: 187). Balancing (or negative) feedback loops are equilibrating, while reinforcing (or positive) feedback loops are self-enhancing, leading to exponential growth over time.

2 For some, a purposefully self-regulating Planet denotes something spiritual. But for us, for now, removing any notion of intent from the purpose, we can consider that it's been our good fortune that the "purpose" of the Planet's self-regulation has to date been to keep the Planet propitious for human life. It is the Planet's self-regulation that created the Holocene, the period of some 10,000 years during which civilisation flourished. Self-regulation is at the heart of James Lovelock's Gaia theory. See Lovelock, 2000.

Unlike the Planet, the economic system is open—that is to say, it exchanges both energy and matter with its host. Materials and energy flow from the natural world enter the socio-economic sub-system, are used, and are then ejected as waste and dissipated energy back into the planetary system. All our resources come from the Planet, and all our wastes go back into it as well. Moreover, the economic system is subject to the same laws and behaviour patterns of its host system. For example, the economic exploitation of planetary resources is fundamentally entropic: transforming valuable, low-entropy materials and energy into unusable, high-entropy materials and energy. This process is linear, and largely irreversible (although it can be delayed through recycling)—this is why we can't reuse oil again and again (Georgescu-Roegen,1975).[3] And, lastly, there are final limits to the material growth of the economic system, since the Planet itself isn't growing: our supplies of freshwater, minerals, timber and fossil fuels are ultimately finite. As Donella H. Meadows observed, "No physical system can grow forever in a finite environment" (Meadows, 2008: 59).

If we conceptualise our society and economy accurately within its environment, our Planet, it might look something a bit like Figure 1.1.

Yes, this is all a bit complex and confusing, but it nonetheless gets at something important. Part of the difficulty with this representation is that it differs so much from how we usually understand our relationship with the environment, which instead looks a bit like Figure 1.2.

This schema imagines our economy as separate from the environment. Sure, somewhere out there, there is something called the environment, which conveniently provides us with resources and an outlet for our pollution. But Nature is there for the picking, and the economy can grow in line with our desires. This view has prevailed since the Industrial Revolution, and it gives us an instrumental, anthropocentric view of the natural world, where nature is of interest principally as a resource. It is the view that has created the economy of the industrial era, the unsustainable economy that we have inherited, and continue to live with, today—what I call the *legacy economy*. There are obvious limitations to this view, but, for now, let's keep our anthropocentric hat on and try to answer the following question: *what has the Planet ever done for us?*

---

3 Georgescu-Roegen also makes the interesting point that entropy is an anthropocentric measure, measuring energy availability to humans.

Figure 1.1 **The economic and planetary systems**

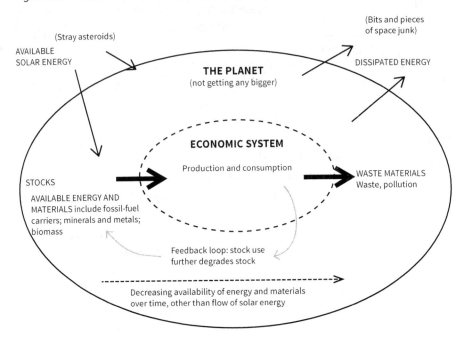

Figure 1.2 **Common misconception of the relationship between the economy and the environment**

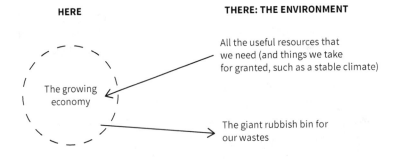

This diagram is inspired by Figure 1 in Rees, 2011.

The Planet creates the opportunity for economic activity through resources, sinks and natural regulation

Our Planet supports our economy in three ways: by providing us with the *resources* that we need, by providing *sinks* for the waste we produce, and by providing viable conditions in which to conduct our activities, through its *regulatory capacity*.

The most obvious way in which the Planet supports our activities is through resources—these are the planetary stocks I mentioned earlier. Resources provide the *material basis* for *all* business activity. Even services are more reliant on "stuff"—on natural resources—than their name suggests. A trip to the hairdresser will require cotton to clothe the hairdresser, fossil fuels to make and power the hairdryer, and wood for the customer's chair. There are four broad categories of resources: biomass, construction minerals, fossil energy carriers, and ores and industrial minerals.[4] As all economic activities require some resource use, in general *a growing economy requires growing resource use*. And all evidence suggests this is true. Since the beginning of the Industrial Revolution, global consumption of these resources has grown at an unprecedented rate, with a further dramatic increase since the end of the Second World War and an 80% growth in the last 30 years alone (Dittrich *et al.*, 2012). Globally, we now use between 60 and 70 billon tons (Gt) of materials per year, or in the region of 9.2 tons per capita, representing an *eightfold* increase in the last 100 years.[5] We are munching our way through planetary resources at an extraordinary speed. This raises a critical question: will resources be able to support forecast

---

4 The four categories of resources are identified in Krausmann *et al.*, 2009. Biomass includes the products of agriculture, forestry, fisheries and hunting, often products that end up on our plate or furnish our homes. Biofuels are another use of biomass products. Construction minerals are used in construction activity. These include limestone, sand, clay, gravel, silica and gypsum. Fossil energy carriers are the fuels that we use to power our economy: the triumvirate of oil, coal and gas. It also includes peat. Ores and industrial minerals are ferrous and non-ferrous metals, or metals that contain steel. These include aluminium, copper, nickel, tin, zinc, titanium, lead and brass; precious metals such as silver, platinum and gold; and rare metals such as mercury, cobalt, indium, niobium and others.

5 Data is from 1900 to 2000. In that time, construction mineral consumption increased by a factor of 34, ores and industrial mineral consumption by a factor of 27, and fossil fuel consumption by a factor of 12 (Krausmann *et al.*, 2009).

growth, or will the economy ultimately be constrained by the finite nature of the Planet and its stocks?[6]

The answer varies from resource to resource. Given the central importance of fossil fuels in our economy, much effort has been expended to figure out if—or when—we will run out of oil. Attempts to estimate oil reserves go back to the 1950s, when M.K. Hubbert predicted that oil production in the United States would "peak" between 1965 and 1971.[7] But attempts to predict the timing of peak oil production have not been easy thanks to the ongoing discovery of new fields and the exploitation of "unconventional" sources. Some now give a date of 2020; but, in the meantime, we are actually in the midst of an oil and gas boom. In other words, we are not "running out of oil" in the immediate future; rather, according to BP, we have at least half a century of *proven* reserves ahead of us, to meet the needs of global consumption.[8] As for other fossil fuels, we have at least 64 years of natural gas and 112 years of coal. Since these figures refer only to proven reserves, they are likely to be massive underestimates. The situation for metals and minerals varies significantly depending on the particular material. Some, such as aluminium, iron and magnesium, are plentiful in the Planet's continental crust. Construction materials such as sands, gravel and limestone are also plentiful. For other metals and minerals, estimating remaining reserves can be difficult. These are sometimes revised downward as ore is mined and extraction becomes more difficult. More frequently, they are revised *upward* as new deposits are discovered, or as the potential to exploit existing deposits is increased. Estimated copper reserves in 2012, for example, were more than double the 1970 estimate (US Geological Survey, 2013). "Rare metals" are, obviously, scarcer, but, as for fossil fuels, any economic constraint due to scarcity of metals and minerals does not seem imminent.

The situation for biomass is considerably more alarming, and we are already in what one study describes as a situation of "ecological overshoot": that is to say, globally, our use of biomass is so great that it is undermining

---

6 The question of resource constrains goes back to the 18th century, with Malthus's work on population. More recently, the Club of Rome's landmark 1972 report models limits to growth in systems (see Meadows *et al.*, 2004).

7 Peak oil refers to the maximum rate of oil production to be reached, after which it would decline (see Hubbert, 1956).

8 Reserves-to-production (R/P) ratio is measured as follows: the reserves remaining at the end of any year are divided by the production in that year. The result is the length of time that those remaining reserves would last if production were to continue at that rate (BP, 2012).

its replenishment. On a regional level, there is also considerable mismatch between biomass endowment and consumption. Most European countries "ran out" of biomass centuries ago, supplementing home production through trade or conquest. The latest version of this transfer of biomass from poor to rich are modern-day "land grabs": foreign companies and countries purchasing large tracts of productive African lands to supply their customers or citizens, often with devastating effects for local populations (ETC Group, 2011).

The second way the Planet supports economic activity is by providing *sinks.* The Planet acts as a sink when it absorbs our spent energy and used materials that have left the economic sphere and re-entered the planetary system as waste and pollution. Remember, as the Planet is a closed system, *there is no outside—nowhere to put waste and pollution away:* it stays within the system. While we have to date not spent much time thinking about the Planet's sink capacity, it is becoming clear that pollution and waste are now reaching extraordinary volumes, with devastating consequences for some ecosystems (think of the plastic islands floating around the Pacific Ocean, or the contamination of rivers and landscapes around mining operations). This is in turn affecting resource availability and quality of future resources, as well as interfering with the Planet's third function.

Perhaps the most serious impact of resource extraction, pollution and waste is on the Planet's *regulatory capacity:* that is to say, on the stable condition, the natural cycles that enable life on Earth. Much like the Planet's role as a sink, we have pretty much taken this capacity for granted, and are only starting to notice it as it appears not to be working quite so well. For example, we now know that the use of neonicotinoid pesticides has had devastating impacts on bee colonies, affecting the yearly cycle of crop pollination. The global cycles of nitrogen and phosphorus may not be as visible as the honeybee, but they have been seriously disturbed by intensive agriculture, and this will affect future biomass resources. Climate change, belatedly recognised as the greatest challenge of our time by all major world leaders—described by Barack Obama as the "one issue that will define the contours of this century more dramatically than any other", and by Ban Ki-moon as the "defining issue of our age"—is itself a problem of the Planet's regulatory capacity.[9] The failure of climate regulation is caused by the

9 Remarks made to the UN General Assembly at the 2014 Climate Summit in New York City, 23–24 September 2014: http://www.un.org/apps/news/infocus/ sgspeeches/statments_full.asp?statID=2355#.VCVYXRZb66k.

inability of a sink (the atmosphere) to absorb the pollution output (CO_2 and other greenhouse gas [GHG] emissions) generated through intensive use of a resource or stock (fossil fuels [with land use changes also contributing to increases in CO_2 concentrations]). Global GHG emissions due to human activity have grown significantly since the Industrial Revolution, with an increase of at least 70% in the last 40 years (IPCC, 2007).[10] The last time the atmosphere had so much CO_2 in it was 8,000 years ago, when the Planet was a very different place. So, accuracy of reserve predictions aside, it is not shortage of fossil fuels that may constrain their use, but limits to the Planet's sinks and the effect of overloading those sinks on its regulatory capacity. Even the International Energy Agency (IEA), not exactly known for its radical environmental agenda, pointed out that "no more than one-third of proven reserves of fossil fuels can be consumed prior to 2050 if the world is to achieve the 2 degrees Celsius goal" (IEA, 2012).[11] Two degrees is recognised by the UN as the upper permissible warming level, with 1.5° warming agreed as the safer aspiration in the 2015 Paris Agreement. Exceed this and even conservative projections predict catastrophic human suffering. In other words, we cannot use the fossil fuels we know we have if we have any ambition of stabilising the climate and avoiding devastating impacts on water supply, ecosystems, food, coasts and human health.

The legacy economy, which requires *unprecedented and growing* resource use, results in *growing and unprecedented* creation of waste and interference with the Planet's regulation capacity. The situation is now so dire that there is widespread consensus that our "planetary boundaries" have been breached—that is to say, we have degraded the environment so badly that it may no longer support the ecological conditions required for human life.[12]

---

10 The 70% increase refers to the increase between 1970 and 2004.

11 The Agency adds "unless carbon capture and storage (CSS) technology is widely deployed" but then proceeds to tell us that "its pace of development remains highly uncertain, with only a handful of commercial-scale projects in operation".

12 Our interference with the Planet's resources, sinks and regulations since the Industrial Revolution has been so great that we are breaching "planetary limits". These boundaries identify the upper permissible limits of environmental degradation brought about by human activity to retain the ecological conditions necessary to support human life. Of the nine planetary boundaries—the phosphorus cycle; stratospheric ozone depletion; ocean acidification; global freshwater use; change in land use; atmospheric aerosol loading and chemical pollution; biodiversity loss; climate change; nitrogen loading—the last three have already been breached (see Rockström *et al.*, 2009).

There is no way for the global economy to keep growing on the Planet

This is all rather gloomy: surely, there *must* be a way to disentangle our growing use of resources from dangerous environmental degradation? Surely some of the world's greatest minds are on the case? Those seeking their way out of this conundrum usually think technology will save the day—despite all evidence pointing to the contrary. Nonetheless, techno-optimists often suggest that the growing use of resources can be sustained through *substitution* and *decoupling*.

Substitution suggests that we could simply replace scarce natural resources, and those that involve high environmental impacts, with more plentiful, less harmful alternatives: say, gold for copper.[13] Problem solved. Alas, substitution between these different materials is not always possible. For energy, while some sources could be substituted for each other, the abundance and sheer muscle of fossil fuels are barriers to meaningful substitution.[14] Even if we cracked the energy problem, and created clean, human-made energy from scratch (some claim that widespread, safe, pollution-free hydrogen or nuclear fusion is just around the corner—even if commercial deployment is still uncertain and far away), this would still not solve the problem of our finite stock of materials, or the significant environmental degradation and waste pollution that comes from their use. To resolve the latter, "substitutionists" often suggest replacing materials for existing human-made artefacts, through recycling and repurposing. While material reuse has a clear role to play in slowing down the pace of resource use, it cannot provide a complete solution. Sure, a new table could be made from the materials of an existing one, but that is simply replacing one artefact with another. Making a new table would require new materials.

Decoupling involves reducing the environmental resources needed for each unit of economic activity, increasing the efficiency with which natural resources are used to generate economic value. The plan is to continue

---

13 Substitution gives rise to two versions of sustainability: "weak sustainability", whereby we assume that human-made capital (or artefacts) are substituted for natural capital, and "strong sustainability", which posits that no such substitution is possible.

14 Renewable energy only accounts for 2% of global energy use, while coal use is increasing (BP, 2012). While electricity can be generated from non-fossil-fuel sources, the feasibility of replacing liquid fuel used in transport, which accounts for over half of global oil consumption and is set to increase further, is less clear.

growing our global economy, without the growth in resources it has hitherto relied on. Historical evidence suggests *some relative* decoupling is possible. In fact, economic growth outpaced resource use by a factor of three during the course of last century (Krausmann *et al.*, 2009). But, given the *finite* stock of planetary resources, we would need *absolute* decoupling should we wish to continue growing the economy indefinitely. That is to say, we would need a situation where the rate of resource use stays steady or declines, regardless of the growth rate of economic value.[15] Under these circumstances, we could keep growing the global economy. But this appears simply impossible, since we know economic activity *always* requires *some* resource use. In fact, there are *no* examples of economies that have grown while capping their environmental resource use at a low constant level. Indeed, resource efficiency, the basis for relative decoupling, is itself a barrier to absolute decoupling. This is due to an old, but critically important paradox, first identified by William Stanley Jevons in his 1865 book *The Coal Question* (Jevons, 1866; Alcott, 2005). Studying coal use in the Industrial Revolution, Jevons noted that any increase in the efficiency with which a resource is used tends to *increase* rather than decrease the rate of use of that resource. Technological progress that increases the efficiency of resource use simply reduces the cost of that resource, stimulating its demand elsewhere and increasing its use overall. This paradox constitutes a classic, pervasive rebound effect. So, while new technologies are crucial in reducing resource use and the pollution emissions of economic activity, and have resulted in some decoupling, technology alone cannot dissolve the link between growing use of resources and economic growth. The limits to decoupling do not mean that we shouldn't seek to use resources more efficiently, recycle, and substitute where possible; but none of these solves the underlying issue: *we do not know how to grow the economy without growing material resource use.*

Finally, technological approaches have usually been framed around solving the issue of resource constraints. But, as we have seen, resource constraints are not really the problem: we have already dangerously compromised planetary sinks and regulatory systems long before we've begun to run out of resources. These approaches miss the point. The question isn't so much "What should we do about resource depletion?" but "Should push come to shove, could we create a life-sustaining planet from scratch?" Even the most enthusiastic techno-optimist must recognise the answer is "not

---

15 For more information on different types of decoupling and their feasibility see UNEP, 2011.

any time soon". "Creating Planet Earth" would require humans producing an atmosphere, a hydrological cycle, photosynthesis, stable climatic conditions and biomass, among other essential features of life (Ayres, 2007).

To date, the Planet has provided us with resources, absorbed the waste we produce and maintained stable conditions propitious to life. But our economic activities have dangerously overloaded these sinks and eroded these conditions. We now have a legacy economy that is ecologically precarious. What we need are economic activities that are consonant with their location in the planetary system.

Sustainability requires an economy-in-Planet

Sustaining the conditions for human activity on Earth requires understanding and implementing what I call an *economy-in-Planet*. Understanding the economy-in-Planet requires asking two principal questions: first, how would this economy interact with its host system? In other words, what happens at the (permeable) boundaries between the ecological and economic systems? And, second, what happens within the economy?

The boundaries of the economy-in-Planet can best be understood as the moment natural material or energy leaves the ecosphere and becomes a resource in the socio-economic sphere; and, after transformation, use and disposal, the moment it leaves this sphere and goes back into the natural world as waste. The boundary is crossed when a tree becomes timber, and when a wooden table is discarded. The parameters of the boundaries *are determined by the rate of inflow into the economic system from the planetary system, and outflow from the economic system into the planetary one.*

As we have seen, there are limits to how much material an economy can use and still "fit" within its planetary host. We can say the material aspect of the economy would be optimally sized when it utilises energy and resources at a rate and in a manner that keeps its host environment functioning to support human life, on indefinite human time-scales. At this size, the material economy's operation would be consistent with the self-regulation of the overall planetary system—in a way so as to support conditions propitious for human flourishing. Defining the optimal size of the material economy therefore requires the defining of optimal rates of materials and energy throughput. Herman Daly did just this in his seminal work in the 1970s, coining the term "steady-state" economy—that is to say, an economy "with constant stocks of people and artefacts maintained at some desired, sufficient levels by low rates of maintenance throughput"—or low energy and material use throughout production (Daly, 1991).[16]

In other words, as many ecologists have argued, what planetary maintenance ultimately requires is an economy that *does not grow*. Note how the idea of an economy that *purposefully* does not grow is anathema to our politicians, economists and business leaders (even those who claim to be engaged in sustainable business)—indeed, growing an economy or a business is their yardstick of success. But it is nonetheless a central, non-negotiable aspect of sustainability. The steady-state economy is maintained at optimal size through certain, low rates of resource flows—with the precise rate depending on the resource. For example, in the steady-state economy, the maximum harvest of biomass would be limited both by the need to ensure the harvest's complete subsequent regeneration, and by the need to keep waste associated with the harvest within the Planet's sink capacity (Daly, 1990). With *non-renewable resources*, or at least those not renewed on a human time-scale (groundwater can take thousands of years to accumulate, and the next batch of fossil fuels will be ready in 300 million years), any use of these stocks *necessarily* limits future use, leaving us with a choice between using all the stocks now or saving some for later. Daly suggests pairing exploitation of non-renewable resource with investments in renewable substitutes, with the overall ambition of developing renewable replacements by the time the non-renewable resource is depleted (Daly, 1990). Daly's principle works better in theory than in practice, as it assumes a high level of substitution between renewable and non-renewable resources which may not exist, or be too costly—it is hard to imagine, for example, replacing all fossil fuel energy with renewable alternatives.

More importantly for our present crisis, however, are the problems of sinks and regulation. Given the difficulties in defining appropriate rates of consumption, and the clear limits to effective substitution, the specific *purpose* driving the use of non-renewables should also be considered alongside rate. In very general terms, we could say that non-renewable resources should be used for the meeting of immediate and future human need—if sustainability is the goal. This suggests, for example, preferentially allocating resources towards essential, durable infrastructure instead of towards

16 Daly imagines "the lowest feasible flows of matter and energy from the first stage of production (depletion of low-entropy materials from the environment) to the last stage of consumption (pollution of the environment with high-entropy wastes and exotic materials) (Daly, 1991: 17).

one-time consumption: choosing, say, solar panels over fast lifestyles. But what constitutes appropriate use of our non-renewable stock remains an open, ethical and tricky question.

Things were far, far easier in the legacy economy! In the legacy economy, resources enter the economic system from the ecological one if there is a buyer, and if a price can be agreed. Whichever entity—an individual, a state, a company—claims an ownership stake on the resource will then gladly sell it, regardless of consequences of its use on planetary systems. It really is that simple. As Nicholas Georgescu-Roegen reminds us: "Let no one, economist or not, forget that the irresponsible deforestation of numerous mountains took place because the price was right" (Georgescu-Roegen, 1975: 377).

In the economy-in-Planet, the flow of resources from the ecosphere into the economy and back out again is held steady at optimal scales. *Within* the economy-in-Planet, however, a different dynamic prevails. In a sustainable economy, sustainably extracted resources must be transformed and consumed in a *slow, circular* fashion. Resources are used for as long as possible, often by many different users; a system functioning in this way is known as a "circular economy".[17] These circular resource flows are quite different to the fast, linear resource flows characteristic of the legacy economy, where resources are extracted, transformed, consumed and then promptly discarded back into the environment. In a circular economy, the use of resources is optimised and the time resources spend within the economic sphere is lengthened as much as possible. By doing this, premature consumption of further resources is avoided. Fewer resources enter the economic sphere, and, consequently, less waste is created, and at a slower pace. This is what resource flows in a sustainable consumption and production system look like. Slowness and circularity within the economy are as essential as steadiness and sustainable flow rate at its boundaries. In comparison to the legacy economy, the economy-in-Planet looks something a bit like Figure 1.3.

17 For a definitive account of the circular economy, see Webster, 2015.

Figure 1.3 **The legacy economy and the economy-in-Planet**

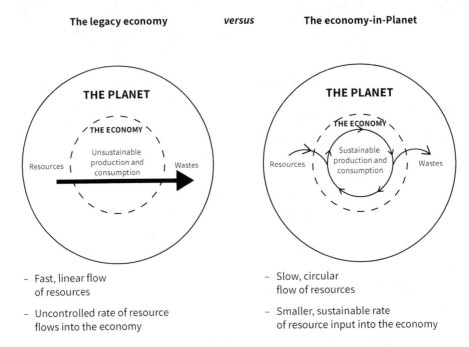

- Fast, linear flow
  of resources

- Uncontrolled rate of resource
  flows into the economy

- Slow, circular
  flow of resources

- Smaller, sustainable rate
  of resource input into the economy

Sustainability requires an economy-in-Planet. We now know what we're aiming for, but how do we get there from where we are today?

2 The transition to the economy-in-Planet

In Chapter 1, we defined a sustainable economy, an economy-in-Planet, in contrast with the legacy economy that created our dire ecological predicament. In Chapter 2, we consider how to make the shift from today's legacy economy, to the economy-in-Planet.

Human development and prosperity require resource use; yet over-use of resources in the legacy economy has already led to the breaching of planetary boundaries

The over-use of resources—and, more specifically, the impacts on planetary sinks and regulation that come from resource use—have created conditions of unsustainability. (When I talk of resource use, I am more accurately referring to "resource use with associated impacts on planetary sinks and regulation". For example, it is less useful to think of using fossil fuels as a resource, which are relatively abundant, and more important to think in terms of the capacity to burn fossil fuels, which, if we are to mitigate climate deregulation, we must regard as very scarce. But, because impacts on sinks and regulation are a consequence, specifically, of resource use, resource use is a good shorthand for both resources and all their impacts, and, most of the time, reducing resource use also reduces impacts on sinks and regulation.)[1]

---

1 Thinking in terms of "resources" has the added benefit that it is far easier to understand resource use than sinks and regulations: we can visualise, touch, use a barrel of oil, but it is far harder to understand the effects of the barrel on the climate system.

While overall resource use has had nefarious impacts on planetary systems, affecting everyone, resource use itself, and the economic activity it supports, have not been distributed equally from country to country (and, indeed, from individual to individual within countries). Citizens living in the countries with the lowest per capita consumption of resources consume two tonnes of materials per person per year for their food and shelter; while those living in countries with the highest per capita consumption use 60 tonnes of materials per capita per year[2] (often for skyscrapers, artificial islands and desert snow-domes.) Note as well that these figures refer to yearly consumption; citizens of higher-consuming countries also benefit from enormous amounts of resources consumed in the past, embodied in our cities and infrastructure. This inequality in resource use reflects inequality in the maturity of the legacy economy, and correlates very strongly with human development. In fact, the link between resource use and development couldn't be clearer: the bottom 30% of countries with the lowest score on the United Nations Human Development Index (HDI) all consume less than 10 tonnes of materials per capita.[3]

We face a bit of a conundrum. We know that economic growth is behind material prosperity. It is what enables us to live comfortable lives in rich countries (those that consume a large share of planetary resources). The correlation between economic growth and poverty alleviation is very strong in countries that use a small share of planetary resources—in fact, economic growth is currently the *only way* we know to lift people out of poverty. At the same time, we know that economic growth requires using the Planet's resources; that their quantity and quality is declining over time; and that, more alarmingly still, resource use is dangerously interfering with planetary sinks and regulations. In short, economic growth lifts people out of poverty and sustains material prosperity; yet it is reliant on the use of declining resources and results in unacceptably dangerous environmental impacts, and the breaching of planetary boundaries. We cannot rely on global economic growth for long-term development and prosperity.

What is the way out of this conundrum? As growing populations require further resource use, population reduction and stabilisation is often

2 Inequality in resource consumption also exists *within* countries, with wealthier citizens typically consuming a greater share of resources compared to poorer ones.

3 The relationship between material consumption and wellbeing only holds up to a point, after which the correlation is less strong, with some countries achieving high levels of wellbeing with relatively low levels of material consumption.

presented as the panacea to sort out our ecological mess. A reduced global population would clearly require fewer resources for its material comfort— and it is true that the massive growth in resource use of the legacy economy is linked to the global population explosion. Just 200 years ago, total world population was 1 billion; during the course of last century, population quadrupled; today, there are more than 7 billion of us. These numbers are unprecedented in planetary history: so much so, that high population num- bers is a defining feature of our time—we truly live on a *Crowded Planet.* But what global population numbers would be ideal today? This would clearly depend on the level of prosperity of said population, or the amount of resources that would be required to sustain its economy and way of life: with low economic development requiring minimal resource use, the Planet could support many.[4] Different attempts have been made to estimate an ideal population size. For example, the UK land mass could support some- where between 17 and 27 million souls, with today's affluence, derived with today's technologies. With that same lifestyle, the Planet's optimum global population could be as low as 2 billion.[5]

But that ship has long sailed. With a projected population of 9–11 billion in the next 30 years, we would need to get rid of 7–9 billion humans to achieve sustainability through population reduction alone. While access to repro- ductive choices is critical in stabilising global population numbers, and improving the lives of millions of women and their families, it can clearly not reduce population on the scale required to lower projected forecasts by some 7 billion. Moreover, those in the Global North advocating "population control" in the Global South as a means to reduce environmental impact ignore the fact that population reduction in high-consuming countries, in the Global North, would be a far more effective intervention than popula- tion reduction among low-consuming regions of the world.

---

4 The notion of "carrying capacity" is useful to understand the relationship between population numbers, affluence and technologies. The Planet has a "carrying capacity"—that is to say, it can support a certain number of people, living at a certain level of affluence, derived from the use of certain technologies (or "technological intensity') in their economic activity, without degradation. The three variables for sustainability of population numbers, technology and economy are also captured in the famous IPAT equation: Environmental Impact (I) is equal to Population (P) multiplied by Affluence (A) or income level multiplied by technological intensity (T) of economic output—or $I = PAT$ (The Sustainable Scale Project, n.d.).

5 Desvaux, 2011. This research assumes a 2011 level of affluence.

To make matters worse, we can expect increased resource use overall, and per capita, and different types of resources being consumed, by the growing populations of poorer countries: the so-called "Global South". As economies grow, the use of fossil fuels, ores, and construction and industrial metals and minerals increases significantly, lifting populations out of poverty and increasing their material comfort—but with serious impacts on planetary systems.[6] This situation is exacerbated further still by the fact that the countries experiencing some of the strongest economic growth are also those with the fastest-growing populations.

Resource use and the threat to the planetary systems it has created will get worse, unless radical changes take place in over-consuming, Global North economies. These need to massively reduce their resource use, which will require economic "degrowth".

The shift to the economy-in-Planet requires significant resource use reduction and degrowth of Global North economies

Degrowth is the name given to the *planned, deliberate* process by which we can transition from an economy in ecological overshoot to one that operates within its host planetary environment. One definition would be the "equitable downscaling of production and consumption that increases human well-being and enhances ecological conditions at the local and global level" (Schneider *et al.*, 2010). The goal of degrowth is a stark reduction in global resource use, with eventual stabilisation at a sustainable level. Reducing resource use is an imperative, since, as we saw in the previous chapter, our current overuse of resources has led to a dangerous degradation of our planetary systems. Since resource use and economic activity are linked, with a growing global economy requiring the growth of resource use, the reduction of resource use requires degrowth of the global economy. It would be disingenuous to suggest that the imperative to reduce resource use could be achieved without it. The idea of *deliberately* degrowing the global economy may sound outlandish, but it has nonetheless gained considerable traction

---

6 Economic growth has led to a striking shift from biomass consumption to non-renewable mineral resources and fossil fuel extraction: biomass represented 75% of resources consumed in 1900 and only 30% by the beginning of this century (Krausmann *et al.*, 2009).

in academic circles in recent years.[7] Let's clarify what degrowth is, and what it isn't.

Degrowth requires rethinking our understanding of prosperity. Essentially, it requires a move away from high-resource-consuming and high-greenhouse-gas-emitting lifestyles, to decarbonised, low-materials lifestyles. Note that many of our politicians are increasingly on board with the need for full decarbonisation of the economy (or the move away from fossil fuels); but have not yet begun, or are only just starting, to grapple with the need to significantly lower use of *all* materials as well (no less because materials often require energy-intense processes in their transformation). Crucially, degrowth only applies to those countries that consume an overly large share of the world's resources (whose citizens enjoy an affluent life-style reliant on high levels of resource use). It aims to remedy the fact that some countries (and their citizens) "utilise" a far greater share of Planet than others to live lives with high levels of material comfort. If all humans had North American lifestyles, for example, we would need somewhere between three and four Planets to have enough resources to go round—and for our multiple planets to act as effective sinks and natural regulators. If we all had the lifestyles of some of the poorest countries, by contrast, we could manage with just the one.[8] In essence, many of us in the Global North have sustained high levels of affluence and material prosperity by consuming a far greater share of materials and fossil fuel energy than poorer countries. Since there is simply not enough Planet to go round—i.e. not everyone can live "Western" legacy-economy lifestyles on one Planet—sustaining our lifestyles requires keeping the poor in poverty. We may not like this, or deny it, but its none-theless pretty much what has been happening to date in the legacy econ-omy. Global North countries' refusal to act meaningfully on climate change is an example of this: we continue to sustain high-greenhouse-gas-emitting lifestyles, while depriving those living in poverty the opportunity to burn these fossil fuels themselves—and, worse, knowing that they will suffer the impacts of climate change disproportionately.

Degrowth is the process by which this global injustice is addressed: if poorer populations of the Global South are to increase their economic activity and material prosperity (albeit *necessarily* following a growth

---

7 In addition to the notion of "degrowth", other thinkers in related subjects have spoken of "postgrowth" or the "end of growth". See for example the works of R. Heinberg, D. Maclurcan or S. Latouche.

8 See the work of the Global Footprint Network: http://www.footprintnetwork.org/en/index.php/GFN, accessed 1 July 2015.

trajectory different to the Global North's industrialised path, which led us into our environmental cul-de-sac in the first place), requiring resource use, the share of global resources consumed by Global North countries must *necessarily* decrease. As a requirement for development of poorer, under-consuming countries (and their citizens), degrowth is an ethical project of global equity. It is also *realpolitik*: ethics aside, economic growth is happening at an unprecedented pace, in a process beyond the control of "over-consuming" countries. Degrowth is *planning* for the implications for Global North lifestyles and economies of the Global South's economic takeoff: the *unplanned version* of this decrease can only mean instability, hardship, and threats to human health and security through lack of access to essential resources.

Reaching a "fair" allocation of planetary resources across countries (and for all citizens) requires a process of "contraction and convergence" of resource use, to a steady, sustainable level, congruent with the requirements of the economy-in-Planet. Contraction and convergence is a notion that was developed by the Global Commons Institute to describe a mechanism to stabilise the climate through a reduction of emissions overall and equal emissions per capita.[9] The same logic would underwrite an expansion of the concept of global convergence to *all* resource use—not just the capacity of the atmosphere to absorb carbon pollution. The contraction required by global convergence can be quite dramatic: for example, a "fair" use of steel and aluminium, given the environmental impacts associated with these metals, would require a contraction of use by at least 80% by 2050 compared to 2005 levels in the UK; for timber, over 70% (cited in Cooper, 2005). And the scale of the reduction in resource use is all the greater, since the planetary boundaries have already been overshot.

At home in the Global North, degrowth is not exactly the most appealing of platforms, with mainstream political and business discourse focused exclusively on growth and the avoidance of recession and stagnation. But degrowth is neither of these. It is not recession, as it is a planned, deliberate alteration, not a malfunction in a growth-based system. More importantly, degrowth does *not* mean "shrinking" all areas of human life or of the economy: it does not preclude qualitative development of human activity: care, arts, sports, appreciation of the natural world. Degrowth applies *specifically* to resource use in the economies of the Global North, the material basis of

---

9 See Contraction and Convergence: http://www.gci.org.uk.

our economy which is the subset of the planetary system (Chapter 1). *The resource reduction imperative requires degrowth, and vice versa.*

The legacy economy now requires the building of resilience in the shift to the economy-in-Planet

If we succeeded in radically transforming the legacy economy through degrowth, would that be enough to achieve sustainability? Spoiler alert: probably not. The unprecedented resource use of the legacy economy has interfered so much with natural cycles that our planetary host has already significantly changed. Our climate has been deregulated and become unpredictable; our aquifers have been depleted affecting abstraction and the water cycle; and we are going through a wave of species extinctions not seen since the dinosaurs met their own unfortunate end. These changes complicate the business of global economic transformation, itself hardly a mean feat, even further. Even if we were to roll up our sleeves and get to work today, we have changed the nature of our relationship with the natural world to such an extent that some geologists argue that we have entered a new geological era, the Anthropocene, which we now need to contend with as we consider the context in which our economy and businesses take place.

The term "Anthropocene" was first proposed by Nobel Prize winner and atmospheric chemist Paul Crutzen in 2000 (Sample, 2014). The Anthropocene is the era in which *human action guides environmental change*, marking a wholesale change in our relationship with the natural world. Up until now, in the age geologists have labelled the Holocene, humans could take existing environmental conditions as background. The environment was a *given*, and humans shaped their lives accordingly. This is not to say they did not seek to shape or impact their environment: the building of settlements and the clearing of land for agriculture has, for example, required significant deforestation over the centuries. But in the Anthropocene, for the first time in history, human effects on their environment have become so significant that they are felt beyond landscape alteration, affecting all ecosystems, the atmosphere and lithosphere. Humans now shape the whole of the planetary system. The term Anthropocene has caught on quickly since it was coined; and there is now widespread consensus that Crutzen and his colleagues are onto something, even if scientists continue to disagree about whether our impacts on the planetary system represent a new *geological* era, and whether entry into the Anthropocene can be accurately dated. Some have suggested the Anthropocene began with the atomic age or the dropping of the bomb. Others have suggested 1784, the year the steam engine was invented, and the year that marks the beginning of our massive emission of greenhouse gases into the atmosphere. Even if largely symbolic, this last date is useful. It reminds us that the Anthropocene is squarely a by-product of the industrial, legacy economy.

What do we know about the Anthropocene? Firstly, it is *not* the Holocene. Our entry into this new era means leaving the previous era behind. The implications of this departure are hard to get our heads around, when we consider that *all* of human civilisation took place during the Holocene (which had been with us for close to 12,000 years)—the Pyramids, the Mona Lisa, the lot. Gone is the era of fortuitous planetary self-regulation, which, while not necessarily making for an easy, entirely rosy life, provided the conditions for life to flourish.

The Anthropocene does not, alas, seem so propitious. Climate change is of course the most visible manifestation of the Anthropocene—and there is now next to no hope of keeping global warming to the "safe" 2° above pre-industrial levels (Friedman, 2015). Unfortunately, climate deregulation is only the tip of the fast-melting iceberg. Other related and unwelcome features of the Anthropocene include resource depletion, biodiversity loss, ocean acidification, freshwater scarcity, and mass species extinction. This is environmental degradation on a *systemic scale*—and it threatens our capacity for decent lives on Earth. But, in this brave new world, we cannot be entirely sure of the severity of the impacts, their knock-on effects, the odds of system collapse—or the timeline in which all these worrying developments might hit home. The era of the Anthropocene is the *era of systemic risk and uncertainty*. Some examples: Extreme weather events mean we may no longer be able to expect timely, consistent supply chains, with massive implications for the movement of goods and foodstuffs. The digital economy (let alone the "internet of things") only works with reliable electricity, which requires the maintenance and reliability of a huge, dispersed and highly vulnerable infrastructure. Worse, our agricultural systems developed with the expectation of certain climatic conditions, a certain access to water, a certain access to petrochemical fertilisers—conditions that are changing and may no longer apply in the Anthropocene. In fact, climate-change-induced food shortage is one of the greatest threats to human life and security identified by the UN's International Panel on Climate Change

(IPCC), with significant drops in wheat and maize yields and fish catches, among other agricultural products, predicted (IPCC, 2014).

In the face of the risks and threats of the Anthropocene, building the resilience of the economy-in-Planet is essential. The focus on resilience is especially critical in the transition to such an economy, with the massive unknowns associated with resource use reduction. After all, deliberately degrowing the economy has never been done before.

Resilience is a notion that has its roots in ecological and systems science. According to the Stockholm Resilience Institute, it is the "capacity of a system to deal with change" and "continue to develop" (Stockholm Resilience Institute, n.d.). A resilient system has three key characteristics: persistence, adaptability and transformability. Whereas a vulnerable system may collapse under internal or external pressure, a resilient system will be pliable enough to survive shocks. A resilient economy would persist or function effectively over time to support a viable society, conducive to safe, flourishing lives. It would continue to provide the goods and services that we need for decent lives, despite the threats and impacts of ecological degradation and population growth. Ultimately, it would adapt to new conditions—in particular, to significantly reduced resource use.

Resilience has become a bit of a buzzword, and much work has been carried out to identify what it looks like in practice, or what characteristics we could expect in a resilient system.[10] Adaptability requires *flexibility*, or the capacity of some components of the system to fail without the whole system collapsing. This itself requires some *redundancies* in the system. A resilient economy could have many different actors providing similar goods or services, many different ways to procure the same item. Redundancies themselves demand a *diversity* of actors, operating in different ways and at different scales. Over-reliance on one model, on one way of doing things, should be avoided. For example, food provision is more secure if provided through a mixture of home-grown, community gardens, markets, small businesses and larger organisations, rather than through a handful of supermarket chains alone. Systems also need to be *reflective*: that is to say, their actors need to anticipate, plan and evolve for change, continuously. And in the face of shocks, risks and uncertainty, they need to be *resourceful* and open to experimentation, and ultimately transformation into something new. All

10 The characteristics of resilience in this paragraph are adapted from those listed in Da Silva, 2014.

this helps to ensure that individual failure does not cascade into a wider, systemic crash.

The threats of the Anthropocene pose significant risks to health, security and prosperity—at a time when an unprecedented decrease in resource use must happen to steer the global economy toward sustainability. In such a context, building of socio-economic resilience is essential in the transition to the economy-in-Planet.

~

In conclusion, Part 1, "The Crowded Planet", has outlined some crucial but overlooked features of the planetary system and its inhabitants, at this point in time, and what it would take to move to sustainability. Understanding these features and requirements helps us define the challenge for the pioneering companies seeking to address the great socio-environmental conundrum that we face.

First, because all economic activity takes place within its host planet, a sustainable global economy must be steady, slow, circular, and scaled within planetary boundaries—it must be an economy-in Planet. Second, since the planetary boundaries have already been breached, the global economy needs to be de-scaled to "fit" within its planetary host. This process will require a significant reduction in resource use in the economy, or economic degrowth. The resource reduction imperative only applies to the richer locations of the world, usually the Global North, which have hitherto consumed a disproportionately large share of planetary resources, contributing disproportionately to the degradation of planetary systems. This imperative is all the more pressing in that global population numbers are at an all-time high—this is the age of the Crowded Planet—and that the "poorer" populations of the Global South must consume an increasing share of resources to lift their populations out of poverty and further their material comfort. Third, we have now entered the Anthropocene, an era characterised by increasing environmental uncertainty and shocks, with the potential to lead to widespread socio-economic disruption. Given this risk, and the further risks posed by the resource reduction imperative, resilience building must be central to the economy-in-Planet and the pathway towards it.

These challenges—*the transition to, and the sustaining of, the economy-in-Planet, the resource reduction imperative, and the building of resilience*—are the key problems of our time. They are what the pioneering company must contend with, and respond to. These challenges and responses are summarised in Table 2.1. They are also the guiding threads of this book. We are concerned with the design of pioneering companies: that is to say, we are concerned specifically with how companies can respond to these three challenges.

Our context	Consequences of the context	Challenge for the pioneering company
Economic activity situated on the Planet.	Sustainability requires an economic system congruent with its planetary host, the economy-in-Planet.	Optimise resource use within economic system, creating slow, steady, circular flows.
		Be viable at a certain steady scale, without the need for growth.
Population numbers are unprecedented.	Use of resources in the under-consuming countries must grow to raise living standards.	Contribute to reduction use reduction.
Resource use, and the prosperity it provides, are massively unequally distributed among countries (and citizens).	Use of resources in over-consuming countries must shrink, sometimes starkly, to enable both the increased resource use of poorer countries and to "resize" the economy within the Planet.	
Planetary boundaries have been breached.		
We have entered a new era, the Anthropocene.	Environmental and socio-economic uncertainty and shocks are to be expected.	Contribute to the building of socio-economic resilience.
	Resilience is central to the economy-in-Planet and the transition towards it.	

To contribute to reduced resource use and the creation of the economy-in-Planet, the pioneering company must design products and services that minimise resource use (Part 2), and build business activities and models (Part 3) and operations and supply chains (Part 4) to support their creation and delivery. Contributing to the steadiness and the "scaling" of the economy-in-Planet, as well as building resilience, requires further innovation in ownership, financing and legal structures (Part 5). The adequacy of the business form itself in the face of these three challenges must also be examined (Part 6). Only by tackling all these issues, in everything that it does, can a company be truly described as pioneering.

Part 2
Products and services

Businesses use resources to provide goods and services to their customers; and it is chiefly through their products and services that firms can contribute to the resource reduction imperative. In the same way that sustainable consumption and production is core to the economy-in-Planet, the *unsustainability* of the legacy economy comes down to *unsustainable* production and consumption. But consumption and production of what exactly? Of *products, goods, objects, items, stuff, artefacts*—terms I use interchangeably and that refer to things that are "man-made" as opposed to "natural": they're the brick to the stone, the house to the cave, the swimming pool to the pond. Food, though of course qualitatively different to products, should also be thought of in this way and included in our analysis. Since products are inherently resource-using—that's what they're made of—the type and quantity of products offered or used by a business has as significant bearing on their overall use of resources. Essentially, our ecological mess is down to the creation, use and disposal of *too many of the wrong kinds of products*. The products of the legacy economy, *"legacy products"* require too many resources, create undue pollution, and result in excessive waste. They're the culprits behind the breaching of the planetary boundaries. And significant opportunities exist to decrease resource use by designing better products. Services, often treated as another category of business altogether, are included here because all services, whatever their nature, require objects, or tools, for their delivery.

To solve the problem of unsustainable consumption and production, and create and sustain the economy-in-Planet, we must move away from legacy products and change the nature of our artefacts. But what would the "right kind" of products—those supportive of the resource reduction imperative, those congruent with the planetary system—be like? This is the key problem we set out to solve in Part 2. I first examine the critical role of product design in supporting the creation of the "right" products in Chapter 3. In Chapter 4, I look at the properties of such products in more detail, and propose a panoply of design interventions to give objects these specific attributes. The resulting products are *"resource-efficient"* and *"resource-sufficient"* or simply *"efficient"* and *"sufficient"*, or *"frugal"*. Collectively, they change the size and type of the material basis of our economy, to make it congruent with our planetary host (Part 1).

Note: this chapter will be relevant to your firm whether or not it is engaged directly in the design and manufacture of products. Thinking through what makes a product frugal, and acting on those considerations, is more particularly a task for the pioneering company engaged in product design. These companies have a *leading* role to play in achieving sustainable production and consumption, because they are responsible for putting new artefacts into the world. But products are also an important consideration for other types of businesses, because *all* companies—even "services"—use products in their activities. An insurance company, for example, may be selling nothing more than a piece of paper, but its core business still necessitates artefacts: the policy required a computer and printer (with a minor environmental impact); should it be claimed, there will be possessions to be replaced, or houses to be rebuilt (with potentially significant impact). So, while the design features identified in this part will be most relevant to companies engaged in product design and manufacture, they can help all businesses guide their procurement choices. *All* companies can help drive demand for products fit for the economy-in-Planet; *all* companies can use these products in their activities; *all* companies have an important role to play in supporting the shift from legacy to frugal product.

3 The purpose and design of products

The economy-in-Planet will only be achieved when the unsustainable production and consumption of legacy artefacts is replaced with the sustainable production and consumption of their frugal counterparts—those that reduce resource use and are congruent with the planetary system.

In this chapter, I examine the leadership role played by product designers of pioneering companies in effecting this crucial change. But, before that, let's quickly remind ourselves why products exist in the first place.

Products work with their users to perform jobs for them

Products exist *to perform a job*. Books are for reading, glasses are for seeing, phones are for chatting (and so on); that's why they were made in the first place. The opposite of nature, products are made by humans, for humans; they are intentionally designed to serve a purpose, and are the result of human labour. Products that are ready to perform their job for the benefit of their user are *end-use* products; and their users (individuals, households, businesses) are *end-users*; the components that go into an end-use product we might think of as intermediate-use products. End-use products are the products I refer to throughout this book: products in their finished form, ready to perform their job, easily recognisable and identifiable as particular "things".

In addition to performing their *obvious, real, physical* job, many objects also do *cultural or symbolic work*. This is especially true of items for which the end-users are individuals and households—"consumers", rather than businesses. Take clothing: it performs the job of keeping its user warm and modest, but fashion and dress can also tell the world a lot about the kind of person we are. Likewise for the books we read (or like to be seen reading), the glasses we wear, the phones we use. Artefacts often act as our *external, materialised,* and sometimes better selves. Their role in identity formation and socialisation is not new, but is of special relevance in the legacy economy, and, more specifically, in the post-war consumer society. There have never been so many products from which to construct our social identity—from furniture to phones, clothes to cars, homes to offices. The products we own and use help define our place in society, arguably more than the traditional markers of class, profession, gender or ethnicity (Jackson, 2005). Our stuff reflects who we are, our stage in life, the people we associate with, who we want to be. Products can even act as a substitute for their owners' time and self—think of the rich, time-poor parent who buys presents rather than attending their child's school show. Objects can likewise represent our self-image and aspirations—an aspiring hiker may purchase expensive outdoor equipment that will rarely be used, but the mere possession of fancy boots provides reassurance that she is indeed a hiker. Many objects send a conscious or unconscious signal to our neighbours about our wealth or social status. Consumption of such "positional products" (Spangenberg *et al.*, 2010) is known as "conspicuous consumption"; and it happens when we aim to emulate or surpass the consumption choices of those around us or on our screens and tablets.[1] Through familiar processes of competition and emulation, more and more people acquire what were formerly prohibitively expensive items, driving the creation of mass-market alternatives, and displacing the object's status meaning onto something else. The cultural role of products in the consumer society thus leads to what seems like a proliferation of "useless" objects (not performing a "real" job, only a symbolic function)—and unquestionably involves significant resource use.

So products often perform one or two jobs for "their" human. But they cannot do either of these alone: product job performance requires human input. We really do have a close relationship with the artefacts we use! Books exist for reading, but for them to actually be read requires a reader; fashionable clothes exist to tell the world we're on top of the latest trend, but someone must wear them, and so on. Sometimes, our involvement with products

1 Juliet Schor found that television viewers tried to keep up the lifestyles of television characters and celebrities rather than their neighbours (Reisch, 2001).

feels like hard work, when objects are the tools, machinery and equipment that we use in the workplace (Chapter 8). Sometimes, the human activity required for the object to perform its job is leisure: drinking a cup of tea, watching a film. Either way, product job performance requires a mixture of "product" and human activity. The exact mix depends on the type of product, and, importantly, its design.

The resource reduction imperative requires the design of products that minimise the use of resources throughout their lifecycle, and overall

The shift to the economy-in-Planet requires both *a new goal and a new approach* to product design.

Starting with the *new goal*: whereas, in the legacy economy, objects are typically designed with functionality or aesthetics—and revenue potential—in mind, creating sleek objects with high-sales potential is not enough (and is likely problematic) for the designer seeking to create frugal products. She must also specifically aim for resource use reduction. To do this, thinking of objects in terms of their jobs is useful: for example, it can help the designer consider how the same job could be done producing less waste or using fewer resources. The goal is, then, to *minimise resource use (and associated planetary impacts), without impairing the object's ability to perform its job.* Minimising resource use is usually understood to mean "improving the resource efficiency of products"—that is to say, reducing resource use (and pollution and waste generated) *per product unit.* But as we have known since Jevons (mentioned in Chapter 1 and to which we return to throughout this book), improving the resource efficiency of *individual items* is likely to increase resource use *overall,* lowering the price and "freeing up" resources to use elsewhere. To "truly" minimise resource use, product efficiency is insufficient and may backfire—in fact, I would argue that environmentalists promoting resource efficiency exclusively have been barking up a woefully wrong tree. To make up for the shortcomings of resource efficiency, frugal product designers must also aim for *"resource sufficiency"*—that is to say, products that help reduce resource use *overall,* and are not simply a more efficient version of another object.

This may seem somewhat implausible, inasmuch as objects, by their nature, require the use of resources! But it can be done: to create a resource-sufficient product is to create a product that *restricts or inhibits the creation of other artefacts*. Resource sufficiency is clearly far trickier than simply designing in features to support an object's resource efficiency—but it is nonetheless the only way to make up for the shortcomings and rebound potential of efficiency. To design a frugal product, apt for the economy-in-Planet, product designers must therefore create artefacts that are both resource-efficient and resource-sufficient; or, in shorthand, *efficient and sufficient products*; or, more briefly still, *frugal products*, to which we return in Chapter 4.

Regarding the new *approach*: despite the fact that objects are created to perform a job, being "on the job" is actually a small part of any product's "use phase" (say, when reading glasses are on the nose rather than in their box); and the use phase is itself just one of the phases of a product's "life" or "lifecycle". A product's lifecycle is a path shared by all objects, which, in the legacy economy, runs from idea and design, to manufacture, distribution, use, and disposal and end-of-life (with a bit of luck, some materials may be reused or recycled when a product's lifetime is over). A typical, if very simplified, product lifecycle looks like Figure 3.1.[2]

Figure 3.1 **Simplified product lifecycle**

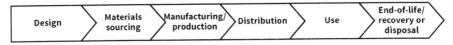

Each lifecycle stage generates direct and indirect planetary impacts: for example, in addition to the materials used in the product itself and the energy used to power it during use, the lifecycle involves fuel use for distribution, packaging waste, or lighting used in retail stores. In fact, for many products, the bulk of their impacts happen in phases other than their use phase, when they're actually doing the job they were created to do. So paying attention to resource use and associated pollution and waste impacts throughout a product's lifecycle is critical if planetary impacts are to be minimised.

This responsibility falls squarely on product designers. Both the exact nature of each stage of a product's life—including the use phase when it

---

2 Note that I use "product lifecycle" to refer to different stages of a product's life, from design to end-of-life. More often, "product lifecycle" is a term used in marketing to refer to different stages of product commercialisation, from introduction, to growth, maturity and decline.

performs its job—and the associated impacts of each phase are *overwhelmingly committed at the design stage*. The designer's impact on a product—and the Planet—persists long after the creative process is done; it affects the whole of the product lifecycle, from the types of materials used in manufacturing, to usage patterns and the potential for materials recovery at end of life. This holds true for all objects, even for items that require a lot of energy for their operation. Take hairdryers, for example: although 90% of the energy expended over their full life occurs during use rather than manufacture, up to 90% of this expenditure is committed at design stage rather than through usage patterns (Tischner 2001, cited in Spangenberg *et al.,* 2010). If your electricity bills are high, you may not be over-drying your hair; it's more likely your hairdryer was not designed for energy efficiency in the first place. Making frugal products doesn't only mean making products that do their jobs with less energy; it also means making products that require fewer resources (and generate less waste and pollution) throughout their lifecycle. This hairdryer at least brings home the point that to design frugal products requires both thinking about how to improve an object's job performance, but also how to make improvements to the other stages of its life.

To design frugal products, a designer must imagine her proposed object's full life from the onset. She cannot simply imagine her object in its finished form, and then "work back" to the manufacturing to make it happen—which was, until recently, the standard approach in the legacy economy. More recently, much progress has been achieved by the more far-sighted companies of the legacy economy on improving lifecycle performance of products ranging from crisps and packaging to office furniture and clothes. To improve the *efficiency* of their products, these companies use a technique called "lifecycle assessment", which provides insights into efficiency by analysing the materials, energy and other environmental impacts associated with each phase of a product's lifecycle. Improvements can then be identified along the way: using responsibly sourced materials in production, maximising energy efficiency during the use phase, and using materials that can readily be reused or recycled at the product's end-of-life. Choosing primary resources that have been certified as sustainable by a third party is an important example intervention. Lifecycle assessment is often used to compare the environmental performance of two similar items—say disposable and non-disposable nappies (Environment Agency, 2005)—to improve products, help manufacturers make environmental claims or to help guide policymakers. The technique requires considerable specialist knowledge of industrial processes, environmental management and environmental systems, as well as time-consuming and costly data collection and analysis. Moreover, the technique requires making numerous assumptions about what happens during the course of the product's life (How will the item be used and for how many years? How will it be disposed of?), arguably undermining the validity of findings. The need for expertise, cash, time and assumptions limits the uptake of lifecycle assessment across products and companies.

For our purposes of *frugal* product design, lifecycle assessment has a further shortcoming: it points toward improving product efficiency only, but tells us nothing about product sufficiency. No amount of lifecycle assessment number-crunching can tell us what a product does to the overall use of resources, outside of the object itself. A lifecycle assessment may conclude that, say, disposable nappies are preferable to reusable ones once all material and energy inputs have been factored in, but it cannot tell us which are more likely to reduce the "nappy need" for infants "overall", now and in the future: this is a cultural change question, clearly outside the expertise of technical lifecycle assessors, and, some may say, barely answerable at all. The best shot may be assembling a team from many different disciplines, from within and outside the designer company: in addition to product designers and environmental specialists, the expertise of social psychologists, anthropologists, sociologists and others could also be useful. Complementing the technical lifecycle assessment, the team would together reflect on the anticipated life of the proposed product, and perhaps use scenarios to deliberate on the potential effects of the product on wider patterns of resource use. Through this process, the designer and her team could identify product features that would support efficiency and sufficiency throughout the lifecycle, and use those features to inform product design. Rather than a "formal" lifecycle assessment, this process could be thought of as a lifecycle *approach* to frugal product design.

The lifecycle of a successfully designed frugal product would look a bit like this: the product starts off in the imagination of its designer; she uses a lifecycle approach to consider the proposed product's efficiency and sufficiency from its conception to its absorption into the planetary system, enlisting the help of colleagues and experts. She then refines product design in light of the findings (or maybe even decides to drop the product altogether). By the time it reaches its end-user, the product's life to date—its primary resources, its manufacture, its distribution—has had minimal environmental impact. During the course of its use, at home or at work, the product is used in such a way as to limit the need for further products, thereby reducing consumption of resources overall. At the end of its life, when it no longer performs its job, its materials are reused, recycled, or readily decompose for absorption by the planetary system. The product's obituary would make it clear that, throughout its life, opportunities to make the product more efficient and sufficient have been maximised.

This lifecycle approach to frugal product design, requiring both technical expertise and multidisciplinary teams, isn't exactly cheap and easy, nor is it foolproof: it has the same difficulties, and more, as a lifecycle assessment, which has consequently enjoyed very limited uptake in the legacy economy. Is frugal product design, then, realistic? Not very—but the good news is there may be some shortcuts. While the exact way to make objects efficient and sufficient will vary from object to object, frugal products nonetheless share some attributes or properties. To help guide the work of the frugal product designer, we can therefore usefully *identify the properties of efficient and sufficient products*, to see if she could integrate all or some of these into her proposed objects. We turn to these now.

4 Properties of efficient and sufficient products

The pioneering company engaged in product design contributes to shifting the stock of planetary artefacts from legacy to frugal products by designing and creating items that are resource-efficient and -sufficient—that is to say, that use minimal amount of resource per unit, and contribute to resource use reduction overall (as well as minimising the impacts on sinks and regulation associated with resource use). To do this requires creating products with specific properties; and fostering these through specific design interventions. These properties and interventions are the subject of this chapter: efficient products are *"resource-sparing"*, *"nature-inspired"* and *"user-centred"*, while sufficient products are *"long-lived"* and *"shareable"*.

A product is resource-sparing when it uses the least amount of resources possible in order to perform its job

To design a resource-sparing product is to create a product that uses minimal amounts of materials and energy, while still performing the job for which it is intended. Interventions for "resource-sparing" include *mass minimisation, energy optimisation* and *multifunctionality*.

Most of the time, the smaller the mass of resources used, the smaller the planetary impact—the link between resource use and impact on planetary sinks and regulation is so strong that the first can usually be used as a proxy for all ecological impacts (see Chapter 2). A first challenge for the frugal product designer is therefore to minimise the mass of a product as much as possible without undermining job performance, in a process of "dematerialisation". The most obvious and straightforward way to do this is through *shrinking its size—miniaturisation*:[3] creating the smallest possible artefact, to the point where any further size reduction would render the object less useful or useless. A small wooden table still large enough to hold a meal for four is clearly environmentally preferable to a larger wooden table that could sit eight, when half of the guests have failed to show up. *Digitalisation* is sometimes an appropriate method of "ultimate dematerialisation". A webpage for a retail company could be thought of as a "dematerialised shop" performing the job of "showing wares to customers". Of course, webpages are not fully dematerialised—memory chips sitting on a server in a warehouse, energy and internet infrastructure, and personal computers replace the bricks and mortars required for a "real" shop—but the "spared" resources from an online shop can nonetheless be considerable compared to its physical counterpart.[4]

For energy-using products, a further intervention for resource-sparing is *energy optimisation*. Optimising energy use is clearly most beneficial when energy sources are polluting; but it is still a beneficial intervention in a future decarbonised energy system, which will still require material-using infrastructure, regardless of the energy source. Energy optimisation first consists of increased *energy efficiency*—often achieved through changes in technology, such as the hybrid car. Without significant change in an item's technical specificity, other roads towards energy efficiency include automation, such as sensor-activated light bulbs, and immediate feedback mechanisms or default settings, such as instant information on fuel consumption while driving, or on unused capacity in washing machines or kettles. These features have been shown to encourage product users to use products in a more energy-efficient way (New Economics Foundation, 2005), and there is hope that the "Internet of things", or the potential connection of everyday objects to one another to share data on activity, could also play a part in saving energy by optimising the use of household appliances. Better still, moving beyond energy efficiency, the frugal product designer can create items

---

3 Howard J. Brown, Kathryn Lewis and Kristin Aldred Cheek talk of "naked value" to refer to the "essence" of an item "after stripping away all unneeded resources" (Brown *et al.*, 2012: 3).

4 At the same time, factoring transport impacts of goods, the benefits of direct retail through digital shops may depend in part on customer density.

that *produce and store energy* as they perform their jobs, as many solar operated gadgets now do.

Interventions to dematerialise and optimise energy use benefit the single object under design. But products exist in a world of artefacts; so designing products that are *multifunctional* can help "consolidate" disparate items" jobs into a single artefact. By designing an object that performs multiple jobs, the frugal product designer streamlines resource use, with each job's resource footprint much smaller than if it were delivered through multiple objects. Multifunctionality is particularly relevant for digital technologies: our tablets are all-in-one cameras, phones, GPS, sound systems and movie players. While newer technologies have always displaced old products, digital technologies have taken this a step further by concentrating the functions of many different products into a single device: think, for example, of the quick demise of the dashboard GPS, which has been blamed on the smartphone. The job consolidation achieved through multifunctionality supports efficient job performance—provided the multiple functions are actually used; if not, a multifunctional object risks using more resource than a single function one, unnecessarily. All going well, a multifunctional object could also help avoid the need for other artefacts altogether, and can as such also be considered a measure for resource sufficiency.

A product is nature-inspired when its impacts on planetary sinks and regulation are minimal

While minimising resources embodied in a product *usually* minimises impacts on planetary sinks and regulation, this link does not always hold true. For example, the trend toward "miniature" electronic items makes material recovery at the end of the gadget's life difficult, both technically and financially: it is possible that a larger gadget would actually be preferable for resource use overall, if larger components are more likely to be retrieved and are more readily recyclable (Ayres, 2007). A large table made from accredited, certified pine is likely to be *less* environmentally pernicious than the smaller table made of tropical hardwood—regardless of the number of guests. Small amounts of manufactured chemicals are likely to be more effective than larger amounts of their natural counterparts (think bleach versus lemon); but such chemicals are generated through industrial processes with considerable environmental impact, creating waste pollution that is not always easily broken down by the Earth's sink capacity (although we would also need to think carefully about the agricultural impacts of lemon growing for a like-to-like comparison).

Alongside the general principle of mass minimisation, there is a further principle for the design of efficient products: the *inspiration from nature*. Note that I am not advocating for "natural products" but "nature-inspired" ones: human-made artefacts are de facto the opposite of natural. There is no such thing as a "natural artefact". But natural processes can nonetheless be a powerful educator as we figure out how to make artefacts that are *as natural as possible*, while still performing their job effectively, and therefore as congruent as possible with their planetary setting. A nature-inspired product is designed, then, to have benign or even beneficial impacts on planetary sinks and regulation throughout its lifecycle.

Ecological design, or imitating nature in the design of products and manufacturing processes, is the approach through which such products are created. Ecological design is well established and has been conceptualised and implemented in several different ways. Here are three examples. "Biomimicry", a design concept developed by Janine Benyus, looks to the environment for inspiration for new inventions, replicating natural patterns and systems. For example, Velcro mimics the tiny hooks of the seeds of many plants (Benyus, 2002). William McDonough and Michael Braungart's "cradle-to-cradle" design aims to improve products from their inception to their future lives in a cyclical process, by innovating in material use and reuse, and prioritising renewable energy and responsible water use in their supply chain (McDonough and Braungart, 2009). "Permaculture", a broad design discipline developed by Bill Mollison and David Holmgren, focuses on designing nature-inspired, self-sustaining systems that require very little maintenance for their continuation. Often used in the design of agricultural systems, permaculture can also be used in product design, helping the designer position objects within the system in which they are being used (Mollison, 1988). What these approaches have in common is a commitment to observing ecological systems, and trying to build the characteristics of the natural world into our products and processes.

This is, however, far easier said than done. There are often good reasons why the design of legacy products is anything but "ecological" in its approach. You can't, for example, always use a "natural" material over a petrochemical or "man-made" one without undermining job performance. Some would argue that pesticides have been more efficient at protecting crops than organic methods. Replacing a legacy object with a frugal one will often require *materials substitution*—and yet substitution is not always feasible or practical. The best, cheapest, most readily available and most suited material for the job is no doubt already being used: there are some very good reasons why Manhattan was not built with bamboo. Nonetheless, it is the task of the frugal designer to choose materials that, as much as possible, have minimal impacts on the stock of resources, are easily absorbed by sinks, and do not affect regulation. For example, biomass materials ought to come from sources harvested at their replenishment rate; manufacturing could rely on solar energy and generate no waste (we return to these processes in more detail in Chapter 8). Since they "embody" nature-inspired materials and production processes, at the end of their lives the components and matter of nature-inspired objects are easily recoverable for reuse or recycled (nothing is wasted in nature). And, when no further use can be derived from them, nature-inspired products decompose and are *absorbed by the Planet's regenerative capacity*—again, sharing the same fate as natural entities.

A product is user-centred when it optimises the activity required in its job performance, paying attention to the quality of human experience

As we saw in Chapter 3, product job performance requires a mix of "product" and input from its user. The mix depends on the item and job at hand: a highly automated product requires less human input than a less-automated, "manual" alternative. We might say that less-automated products have higher "human intensity". And, because they are less automated, they are likely to expend less energy and materials in use (as well as in manufacture). Therefore, finding ways to "increase the human" in the human–product mix, or reducing undue automation, can help get the job done with greater resource efficiency. The frugal product designer then, seeking to create an efficient product, must find ways to increase human input, or decrease product input in job performance. Tilting the mixture in this way requires paying close attention to the *nature* of human activity required: specifically, the *quality of the experience, of the time* spent with the product, and the *skill* required for its effective operation. The frugal product designer must "optimise" the required human activity, designing objects that are *user-centred*.

Products that prioritise human input over energy use employ what E.F. Schumacher calls "intermediate" or "appropriate technology" (Schumacher, 1973). This type of technology uses low amounts of resources, usually readily and locally available. It is often labour-intensive, but has the advantage that the labour expended is autonomous, sometimes simple and sometimes skilled. In the kitchen, for example, shifting to intermediate technology might mean using time-intensive, manual equipment, instead of time-saving electric gadgets, to prepare meals. Nice idea, but, much like materials substitution as a way to create nature-inspired products, this approach may work better in theory than in practice. Many products exist precisely to save us hassle: sure, we *could* beat egg white with a hand-whisk, but electric mixers save us from this tedious task. To design products that *deliberately lengthen* the time spent on a task seems odd to say the least, since so many products were created specifically to *save* time. Moreover, many of our high-tech gadgets can't easily be replaced with more "appropriate" alternatives: no one wants to go back to handwriting with a quill instead of typing on their tablets.

So does the idea of a user-centred product have any legs to stand on? Let's think first about objects *as time-savers*—since this is often why we have automated products in the first place (we could in fact think of many objects' primary job as saving time: a laptop is a fast way to write and file). While no one would seriously dispute the time-saving benefits of many objects, we can note that there has been a bit of a backlash against "time-saving". The "slow movement", for example, is a reaction against our "fast society". It argues that a certain quality, which comes from time expended, has been lost due to time-saving. Slow Food, for example, promises pleasure in food preparation and consumption (while sometimes overlooking the many reasons why our relationship to food is often so harried).[5] Ivan Illich's notion of "counterproductivity", which observes the point at which objects (and institutions) compromise their own purposes, is useful here. The promise of time-saving, Illich suggests, has been oversold: we may think of cars as travelling, say, at 60 miles per hour, but, once you factor in traffic jams, the time at work required to purchase your car in the first place, any time lost to ill health due to crashes and sedentary lifestyles, a car's "true speed" is in fact considerably slower (Illich, 1974: 18-19).[6] Finally,

5 http://www.slowfood.com, accessed 30 March 2016.
6 Thank you to André Reichel for highlighting the relevance of Illich's counterproductivity in this section.

we could also argue that there are limits to the time-saving itself: in reality, time cannot be "saved". When we "save time", we actually just spend it doing something else. Time-saving products help us save time on long, tedious or disagreeable work, and, if we're lucky, give us time for entertainment, fun or relaxation instead; or, if we're less lucky, more time to spend at work. Often, time-saving devices may free up time that is spent on activities that further resource consumption: either through objects used in leisure activity, or through spending more time at work, enabling future consumption (but not necessarily either—it may free up time for a walk in the park). If, rather than saving time, *objects supported the expenditure of time* in ways that did not involve further resource use (beyond the item at hand), this might be environmentally beneficial. Put simply: from a resource use perspective, it is better to spend one hour whisking eggs, compared to five minutes followed by a shopping trip.

To make the former more desirable than the latter would require the time spent "with the object" to be agreeable, fun and enjoyable. This is likely to be tricky, since so many products exist to help us avoid unpleasant tasks. But *designing for slowness*, designing products that *support high-quality time*, a high-quality experience, for their user, is nonetheless the challenge for the designer seeking to create a frugal product.

Along with an increase in the labour required to get the job done, user-centred products often employ human skills: the frugal product designer must aim to create products that require relatively *skilled human input.* This has the dual benefit of resource efficiency—minimising the share of the work done by resource-using artefacts—and of making the interaction with the object more enjoyable. Bikes, rather than legs perhaps, are the ultimate "intermediate" or "slow" cars. They perform the job of mobility with comparable or better performance to the car in urban areas; cycling is a skill, but can be mastered by a majority of people, is an agreeable activity and considered by many to be *"time well spent"* (although it could be someone else's idea of hell! Designing skill-using objects for time well spent is clearly not that straightforward).

Finally, in the same way that the frugal product designer must consider "natural inspiration" in the early stages of a product's lifecycle, to design a user-centred product requires understanding that an object "embodies" human labour in the same way as it embodies material and manufacturing resource use. The frugal product designer must therefore not lose sight of the nature of the human labour required in the making of the product, to ensure the product is user-centred throughout its lifecycle, including in the earlier phases, during manufacture. I return to this topic in Chapter 8.

In Table 4.1, I summarise design interventions and questions to help create efficient products through resource-sparing, inspiration from nature, and user-centredness.

Table 4.1 **Efficient product design interventions and questions**

Resource-sparing	Uses the least amount of resources possible in order to perform its job
Mass minimisation	• Could the object be smaller, yet still perform its job effectively? • Could the object be digitalised?
Energy optimisation	• Could the same job be performed with more energy-efficient technologies? • Could the product benefit from automation? • Could the product provide its user direct feedback on energy consumption? • Could the product generate and store its own energy?
Multifunctionality	• Could the object consolidate the jobs usually done by separate devices in one?
Inspiration from nature	**Has minimal impacts on planetary sinks and regulation**
Ecological design	• Are there ways in which the product could work by seeking inspiration from natural systems and processes? • Are the materials used ecologically benign? • Does the product embody nature-inspired manufacturing processes? • Are product materials recoverable? • Could decomposable materials be used?
User-centredness	**Optimises the human activity required in its job performance**
"Appropriate technology"	• Can the object be operated simply, autonomously by its user? • Are there ways to improve the quality of the time a user will spend with her product? • Does the product required skilled, enjoyable user input for its operation? • Does the product embody a manufacturing process that was itself user-centred?

The best way to manage the risk of product rebounds is through design measures for sufficiency

In the same way as resource efficiency tends to lead to an *increase* in resource use, the design approaches described in this chapter are not guaranteed to reduce product numbers; in fact, we could imagine some leading to more products, creating "product rebounds". A "dematerialised" object, for example, could "create the space" for further items: going for a small table over a large one does not lead to resource use reduction overall if there's now space in the room for a matching side-table. The rebound effects of digitalisation on wider resource are potentially far greater: digital stores may have saved on construction materials, but they have also created essentially unlimited shelf space, allowing 24-hour shopping for everything one could desire just a click away—leading to flurries of rash purchases, as well as massive resource use embodied in these soon-to-be-regretted items. Digital pictures require fewer resources than their physical counterparts (no extra cameras, no labs, no chemicals)—but at the same time, many of us now take hundreds of pictures, all requiring digital storage, when in the past we may have taken one. The resource benefits of digital photography are perhaps not quite as clear-cut as they may first appear.

To counteract this risk of "product rebounds", the frugal product designer must instead aim for product "debounds"[7]—that is to say, integrating design interventions in her product *that will reduce the need for further artefacts, contributing to resource sufficiency.* An example: the single best measure to reduce resource use associated with a house may be to shrink its size. Not only will the house itself be more resource-sparing that way, but it will be filled with far fewer, and smaller artefacts than are likely to be found in a mansion.[8] But accurately predicting how a new item will affect other objects in the world of artefacts is not straightforward. Do laptops create debounds? Sure, they remove the need for desktops, offices and commutes; but they may create the need for a home-office, and lead to less frequent but longer commutes (with worse transport impacts overall), now that occasional homeworking is possible. And the home-office could really do with a desktop and a printer . . .

---

7 Schneider (2012) uses the term "debound".

8 For an interesting study on the link between house sizes and resource use, see Wilson and Boehland, 2008.

Is it actually possible to *design products in a way that will certainly, or almost certainly, result in fewer artefacts overall*? To complement measures for efficient products, and make up for the well-known shortcomings of resource efficiency, we need design interventions for *sufficient* products. In addition to properties for efficiency, the frugal product designer must give objects properties that contribute to absolute resource reduction.

Sufficient products share two qualities: *"shareability"*—which is a capacity to reduce the number of artefacts needed *now*; and *"longevity"*[9]—which is a capacity to reduce the number of artefacts *over time*.

Shareable products reduce the need for duplicate objects now; long-lived objects reduce the need for duplicates over time

One important way to create sufficient products that reduce resource use overall is to make it possible to share a smaller number of products among a larger number of users. Not all objects can be easily shared; objects that can be shared we will call *"shareable"* or say that they exhibit the property of *"shareability"*. Shareable products can be used by many different people; thus many different users can derive benefits from the product with fewer artefacts overall in the world. One way to describe the impact of shareability is to say that it increases a product's "use intensity" (Spangenberg *et al.*, 2010)—that is to say, increasing the amount of time a product spends actually doing its job. As we know, objects exist to perform jobs for their user; between jobs, they sit idle. If they worked full-time, many people would derive benefit from their use, with fewer duplicate items in the world. Use intensity cannot be increased for all products: it won't work, for example, for single-use products, those already used all the time, frequently or repeatedly, or those that *really* cannot be shared. But for many products used occasionally, whether sporadically or regularly, increasing use intensity through sharing presents a dramatic potential to increase product sufficiency.

Longevity, the second intervention for sufficiency, works by reducing the need for duplicate artefacts *over time*. Longevity avoids the need to create new objects altogether. Long-lived products perform their jobs for longer

---

9 Longevity is the term used by Tim Cooper to denote the quality of products with extended lifespans (Cooper, 2010).

before disposal, thereby avoiding frequent replacements—and the future resource use required for those replacements. Long-lived products significantly reduce pollution from avoided production, and curb waste by reducing the number of products thrown away. Longevity really has the potential to be resource sufficiency's silver bullet, albeit with some important caveats, which we return to later in this section.[10]

Let's consider two (hypothetical) examples to examine the benefits of shareability and longevity: German cars and British toasters. First, the cars. According to one study, the average car in Germany is used on average 29 minutes a day, or a total of 3 months over 12 years. While being used, the car does its job as a "provider of mobility"; the rest of the time it is simply metal gathering dust. Rather than having 11 years and 9 months off over 12 years, Germany could, theoretically, get by with a tiny fraction—as low as 2%—of its current stock of cars if the remaining few were on the job all the time (Bund and Misereor, cited in Spangenberg *et al.*, 2010). Cars, of course, do degrade with use, but proper maintenance can extend vehicle lifetimes long beyond what households usually achieve. What about the toasters? There are currently 26 million households in the UK, and they, most probably, pretty much all have a toaster. Say a toaster is kept on average for 4 years before replacement. Over 12 years, as our German car gathers dust in its garage, those 26 million households will buy 78 million new toasters (Defra, 2011a).[11] But if toasters had longer lifespans—say, if it were doubled to 8 years—the replacement rate of toasters would fall significantly. Rather than working their way through 78 million toasters, UK households would only need 39 million toasters for the same job of toasting toast. So, over 12 years, shareable cars and durable toasters could get Germans around the Autobahn and fill Britons up with toast—but with 2% of the cars and 50% of the toasters compared to the baseline. Such changes would require durable objects that work continuously for long periods of time, and, in the case of the car, mechanisms to enable sharing—for example, by making sure cars

---

10 All the section on longevity draws heavily on some work I did with Jackie Downes and Bernie Thomas at Environmental Resources Management for the Department for the Environment, Food and Rural Affairs (Defra). This includes the example of toasters and washing machines, some of the complexities associated with achieving product durability, and some of the possible design interventions later in the chapter (Defra, 2011a).

11 In this study (Defra, 2011a), toasters are assumed to last 3.5 years; for simplicity, and to enable alignment with the German car example, I have here made an assumption of 4 years.

are in the right place at the right time, all the time. Increasing the shareability and longevity of products would help dramatically lower the number of artefacts we need to provide the same level of benefit to users.

The creation of a long-lived and shareable product is the goal of sufficient product design. But, as mentioned above, not all products can be shared. Here it is useful to distinguish between what I call *"user-owned"* and *"user-accessed" items. User-accessed products are items for which access alone* allows the product to perform its function, conferring benefit on the user. For user-owned products, by contrast, *ownership* is integral for job performance.

Clearly some products *need* to be owned by their user: communal toothbrushes, anyone? Hygiene-related products, or items that are in more or less continuous use, such as beds at home or computers at work, are also hard to share. Likewise for items that contribute to our sense of security and wellbeing: for many people home ownership has wellbeing benefits beyond "the provision of a roof over one's head", a function that, on paper, could equally be achieved by a rental property. But it is equally clear that many items that are owned today *could* instead be shared, user-accessed items. These include items that are widely owned but rarely used; the household power drill is a case in point, used at most for a few hours (or even minutes) a year, and yet occupying pride of place in the toolbox of most households. For many items, the added value of ownership over mere access has a *cultural basis*, often traceable to the work of advertisers. Arguably, this is also the case with home ownership, which might not be so highly prized if lifelong rental were the norm.

Since sharing is an integral part of sufficiency, a primary goal for product designers is to *design user-accessed items for sharing*: that is to say, to integrate object features to ensure items that could be shared are actually shared. But our culture's preference for ownership demands that designers interested in sufficiency pursue a second goal as well: product designers should also find ways to increase the number and type of shared items, *supporting a cultural shift from user ownership to user access*. This goal often requires a weakening of the cultural significance of owned products—that is to say, weakening the cultural job of artefacts described in Chapter 3.

Easier said than done: it is hard to predict in advance what social significance items take on in the social system. Nonetheless, a cultural change towards reduced product ownership is necessary to reduce the number of artefacts. The link between product ownership and identity or social position must be attenuated: as far as possible, *transferred to product access,* or, better still, to less resource-intensive aspects of human experience. This cultural shift is a tall order, but possible—the idea of what *can* and *should* be owned has clearly evolved significantly over time. (In previous centuries, it was thought that humans could be owned by others as slaves.) This shift can be supported through product design, and, importantly, through business activities, to which we return in Chapter 6. To increase longevity and share-ability requires technical and aesthetic design interventions.

Technical features for product longevity should be included in all products, cautiously; and technical features for shareability should be included in user-accessed objects

Given the massive benefits associated with longevity—potentially large reductions in resource use, pollution and waste—a first goal for the frugal product designer is, as a general rule, to make objects that are as long-lived as possible. Unfortunately, creating a long-lived product through techni-cal design interventions, or *interventions for product durability*, is not as straightforward as it may seem. A durable product is one with the technical specificities for longevity. Testing for durability is a challenge, often involv-ing laboratory experiments intended to mimic years of repeated use over days or weeks of testing. In practice, of course, the machine is not used in a laboratory setting but in a household, not continuously but sporadically over time, and probably not strictly according to the instruction manual. Durability is hard to design when use conditions cannot be re-created. This inability to guarantee durability should nonetheless not deter designers from pursuing it. Durability first requires *choosing the most robust possible materials*. Again, this is a general rule: a durable product may require more resources than a disposable or semi-durable product that performs the same job, so this greater use of resources will need to be considered in rela-tion to potential waste avoided. Sometimes, the most durable product may have worse planetary impacts than its less durable alternative (platinum is more durable than aluminium, for example, and has worse planetary impacts). Nonetheless, for most products, the benefits of durability will out-weigh concerns about what could be, for example, a more energy-intensive manufacturing process. It is also essential for the frugal product designer to integrate features that extend product life during the use phase. A way to achieve use phase extension may be *modular design*, which requires objects that are *easy to disassemble and reassemble*, and relatively wide *availability of spare parts*, supporting ease of *maintenance and repair*.

Technical durability is not without its pitfalls, and the problem of path dependency is a strong argument *against* seeking to achieve product longevity. We're in a situation of path dependency when our choices are constrained by decisions taken in the past, regardless of whether these decisions would still be made today. Path dependency ties us into certain products. A classic example is road construction, a massive infrastructure investment that locks us into cars as a mode of transport—road networks help make cars necessary, and prohibit the widespread development of competing alternatives, such as railroads. Similarly, durable products can lock us in. This can be especially problematic for energy-using products. As energy efficiency improves, durable products can lock us into artefacts that are less energy-efficient than later models—whereas less durable products enable us to reap the benefits of newer, more energy-efficient alternatives. Our 30-year-old washing machine is likely to be considerably less energy-efficient than a model from last year. To counter this risk, the designer should aim to create what I call *path-independent* items—the opposite of their *path-dependent* counterparts. The aim is to avoid, as far as possible, being locked in to less efficient alternatives when a better, more resource-efficient item comes along. For some products, the simplest way to avoid lock-in may be to design products that are, as far as possible, *stand-alone*: which do not require a supporting constellation of products to function effectively. In practice, most items are used in conjunction with others. For those, the main aim is to design items that can be *readily upgraded* or *retrofitted*: products ought to be durable, but also *flexible, convertible*. The frugal product designer should keep the best-case scenario in mind—one where a better technology with reduced planetary impact will one day become available to perform the job. Will there be ways to adapt the current object to this development? Those experimenting with engine conversion to run diesel engines on used oil from frying potato chips can be a source of inspiration here.

In addition to durability, shareable products need additional features to support their use among multiple users. Clearly, they need to be *tested for use intensity*, for near continuous or frequent use. Specific attributes for sharing could also include *location tracking*, or *locking features* for multiple users—such as passwords, and card or smartphone locks rather than keys.

Long-lived and shareable products also require design interventions for "social durability'

Designing durable products is actually designing *potentially* long-lived objects. It is not enough to ensure that products will indeed be long-lived, as products may be disposed of before they cease to be functional, all at the discretion of their owners. In fact, premature disposal of objects happens all the time. According to one study, a third of household appliances are in working order when they are thrown away; a further third are disposed of when in need of repair (as opposed to beyond repair). In other words, two-thirds of household appliances are discarded prematurely: perhaps because we do not know how to repair them, or do not want to, or maybe just because we no longer want them (E-Scope Survey cited in Cooper, 2005). Premature disposal is a strong argument *against* designing for durability, since durable products may have bigger impacts at production stage than their semi-durable or disposable counterparts. Durable products are often only environmentally preferable to their short-lived alternatives if they are, in fact, used to the end of their lives. Therefore, designing in durability is not enough: a product *actually needs to be used for its full life.* For this to happen, the designer must incorporate some features into products that *allow, encourage or nudge the owner into continuing to use her product* until it can no longer perform its job at all. I call this *"social durability"*: it is about creating products that owners *want to retain* for their full lifetime.

For all objects, social durability, staying power, is supported by *ease of repair*—remember, a third of household appliances are discarded when in need of repair. Maintaining products in working order, and repairing them, must be a *cheap and easy* option for product owners and users. Ideally, products should be easily repairable by their user (lack of skills is one of the main reasons young people don't undertake repair work on their appliances) (Defra, 2011b). *Skills* required for repair need to be accessible to many and—ideally—doing the repairs should itself be enjoyable (if at all possible, while recognising the opportunities to do so may be the exception rather than the rule). Maintaining bikes, for example, is often a hobby rather than a chore. This ease of repair, when enjoyable and skill-using, can be thought of as empowering to product users, as opposed to the all-too-common frustrating experience of being unable to repair complex objects. When repairs do require professional skills, proximity to user and low cost are essential: repairs must be less of a hassle and cheaper than replacement (this requirement clearly goes beyond design, and we return to it in Chapter 6).

But what about the third of objects that are discarded when still perfectly functional, "just because"? Weakening the cultural role of product ownership can help ensure product retention. Without this role, products are simply functional, rather than linked to identity—and therefore less susceptible to being discarded with a change of one's circumstances or on a whim. Designers could aim to *emphasise product function over distinctiveness or aesthetics*—treating products simply as "workhorses", dedicated to performing their "real" job, rather than fulfilling any symbolic role.[12] This approach is quite different to current ideas of design, which tend to emphasise the importance of a product's distinctive character. *Generic, functional products* limit the opportunity for linking products to identity formation. For the same reason that they are less likely to be discarded for reasons of fashion, "workhorse" products are easier to share: because they are less distinctive and less strongly linked to personal identity, they are easier to treat as user-access items. As an example, let's compare cars for ownership, and cars for sharing. Cars for ownership require a particular key to open them (as anyone who's lost their key is painfully aware of). Different car models have their own distinctive features, and can be further personalised with special features like cup holders or one's preferred colour. They are marketed to suggest that owning a particular car confers certain character traits to their owners: adventure, independence, responsible parenting. Cars in sharing schemes, on the other hand, have features like membership-card locks and location tracking, to support use by multiple users. They are not overly personalised—they are unlikely to come in hot pink, nor do they have "humorous" number plates—making them attractive neither to thieves nor to niche consumer groups. These technical and aesthetic features are both essential for supporting car sharing and getting cars off the road.

For many user-owned items, however, generic or functional design is not suitable. Most of us see a difference between our boiler (likely user-owned, but could be user-accessed) and our favourite sofa (likely user-owned). For user-owned products, where ownership is inherent to the object's job performance, creating staying power requires integrating design features that encourage an "investment mind-set" (Defra, 2011b) among their owner-users. Investment items are user-owned items, but, unlike "fashionable" items (Defra, 2011b), they are less likely to be discarded prematurely and more likely to be maintained, repaired and kept until the end of their useful life. Typical investment products are usually larger, household items, but

12 The term "workhorse" product was coined by Brook Lyndhurst (Defra, 2011b).

this mind-set could be expanded to all durable and semi-durable consumer goods. Investment products are usually more expensive than their fashionable counterparts, but they come with the expectation of an extended lifespan and are therefore "worth it" (Defra, 2011b). The product designer can help foster this mind-set by *emphasising high-quality materials* and *timelessness in design*. She should also find ways to help keep the product looking in good shape and up to date. Patterned design or darker colours, for example, could help do this. Table 4.2 summarises design interventions and question for sufficiency.

Table 4.2 **Sufficient product design interventions and questions**

Longevity	Reduces the need for duplicate objects over time
Technical durability	• How can we replicate long-term use in product testing? • Could the object be made of more robust, longer-lasting materials? • Could the object be modular? • Is the object easy to disassemble and reassemble? • Is the object easy to maintain and repair? • Will spare parts be available?
Path-independency	• Would the object be easy to upgrade? • Could the object be retrofitted? • Could the object be converted to support a more resource-efficient alternative should technology improves?
Social durability	• Are repair and maintenance activities cheap and easy to access? • Can users repair their own products, using basic skills? • For workhorse products, does design emphasise functionality? • For investment products, does design emphasise quality and timelessness? • For investment products, could materials be used to keep the product looking good for as long as possible?
Shareability	**Reduces the need for duplicate objects now**
Technical shareability	• How can we replicate intense use in product testing? • Could the object benefit from location tracking? • Could the object have other features that support use by multiple users?
Aesthetic qualities	• Is the product generic rather than distinctive or individualised?

In this chapter, we have seen how the product designers of pioneering companies can help create the frugal products at the heart of sustainable production and consumption. They do this through design interventions, both technical and aesthetic that support efficient and sufficient resource use. For some items—those that are inherently short-lived and simply cannot be shared—only measures for efficiency apply. I realise it would be useful to provide a table outlining the applicability of different types of intervention for different types of products. But this table cannot be drawn: the scope of applicability of interventions for the creation of frugal product defies "typical" categorisation. For example, thinking of "consumer electronics", some consumer electronics can be made "resource-sparing" through miniaturisation (compare '80s boom boxes and cassettes to today's chips supporting endless music collections), while, for others, size shrinking would overly impair job performance—a tiny TV would be cute but useless. So, rather than assigning intervention applicability to different product types, the frugal artefact designer must instead think of potential approaches to support resource efficiency and sufficiency on a product-by-product basis. This chapter has hopefully highlighted the panoply of features to consider as she imagines new items.

≈

In Part 2, we have examined the central role of product design in achieving the resource use reduction required for the transition to the economy-in-Planet.

Efforts to reduce the resource use associated with artefacts are already well under way in the legacy economy, including a growing trend to consider the full lifecycle impacts of products. But the efforts of even the most far-sighted companies have focused on improving the resource efficiency of the items they create: a laudable effort doomed to failure if the goal is absolute resource use reduction. In addition to designing efficient products, the pioneering company must also create sufficient products. And, while designing efficiency into products is relatively easy, often through technical changes, sufficiency is clearly a far tougher nut to crack. Designers can only create products that *encourage or support* sufficiency rather than create it: whether a durable and shareable product is kept until the end of its life and used by multiple users depends on the item's owner, during its use phase. Ensuring that products designed for sufficiency actually contribute to resource use reduction is a challenge.

But the features of durability and shareability, if successful, present a more extraordinary challenge still for many companies. Many businesses *rely on the fact that products do not last forever and cannot be shared.* There is no business to be made by eternal things held in common: compare the sun and desk lamps, and springs and bottled water. In other words, if the product designer in the pioneering company achieved her goal of creating "completely extended lifespan" and "entirely shared" products, these "100% frugal" objects would essentially drive her and her firm out of business.

With such a threat to their business, it is little wonder that even the most innovative companies of the legacy economy have paid scant attention to the problem of product sufficiency! But since creating sufficient products is core to achieving the absolute resource reduction required for sustainability, we cannot ignore this issue, and hope it will go away. Is there a way for companies to *ensure products have extended lifespans and are shared— while remaining financially viable?* This is the question we turn to in Part 3.

Part 3
Activities and business models

Ever feel like your latest techno-gadget has been designed to break on you within a few months of purchase? That's because it probably has. "Planned obsolescence" is the term given to any design intervention that *deliberately* limits the lifespan of a product—say through using flimsy materials, or making parts unavailable. While frustrating for the customer, planned obsolescence makes perfect sense for manufacturers and retailers. Their activities *require* short-lived objects to secure frequent replacement and support future sales. These activities also require a high level of *unshareability*: an item that can be widely shared will generate far fewer sales than an item that can't. In other words, companies engaged in manufacturing and retail, with a sales-based business model, have a strong incentive to produce and sell short-lived, unshareable objects—the exact opposite of the long-lived and shareable products that lead to absolute resource use reduction!

There is, therefore, a deep mismatch between the goals of product sufficiency and the activities and business models of the manufacturers and retailers that prevail in the legacy economy. It would be very difficult for, say, the toaster manufacturers mentioned in Chapter 4 to shift from making toasters that last four years to ones that last twice that long—replacement sales would collapse, as would revenue. Likewise, if household toasters were replaced by one giant communal toaster on the village green . . .

In addition to design characteristics, sufficient products also require a shift away from business activities and models for which longevity or share-ability do not pose an existential threat. Pioneering companies must instead develop viable activities and business models the success of which relies on there being fewer products in the world.

Part 3 considers what these may be. Note that our focus is exclusively on activities and models for *product sufficiency,* and not efficiency: efficiency can be "solved" through technical design interventions (not that this is easy), whereas sufficiency can only be *encouraged* through these (and through aesthetic choices). Sufficiency requires specific business activities, underpinned by specific business models—a term used throughout to refer to the channel through which revenue is general—*designed to promote artefact longevity and shareability.* There is scope for many different businesses to support this goal, from those currently engaged in manufacturing, to retailers and service providers.

Activities fall under two banners: *"product stewardship"*, which we examine in Chapter 5, and *"product access"*, to which we turn in Chapter 6. Since these activities are the conduit to resource use reduction, pioneering businesses are either *"product stewards"* or *"product-access companies"*.

5 Product stewardship

Like their legacy economy predecessors, manufacturers and retailers, the product stewards of the economy-in-Planet are in the business of product creation and sales. However, product stewardship aims specifically at working *with* rather than *against* product longevity. Product stewardship activities therefore include not only production and sales, but also product maintenance, retrieval, remanufacture and redistribution. Aiming to reduce resource use through product lifetime extension, product stewardship responds to the resource reduction imperative, and pioneering companies are often engaged in stewardship activities.

Product stewards are responsible for, and engaged with, the items they create during their use and end-of-life phases

Typically, in the legacy economy, goods are made by manufacturing companies, and distributed to customers through wholesale and retail businesses. These firms are in the business of making and selling items, and they make their revenues through sales. To remain commercially viable, the revenue from the sale of the product must be high enough to cover the creation of the original product, and any other expenses incurred in getting the product to its owner. The more these companies sell, the greater their revenue. As the deciding factor for customer purchase is price, most businesses aim for a high turnover of low-cost products (barring a few firms that focus on more expensive, niche markets). Once the customer is out the door with her purchase, it's time to think about the next sale. Companies with *sales-based business models*, including manufacturers, wholesalers and retailers, are successful when they sell *more and more* objects. These models are therefore predicated on short-lived items, requiring frequent replacement and purchase.

A powerful example of the threat posed to such businesses by "undue" durability—or the attraction of "building in" obsolescence, discreetly—is the famous "light bulb conspiracy". The conspiracy refers to the agreement reached in 1924 by the Phoebus cartel, consisting of the world's largest light bulb manufacturing companies, such as General Electric and Philips. The Phoebus agreement had massive implications for light bulb production—and resource use. For one thing, cartel members agreed that light bulbs across the industry should last no less than 1,000 hours. In the relatively early days of electrification, a thousand hours of light would have sounded like an impressive technical feat. But what was really remarkable about the cartel was a second stipulation: that light bulbs should last *no more than* 1,000 hours. Customers impressed with the 1,000-hours guarantee would have had no idea that the technology already existed for much longer-lived light bulbs—offering up to 2,000 hours. Standardising light bulbs at 1,000 hours actually required designing for a *shorter* bulb lifespan. And, indeed, a lot of research effort was expended to ensure the bulbs wouldn't last beyond their prescribed hours, and cartel members were even fined if their bulbs were found to outshine their welcome. The Phoebus agreement worked very well, and light bulb lives decreased by a third over the next few years. At the same time, sales of light bulbs increased nicely—the bulbs, with shorter lives, required more frequent replacements than their now defunct, longer-lived "non-standardised" counterparts. Sales continued to grow until the cartel was dissolved at the outbreak of the Second World War (Krajewski, 2014).

Even outside of sinister monopolies like Phoebus, sales-based business models require short-lived items and lead to the production and distribution of an ever-growing number of goods—driving an ever-increasing use of resources. Making a link between planned obsolescence of objects and resource use, the French government enacted a law in 2015, the first of its kind, aiming to fight planned obsolescence by making information on the lifespans of appliances mandatory (Prindle, 2015). But, unacknowledged by legislators, if the law is successful at driving the production of "really" durable appliances, appliance manufacturers and retailers will be badly hit. Indeed, there is a deep contradiction between the sales- based business models and long-lived items. To be viable, businesses delivering durable items must instead engage in activities other than manufacturing and retail, and must rely on revenue generation channels other than sales. Enter the *product stewards.*

Product stewards are engaged in a broad suite of activities. In addition to manufacturing and distribution, these include maintenance, retrieval, remanufacture and redistribution ... ad infinitum—or at least until an object's end-of-life, when it will be recovered for material recycling or disposal. Together, these activities extend the life of a product as much as possible—thereby creating durable products. (Remember, the *goal* of product stewardship is product lifetime extension.) In addition to taking on many more activities than manufacturing and retail, product stewards also differ from their legacy economy predecessors in being responsible for the objects they create *throughout their life.* Typically, a manufacturer's concern pretty much stops at point-of-sale (usually to a wholesaler), or, for a retailer, on expiration of a warranty. There have already been efforts to extend this responsibility: for example, the EU's Extended Producer Responsibility policy aims to make manufacturers responsible for the recycling and disposal of the items they create, usually by incorporating costs associated with material recovery into the product price (European Commission, 2014). But the product stewardship activities proposed here go beyond financial responsibility for sound disposal. Instead, recognising that a product's use phase, including its potential for extension, and the possibility of material recovery at end-of-life, are determined at design and manufacturing stage, I suggest that the companies that put objects into the world bear responsibility for them at *all* their life stages.[1] Product stewardship denotes this lifelong involvement, *including during the product's use stage*—the very life stage where longevity potential is realised (this is also the case for use intensity, which we return to in Chapter 6). So, whereas for legacy economy manufacturers the point-of-sale is where they part ways with their objects, for stewards this is really just the beginning.

The first activity taken on by product stewards is *manufacturing*: not manufacturing any old junk, of course, but specifically frugal products, with the efficiency and sufficiency attributes described in Chapter 4. Since the stock of planetary artefacts in the economy-in-Planet must be far smaller than today's stock (as required for resource use reduction), the manufacturing

---

1 The term "product stewardship" already exists. While it often denotes responsibility for a product throughout its life, it tends to assume that responsibility for sound use, disposal or recovery rests with the consumer; which is not what I am suggesting here.

sector must be far smaller than today's global junk creation behemoth. The shrinking of manufacturing—less "stuff" being made—is perhaps the most striking way in which a sustainable production and consumption system will be different to its unsustainable equivalent. But manufacturing is just a small part of stewardship. The second activity is *distribution*, or getting products from where they are made to where they are used. Thirdly, product stewards engage in *maintenance*: care activities that specifically aim to lengthen the life of the item, ensuring users derive the full benefit from their objects for as long as possible. Maintenance activities include cleaning, repairs and upgrades, as well as the provision of replacement parts. When maintenance is no longer enough, and the item no longer performs its function, stewards' fourth activity is *product retrieval*. Distribution, maintenance and retrieval arrangements will differ between user-accessed and user-owned items (as we'll see later in this chapter and in the next). Stewards retrieve items for *remanufacture*, their fifth activity. Remanufacture consists of all the *"re"* activities required to get a product in good shape and working order for the next customer: remanufacture, but also refurbishment, reconditioning, retouching, and replacing parts. These activities are at the heart of product stewardship: the idea is that the "re" activities generate significant resource use reduction compared to the manufacture of new items from scratch. In the economy-in-Planet, product stewards are *remanufacturers first and manufacturers second*: they are *primarily engaged in the "re economy"*.[2]

The prevalence of "re" activities compared to manufacturing is a second notable feature of sustainable consumption and production. In addition to the clear resource use benefits, "re" activities have the added advantage that they create further incentives for product design for ease of maintenance, conditioning and remanufacturing. Once back in tip-top condition, the cycle begins again. Eventually, once remanufacture is no longer possible, stewards *recover* all the available materials, recycle as much as possible, and dispose of residual waste.

The multiple activities of product stewardship create multiple, sustained interactions with customers—at point-of-sale, during maintenance, at the end of first use; and again with secondary and tertiary customers. This

---

2 Spangenberg makes a distinction between the "REconomy" consisting of the "re" activities described in this section and the "DEconomy", which is about dematerialisation. The REconomy reduces flows *into* the socio-economic system, while the DEconomy reduces flows *inside* the socio-economic system (Spangenberg, 2012).

Figure 5.1 **Comparison of manufacturing and stewardship activities**

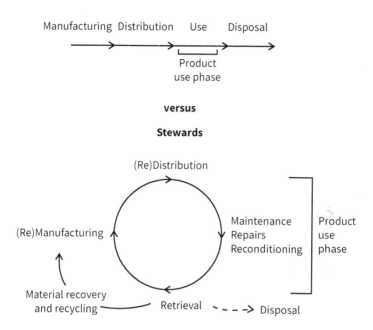

ongoing, relational interaction is different to the one-off transactions some-times favoured by sales-based businesses. Mirroring the life of objects, the business–customer relationship begins rather than ends at point of pur-chase. Today's manufactures may also keep track of a customer, but this is usually to encourage repeat purchase, or to honour warranty commitments, begrudgingly. Stewards on the other hand must have a long-term relation-ship to implement the suite of activities required to lengthen product lives.

Product stewardship activities, then, are varied and complex. This is espe-cially true as some activities take place when the object is not in the stew-ard's possession but with its user. To be successful, product stewards must pay particular attention to the activities that *lengthen product life during use phase*, and to *mechanisms for retrieval*. Without the former, the product's use phase will be shorter than it might otherwise have been; without the latter, the opportunity for a new product cycle is missed. When done well, the activities of stewards, and their effects on a product's lifecycle, look a bit like what's shown in Figure 5.1—nothing like today's businesses engaged in manufacturing and retail.

Whereas the means of revenue generation for legacy manufacturing and sales companies are straightforward—through sales—revenue opportunities for product stewards cannot come from product sales alone. Manufacturing and retail, are, after all, a very small part of what they do; instead, they must generate income across all stewardship activities (while also incurring costs at each stage). Besides, a sales-based business model is inappropriate in that we know it drives product obsolescence—and the stewards are striving for the opposite of obsolescence. Instead, they develop models where success is aligned with the cycle of stewardship activities, requiring and driving long-lived objects.

For user-owned items, stewards can extend product lives through after-sales services and retrieve objects through buy-back options

Despite the fact many more items will be user-accessed in the economy-in-Planet compared to today, user-owned items, which we consider in this section, still exist (when ownership is critical to the object's job performance). Like today, the *manufacturer-stewards* of the economy-in-Planet may sell objects directly to customers; but, more often, these will be brought to customers via retailers. And it is these *retailer-stewards* who will be best placed to conduct the crucial customer-facing stewardship activities of product life extension at use phase and retrieval. Retailer-stewards, selling user-owned items, rely on sales for their revenue—and, as such, like the light bulb manufacturers of the Phoebus cartel, risk being incentivised to sell short-lived items. The challenge for the retailer-steward is to develop a viable business *that does not primarily rely on sales for success*—despite the fact it is in the business of sales!

A first way to address this tricky problem is to find ways to require *fewer* sales for viability, ending up with what we might call a *slow-sales* business model. Rather than on high volumes of sales of low-cost items, a retailer-steward would instead sell fewer, longer-lasting objects, at a higher cost. The high price tag would help compensate for the slump in sales that can be expected with the slowing-down of the pace of purchase of replacement items. Niche legacy retailers that sell high-quality objects, often with durability claims, already use this strategy in the legacy economy. Thinking back to the toasters of Chapter 4, Dualit toasters famously last for decades, but come with a hefty price tag.[3] Durability helps differentiate Dualit toasters from their competitors. But note that this model won't really work in the economy-in-Planet, and can therefore only be a strategy in our transition toward it: under conditions of sustainability, *all* objects are efficient and sufficient—that is to say, we would expect *all* steward-retailers to be selling toasters with Dualit lifespans, and the slow-sales retail model to be standard.

The model, moreover, does not counter the risk of premature disposal. Slow-sales business models may contribute to sufficiency and may attenuate the object proliferation risks of sales-based models, but they do not resolve these issues. To do so, the retailer-steward must develop alternative revenue streams linked to stewardship activities, especially *service fees* for product maintenance, adopting a *model based on a product after-care service fee.* After-sale *maintenance* services can help to extend the life of the object, and ensure its owner derives full benefit from it. These services include cleaning, troubleshooting, repairs, reupholstering, upgrades—anything that helps extend the time the owner keeps hold of her object. For the steward-retailer, the service fee presents a welcome additional revenue stream in the face of reduced sales; for resource sufficiency, product servicing helps extend product job performance. In addition to maintenance services, retailer-stewards could also offer both new and pre-owned items as standard, relying on a *secondary-sale model. Managing secondary and tertiary markets*, retailers retain a model that is inherently sales-based. But resource benefits are still generated: wares are not manufactured from scratch for each new customer, and secondary and tertiary sales "launch" the second and subsequent lives of items, and cycles of product stewardship activities. The life of an object is thereby extended through multiple successive owners.

Some of the activities of stewardship already exist. Secondary markets, for example, are widespread—charity shops, online auctions and jumble sales—and for some products, household-to-household exchange is thriving: for example, in some countries, the majority of baby equipment is procured through these informal arrangements.[4] Some legacy companies also already retrieve, refurbish and resell products, alongside new models: we can already buy repurposed computers, kitchen appliances and cars. For

3 https://www.dualit.com/products/classic-toasters, accessed 6 August 2016.
4 Sales of pre-owned prams, for example, account for about seven out of ten pram purchases in Sweden (Mont *et al.*, 2006).

those companies, making the leap from being primarily a manufacturer to primarily a remanufacturer may not be quite as daunting as it might initially seem. But, nonetheless, most retailers today only sell new items. The challenge for the retailer-steward is to expand secondary and tertiary markets to include as many user-owned items as possible, retilting the share of new and pre-owned product sales in favour of the latter. For items for which a secondary market does not yet currently exist, selling pre-owned items creates an additional revenue stream for these companies; for items already "informally" exchanged once their owner no longer wants them, "re-retail" enables retailer-stewards to capture the second-sale income currently lost to their first, and only, customer (this is a loss from a business perspective only; whether a sale is "formal" or "informal" is neutral from a resource perspective, and clearly preferable to premature disposal).

We have gone slightly ahead of ourselves; before creating a secondary or tertiary market, the retailer-steward must retrieve the object from its first owner, once she no longer derives value from it. Ways to do this include *deposit* or *buy-back schemes*. While these schemes represent a cost to the retailer-steward, they must be weighed against the revenue generation opportunities presented by secondary retail. Before this secondary retail happens, the retailer-steward will take on maintenance and reconditioning, or, if need be, could return the object to the manufacturer-steward for further work. This would require buy-back and sell-back schemes, between retailers and manufacturers.

These retrieval mechanisms, product conditioning and other "re" activities are likely to be costly for both retailers and stewards. But, if these schemes can be made to work financially, they are likely to carry environmental benefits. The opportunity to "sell the item back" could coax customers into purchasing particular, frugal products (in the world where objects are not yet all frugal)—perhaps even if they come with a higher initial price tag. It helps avoid household hoarding of products that sit idle (not producing any benefit for their owner), and lose value as they become outdated, as well as reducing the likelihood of premature disposal.

But buy-back or deposit schemes are not guaranteed ways to reduce resources either: removing the responsibility of disposal from the end-user or creating an income opportunity for her through buy-back may create a product rebound effect and could lead to further sales, now that customers are safe in the knowledge they can simply sell back objects once they tire of them. There is also another obvious limitation to buy-back or deposits of user-owned items: the very fact that they're user-owned suggests that ownership is integral to job performance. A newly-wed would no doubt be less than delighted to find out his wedding ring has been purchased with a buy-back option . . . The scope for retrieval options for user-owned items, and therefore the possibility of secondary and tertiary markets, should not be overestimated. Figure 5.2 illustrates possible products and revenue flows for user-owned items.

Figure 5.2 **Possible product and revenue flows for user-owned items**

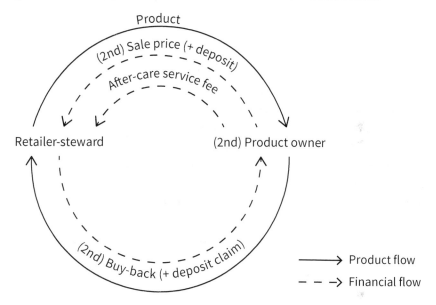

Product stewardship activities both help create the slow, circular economy, and the cultural context required for its acceptance

So why are product stewardship activities so important for the economy-in-Planet? As we saw in Chapter 2, once resources have entered the socio-economic system, sustainable production and consumption requires a radical change in the way resources circulate in the economy, from the fast linear flows of the legacy economy, to slow, circular ones (Chapter 1). There has been much interest, and research, in how these resource flows can be supported through "circular or "resource sufficiency" business models (see e.g. Bakker, *et al.*, 2014; Bocken and Short, 2016). Here, I would like to suggest that these flows are most usefully thought of as *product* flows, and that the business models that support these flows are models for *product sufficiency*: more specifically, for product longevity in this chapter and product shareability in the next. We use resources to make artefacts, we experience resource use through artefacts (I think of a washing machine as such, and not as a particular configuration of steel, porcelain, plastic and so on); it is therefore preferable to think of artefact rather than resource journeys when we think of the slow, circular resource motion required for sustainability. For objects, this means replacing the legacy journey that typically runs from manufacturer to rubbish bin via retailers and consumers, with one that yo-yos for as long as possible between manufacturers, users, remanufacturers, and secondary and tertiary users. By thinking of objects rather than resources, we more clearly identify the resource-saving opportunities of product longevity. We think of "freezing" a resource in its particular product form before recovering and reusing any materials for its next "embodiment". Since the conversion process to the next object is not energy-free, and the quality of the materials degrades at each "conversion", retaining objects in their current form for as long as possible puts the "slow" in "slow circularity", and this slowness further reduces resource use. So, significantly, the slow cycle of product stewardship activities and their supportive business models create *circular* artefact lifecycles. Established economy-wide, these cumulatively create the slow circular resource flows required for a sustainable socio-economic system. This is the opposite of what is created through "traditional" manufacturing and sales activities, where the lifecycles of all legacy products together create the fast, linear resource flows characteristic of the legacy economy (see Figures 1.3 and 5.1).

In addition to the "real" resource impacts of stewardship activities, these activities have the added advantage that they can help drive the social durability of objects. They do this by making interventions that lengthen product lives part of our lived experience of consumption. For example, retail of pre-owned items by "regular" retailers as standard would help to normalise the purchase of second-hand products, reducing any social stigma attached to purchases from "dedicated" pre-owned outlets. Thriving secondary and tertiary markets would also help redefine our cultural norms around product ownership through supporting the idea that value can be derived from an object as second or third owner—not just as first. Product stewardship of an object can help create product debounds (see page 55) by making the longevity of *other* objects more socially acceptable.

To make product stewardship activities possible and effective requires overcoming significant logistical, organisational and cost hurdles

In a sustainable economy, today's manufacturers and distributors will be product stewards instead. But the practical and commercial difficulties of the transition from one to the other, and the continued viability of product stewardship, should not be underestimated. In fact, these challenges in part explain the slow progress toward the circular economy, despite widespread policy and business support for its principles.[5]

First, the logistics of product stewardship activities and the slow circular motion of objects that these create are mind-boggling. We're talking here about the physical motion of goods from steward businesses to their customers and back, again and again—for maintenance activities, refurbishments, repairs, remanufacture, resale. This to-and-fro of goods calls for both a complex system of logistics and processes, but also *reverse infrastructure, reverse supply chains*—as well as a massive administrative effort to manage the whole thing. It requires a huge reconfiguration of supply chains for activities across the product's circular lifecycle, with radically different supplier relationships. Second, as well as the administration required for complex supply chains, another, equally burdensome, effort is needed to manage the relationship with the customers or product-users. To keep track of products during their use phase also requires keeping track of customers. Managing such an ongoing relationship necessitates a relational rather than transactional approach to exchanges with customers—an approach that is time-consuming and costly, with no guarantee of a future sale. This relational approach also requires an internal culture of service, which is unlikely to exist, say, for a manufacturing firm seeking to develop a service-based maintenance and repair offering. In fact, unsuited organisational culture is often identified as one of the key barriers to the adoption of stewardship activities (Martinez *et al.*, 2010).

Cost is the third major barrier to the implementation of product stewardship activities. The logistical and administrative efforts—haulage, infrastructure, supplier and customer relationships—certainly do not come cheap. To these must be added the costs for product refurbishment and remanufacture, which currently usually outweigh the cost of manufacture

---

5 The European Union for example adopted its Circular Economy Package in 2015 (European Commission, 2015).

from scratch. There are also the significant costs associated with use-phase extension, achieved through maintenance or repairs. Partly because of global wage differences in the legacy economy and the low price of resources, maintenance delivered by staff located close to customers is usually more expensive than new products made by cheap labour abroad. This results in widespread customer preference for new purchases over product care services. Offering extended product warranties merely shifts the cost to the business, which faces the same price problem: in the legacy economy, since replacing a manufactured product is often cheaper than repair, broken items tend to be replaced rather than fixed, even when the product is under warranty. To overcome customer preference for replacement of faulty products over maintenance, repairs could be included in the cost of the product, or spares made available as standard. But this higher cost will need to be passed on to either the retailer-steward or the customer: either way, it's a hard sell.

Fourthly, the time-scales required for the extension of product lifetimes present their own set of challenges. Long-lived products, as we have seen, require a long-term relationship between company and customer. This relationship requires steward companies that are *themselves* long-lived. A product steward may provide an extended warranty for two years, or guarantee maintenance for three—but what happens after that? And what about deposits and buy-back schemes for items expected to last a decade? It is hard to know which companies will still be in business next year, let alone in ten years, so customers are likely to be rightly wary of paying more up-front for items that include the core product stewardship activities of maintenance fees or retrieval options. For such an offer to be attractive would require considerable customer trust both in the company's capacity to deliver on its offer in the long term, and in the *long-term viability of the company itself*. Providing this assurance for a smaller, younger company may be impossible. There may be an expectation of company longevity for an established player, with a long track record of success, in the legacy economy—but these are precisely the companies that are likely to have a "traditional" manufacturing and sales model. The question of time, central to the longevity of products (which is, after all, about reducing objects *over time*), is a massive challenge for both start-ups and incumbents.

One way to confront this challenge would be for the various stewardship activities to be taken on by different companies. Rather than one steward taking on all activities, separate companies could take on maintenance or remanufacture, for multiple manufacturer-stewards—thereby significantly increasing the chances that at least one company will be around two or ten years down the line to provide maintenance or take the object back. Multiple entities working on different parts of the stewardship puzzle is considerably more feasible than one entity managing, and following through a product from inception, to the cycles of use and reuse, through to materials recovery and disposal.

But, while more feasible, such an arrangement *won't* lead to long-lived products, the linchpins of slow, circular resource flows and the very goal of stewardship. The fact is that many businesses in the legacy economy are already engaged in what could be described as product stewardship-type activities. Cars can be purchased refurbished and second-hand, and plenty of garages offer maintenance and repair services. But these "stewardship" activities neither drive nor require long-lived products, which we would need them to do for cars that are as long-lived as possible. Why is that? When multiple companies take on different stewardship-type activities, many of the incentives for product longevity no longer exist. Manufacturers are not incentivised to make products that are easy to repair, if the repair fees accrue to an unrelated company—which is what happens when a local garage benefits from a broken-down car with no warranty. Retailers are not incentivised to sell products that could have a second life, if someone else will cash in on this second sale—which is what happens when cars that have fallen out of customers' favour are flogged on eBay. Product longevity requires clear responsibility for the life of the product to be retained by the designer and manufacturer that puts it into the world. To do this requires an *integration* of product stewardship activities, thereby avoiding the situation where incentives for extended product lifetimes are split among different companies: the problem of "split incentives", which prevails in the current automobile market, and in the fast linear economy more generally (Green Alliance, 2013). The easiest way to do this would be for product steward companies to take on *all* activities across a product's lifecycle—this can happen through buy-back arrangement between retailer and manufacturer-stewards (although, as we have seen, user-owned items are unlikely to be returned frequently). But this brings us back to questions of practical feasibility, and trust in a company's longevity.

There are, then, many hurdles for product stewardship to prevail over manufacturing and sales. We return to these, and strategies to overcome them, in subsequent parts of this book. But, first, we turn to the activities and models of companies distributing user-accessed items on the economy-in-Planet: product-access companies.

6 Product access

In the economy-in-Planet, many more objects must be available on a shared basis than in the legacy economy. In Chapter 5 we examined business activities at the use and retrieval life stages of sufficient, user-owned items; in this chapter we turn to these same stages for user-accessed objects. Companies engaged in these activities are *product-access companies*, and the boom in user-accessed items presents a considerable opportunity for them. Three types of companies that already exist in the legacy economy provide a blueprint for product access on the economy-in-Planet: *rental companies*, *service providers*, and *"platform companies"* of the so-called "peer-to-peer" economy. The customers of these companies either derive benefits from objects *by using them themselves*; or, in the instance of services, benefits are derived when objects *are used as tools on the customer's behalf*. Consider, as alternatives to owning a lawnmower, either renting one from a rental company or a "peer", or using gardening services: in the first instance, you rent a lawnmower and mow the lawn yourself; in the second, someone does it for you. Either way, you end up with a freshly mown lawn without owning a lawnmower—creating a mower-shaped resource saving.

As the facilitators of *product access*, product-access companies have a significant role to play in a sustainable economy, which we examine in this chapter.

Reducing resource use requires increasing the number of objects available on a rental basis or through service provision

For customers, the logic of product access can be compelling. Sometimes owning stuff is just more hassle than it's worth: it costs a fortune, always seems to break down, and takes up way too much room. In these instances, renting provides the benefits of ownership without its cost and inconvenience. Rental of items or spaces that are used only occasionally, or where the value to their user declines significantly after first use, or over a certain amount of time, makes a lot of sense: DVDs (not so fun second time round), wedding dresses (ditto) or video games. Within these broad categories— "expensive", "a hassle", "of declining value"[6]—plenty of items are suitable for rental. Some are rented for use at the customer's leisure "offsite"—cars, bikes, lorries—while others are used "onsite" and the customer comes to them: at gyms, other recreational facilities, or co-working offices, customers rent both the space and the equipment. While many rental companies already exist in the legacy economy, their share in the overall provision of goods must be much greater in the economy-in-Planet. This presents a major threat to retailers, but a tremendous opportunity for rental companies. For some items, the case for ownership remains—and these are brought to end-user owners through retailer-stewards (as we saw in the previous chapter)—but many more user-accessed items reach their users on a rental basis. Rather than the sale price, customers pay a rental fee for one-off access, or a subscription fee for access over a defined time period: product-access companies have a *model based on use fee*. The preponderance of rental companies over retailers is a further defining feature of a sustainable production and consumption system.

The transition to such a system is, fortunately, supported by current social and technological conditions. GPS-enabled smartphones, for example, can help customers locate products they may want to rent, and provide real-time information on their availability (particularly useful for cars and vans). Cultural changes may also support a renting trend: credit card culture, for example, may have encouraged the idea of "having it all now", making renting products more desirable than saving up for many years for the same item. Ditto for changes in work patterns: the rise of the independent worker, for example, is supporting the increase in desk-sharing spaces and shared

6 See examples from Botsman and Rogers, 2010.

business facilities. Furthermore, increasingly urban populations are creating the customer density rental businesses need. With such trends, the prognosis is promising for the expansion of rental companies—and for product shareability. In addition to "traditionally" rented objects and spaces, such as cars or office space, many more items, retailed in the legacy economy, could potentially be rented. New York City-based Rent the Runway, for example rents special-occasion dresses for a fraction of the price of ownership—for an item that will most likely only be worn once.[7] For household customers, opportunities exist for renting sporting equipment, household appliances, and children's toys; for businesses, machinery and specialist equipment. In fact, *all* user-accessed items, and especially those that are pricey, used only periodically, a hassle to own, or of diminishing value after use, ought to be rented rather than owned.

Rentals often refer to short-term access to goods; longer-term access, counted in months or years, is usually referred to as a lease. Commonly leased items in the legacy economy include household cars, manufacturing and industrial machinery, and commercial vehicles. Leasing of business equipment, especially high-tech and specialised equipment, is also common in the legacy economy—Rolls-Royce engines, for example, are often leased rather than sold to airline companies.[8] Leasing is usually considered a good way to promote the longevity of products, and there has been much interest in exploring how to expand these leasing models to household customers. The theory is as follows: as product-access companies retain ownership of the product as assets for use in their value-creating activities, they have an incentive to chose the most durable objects available, and to maintain them and use them to the end of their lives, which, all going well, should increase the lifespans of artefacts. At the same time, while leasing may incentivise good care of assets by businesses, there is no such incentive for care by the product user (in fact, quite the opposite, since the items aren't theirs). Perhaps more damming for leasing models' potential contribution to product longevity is a competing view, born from observation of how leasing works, in practice rather than in theory: Far from driving the extension of product lives, leasing enables companies *already trading in durable goods* to take these off the market, and replace them, before the end of their useful lives. Leased cars, for example, may have a *shorter* lifespan

---

7 https://www.renttherunway.com, accessed 10 September 2016.
8 Rolls-Royce and Partners Finance: http://www.rrpf-leasing.com/about.aspx, accessed 3 March 2016.

than owned cars, if it is more lucrative for companies to scrap an older, functional model, in view of leasing the latest version. In other words, leasing models enable companies with "traditional" sales-based models to *solve* the problem posed by durability (Waldman, 2003[9]). Clearly not what we had in mind . . .

To make sure leasing drives artefact longevity would require designing a leasing model with product lifetime extension as an explicit goal. But examples of companies to point to are few and far between. Mostly, leasing, especially among households, is simply a financing arrangement for customers who cannot afford to buy an item outright. At the end of the contract, rather than refurbishing and re-leasing it to their next user-owner, rented items are simply sold, or, worse, discarded. But the pioneering company should not give up on leasing just yet as a driver of resource sufficiency. Pioneering leasers are committed to long-term ownership of the object, have a strategy for re-lease to multiple successive owners, and prioritise remanufacturing, reuse, and recycling at the end of the product's life.[10] Critically, revenue is generated from the leases (or *use fees*) of the successive owners, rather than treating the initial lease as a pre-payment for a sale. If these conditions are met, leasing activities may be a conduit to resource sufficiency.

For some items, accessing the benefits of the artefact through a service may be preferable to a rental or lease. All service providers share a basic model: they own products or tools, which they use to perform a job for their customers. Often, using the tool requires specialist skill (a dental drill); or using the product is tedious (a vacuum cleaner); or both. Providers charge a service fee, which needs to cover the cost of the tool, maintenance, storage and labour costs; their business model is *service fee based*, and can include one-off transactions or subscriptions. Short-term services are similar to product rentals; but, in addition to a product, you also get a service provider to do the job for you. Using the tool on your behalf (because you don't know how to, or don't want to) is the value proposition. And, through using the same tool with multiple clients, the benefits of artefacts are reaped by many without the need for individual ownership, thus achieving resource savings.

There are important caveats: the planetary impact of a service is contingent on the tool, and the service delivery. Services are not environmentally benign per se—think of aviation—and there is significant opportunity to

---

9 Thank you to Tim Cooper for mentioning this study to me; and the limits to leasing models as a mechanism to promote product longevity.

10 These conditions for a successful leasing model are identified in Mont *et al.*, 2006.

improve the delivery of existing services in the legacy economy by making them more resource-efficient and sufficient. For example, many services, such as cleaners or dry-cleaners, use toxic chemicals, which could be replaced with less harmful alternatives. To support absolute resource reduction through services requires both choosing tools that are frugal (that have the properties described in Part 2) and paying attention to the planetary impacts of service delivery (to which we return in Part 4). This chapter is less concerned with improving the resource efficiency of services (the low-hanging fruit of the economy-in-Planet) than with exploring how services could support resource sufficiency throughout the economy. They do this by making it possible for a single tool to serve multiple users, and the sufficiency gains can be considerable if this tool replaces numerous household-owned items. Therefore, provided the tool and the manner of service delivery are resource-efficient and sufficient, the service providers of the economy-in-Planet play a much larger role than retailers in helping customers secure access to product benefits, a further notable characteristic of a sustainable economy.

Product Service Systems (PSS) or "product services" are a hybrid of a lease and a service. They are billed as *leasing product job performance.*[11] In practice, the product "stays" with its user, who derives benefit from it; but the service provider retains ownership of the item. Since what is offered to the customer is "job performance", rather than the object itself, the deal includes maintenance, repairs, replacements and updates—all activities taken on by the service provider to ensure her customer can keep on reaping the benefits of the object's job well done. In return, the customer pays a subscription for services rendered. A famous example: Interface's EverGreen lease. Rather than a floor, the customer is offered "the job performance of flooring". As the late Ray Anderson, founder and Chairman of Interface Inc., puts it: "We sell only the services of the carpet: colour, design, texture, warmth, acoustics, comfort under foot and cleanliness, but not the carpet itself. The customer pays by the month. In this way we make carpet into a 'product of service.'"[12] In this model, the service provider takes on installation, and all necessary after-care services to make sure the floor remains in top condition. The ongoing maintenance commitment is similar to the servicing arm of retailer-stewards described in the previous chapter; the difference

11 There have been many papers written about Product Service Systems. See for example Mont, 2002.

12 Interface Resource Europe: http://www.interface-resource-europe.com/evergreen.htm, accessed 16 September 2016.

comes from the fact the service provider *retains the product as an asset* (i.e. it belongs to her, rather than to the user). It is also close to product rental; but, in the case of rental, the onus is on the customer to make sure the object performs its job satisfactorily, not on the rental business; in this case the product services firm is responsible for the performance of its asset.

In the legacy economy, Product Service Systems have been used successfully for business machinery and facilities. They require less up-front costs than purchase and, like rentals, can be more cost-effective, and less hassle, than ownership. Instead of a large capital expenditure (say to purchase new machinery), the firm has an ongoing operational expenditure (to lease machinery and have it maintained). Product services can save firms the drain of dealing with equipment, and enable them to focus on the core of their business.

As an amalgamation of a service and a lease, Product Service Systems have the potential to contribute to resource sufficiency by supporting both product longevity and shareability: lifetimes are extended through maintenance activities, and both tools and object parts are spread among multiple clients. Close attention must be paid to the structure of the lease, the financing arrangements and the tools used, to make sure resource savings are realised. Without careful design, things could go horribly wrong ... Smartphones, for example, could be considered a product service: an object performing the "service of communications". To access that service, users pay a monthly service fee, typically on a contract. Under this arrangement, the phone is usually "free"—or, more accurately, its cost is in fact hidden in the monthly service fee. This situation discourages careful use and maintenance by the customer, who has an expectation it will be replaced in a future contract: whereas in fact the handset is far from resource-use-free. But, provided product services are designed with resource sufficiency in mind, pioneering companies could further expand Product Service Systems with business clients, and launch them with household clients as well. PSS could be suitable for larger, functional household items, the "workhorses" of Chapter 4. For example, a household could purchase the service of refrigeration for a monthly fee (rather than purchase a refrigerator). The service provider would provide the household with refrigeration by supplying and maintaining refrigerators: first a compact refrigerator, then a larger one as the family grows, and smaller again for empty nesters. Selling refrigeration services rather than refrigerators themselves could avoid unnecessary, inefficient cooling (by keeping efficient refrigerators in use and taking inefficient ones out of use, and by providing customers with the most appropriately sized unit); and prolong a product's life (through maintenance activities if the unit breaks down and leasing to successive owners). Having said that, bar some quirky examples, such as leasing the "festive services" provided by Christmas trees,[13] household applications of Product Service Systems do not as yet exist, and we return to the significant obstacles to their implementation later in this chapter. For the moment, Figure 6.1 shows the product and revenue flows for user-access items, brought to customers by access companies engaged in rental or service provision.

Figure 6.1 **Products and revenue flows for user-access items of rental companies and service providers**

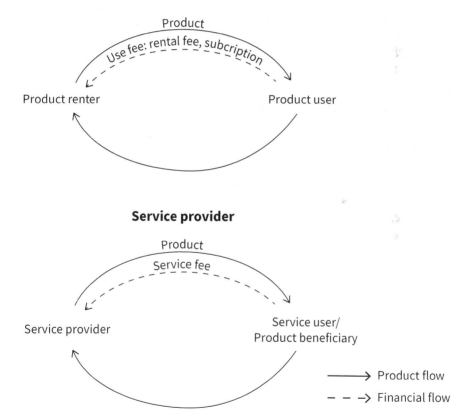

Rental company

Product

Use fee: rental fee, subcription

Product renter

Product user

Service provider

Product

Service fee

Service provider

Service user/
Product beneficiary

⟶ Product flow

--⟶ Financial flow

---

13 Living Christmas: http://www.livingchristmas.com, accessed 10 September 2016.

The platform economy could help increase the use intensity of objects through peer-to-peer exchange

Finally, in addition to rental companies and service providers, a new way of accessing goods on a user basis has emerged in the last decade, through the so-called "peer-to-peer" economy. While peer-to-peer access of goods and services remains marginal in overall economic activity, many proponents of the peer-to-peer economy are very excited about its potential. Companies in this space provide a digital platform for household product renters and service providers to meet with "peer" households, seeking objects or services. This "platform" is central to how these companies operate, and I therefore call these companies *"platform companies"*. Platform companies are essentially introduction agencies for the social-media, smartphone age: nothing new, but digitalisation has massively reduced the transaction costs of peer-to-peer exchange. It has also, crucially, created the space for user feedback on a huge scale; and this feedback, coupled with insurance guarantees offered by platform companies, has near eliminated the uncertainty and potential danger of doing business with strangers. Platform businesses then "sell" both introductions and peace of mind. All going well, if the introduction leads to a transaction, the company charges a commission; these businesses have a *commission-based model*. Unlike rental companies, the company does not own any "real" assets (at the bare minimum, it may simply require servers and an internet connection—and, of course, a strong brand). There are no costs associated with purchase or maintenance of objects. As such, peer-to-peer rental businesses are much cheaper to run than "traditional" rental companies, and are viable provided enough exchanges happen, and commissions are paid. For the customer, procuring an item or service from a peer via a platform business is likely to be cheaper than going through a "traditional" rental company.

When a person procures a good or service that she needs through a peer, a fellow "consumer", she engages in a process known as "prosumption" and becomes a "prosumer"—terms coined by Alvin Toffler in the 1980s (Ritzer and Jurgenson, 2010).[14] Prosumption refers to the ways in which people traditionally thought of as "consumers" also engage in the act of production, as "producers". It is therefore about a blurring of the acts of production and consumption. The dichotomy between the two may have been strongest

14 Thank you to André Reichel for highlighting the relevance of prosumption to my argument.

during the industrial era compared to other times in history (everyone's always done both), but the advent of digital technologies has enabled participation in the production of online media on a mass scale, as well as its commercial application. For example, thousands of travellers participate in online reviews of their accommodation—an activity that would previously have been carried out by a select, lucky group of hotel reviewers (Ritzer and Jurgenson, 2010). Platform companies are the latest iteration of prosumption: online production has spilled over in the real world, with peer "prosumers" engaged in activities that is usually considered the preserve of business.

At face value, the rationale for such prosumption and peer-to-peer market exchange is strong. Most of us have junk that sits idle most of the time: fancy kitchen gadgets, cars, sporting goods and tools. Peer-to-peer rental creates the opportunity to put them to good use. In theory, pretty much everything accessed through rental companies (or through a service provider) could also be provided on a peer-to-peer basis. This includes sporting goods, apparel, household appliances, food preparation, community gardening, travel accommodation, storage space, cars and workspaces. In practice, to date, peer-to-peer exchange hasn't taken off across the board in the way some may have hoped. It has been most successful in the rental of holiday rooms and the provision of car rides—and, to a lesser extent, dog-sitting services. Only companies engaged in these activities, in particular the ubiquitous Airbnb and Uber, have really disrupted the traditional rental models of hotels, guesthouses and holiday homes, and taxi services respectively—to the extent of threatening established industries. For all other products and services, examples of failed companies far outweigh success stories. Successful companies share the particularity that, whichever sector they're in, stakes are high and safety is key—letting a stranger into your home or car, or leaving Rover behind for a fortnight, are pretty high-risk. For these activities, the user feedback and platform guaranteed by the company help increase the confidence of all participants. Perhaps, then, the scope for platform businesses only really exists for high-risk exchanges—otherwise, once two "peers" have been connected, they may drop out of the platform, and any future exchange would simply become an informal arrangement among them. Moreover, the extent of the business opportunity for platform companies may be overly stated, since, unlike for other businesses, it is advantageous to both firm and customer for a single company to dominate its sectors—the benefit of the peer exchange comes through harnessing network effects and having a great number of fellow prosumers to choose and receive feedback from.

Despite the limited number of success stories, and unclear future scope for expansion into other goods or services, "peer-to-peer" enthusiasts often tout the environmental benefits of such exchanges (see e.g. Gansky, 2010). If households access the items they need from other "prosuming" households, this "collaborative consumption" should mean less stuff in the world, they argue. Or, in the language used in this book, the use of a product across multiple users drives its shareability, and resource use reduction potential (in fact, the peer-to-peer economy is also often called the "sharing economy"). In theory, peer-to-peer exchange supported by platform companies is all about using spare capacity—extra time, space or idle products (not dissimilar to those stationary German cars of Chapter 4)—and increasing the use intensity of objects. If a peer-to-peer rental or a service replaces individual ownership, a resource gain has been achieved: say, if I don't buy a car because I know I can easily use a peer-to-peer taxi service instead, or if peer-to-peer holiday room rental clearly avoids the need to build a new hotel. These positive impacts on resource sufficiency can, and could increasingly be, significant; but they must not be overestimated either. For starters, there is as yet no compelling evidence that the emergence of the peer-to-peer market has led to a decrease in individual ownership. Worse, it could create product rebound effects. The opportunity to monetise one's possessions afforded through these models may make us keener to purchase new goods—for example, buying a car specifically to become an Uber driver. To throw another spanner in the works of the "peer-to-peer" economy's potential: peer-to-peer rentals are the rental of user-accessed items *owned* by households . . . precisely the kinds of item that would no longer be commonly owned by household in a sustainable economy. So peer-to-peer exchange may be limited to very specific item categories after all: items and spaces that are usually in frequent or continuous use, but that could be exchanged when there is punctual spare capacity (such as holiday rentals); items and spaces where rental may smooth out "unavoidable" extra capacity (storage space, transport); or perhaps specialist or recreational equipment—products where there is an added value in meeting someone with similar interests (although this model has been tried and has failed, which shouldn't surprise us as these items are only occasionally used, meaning transactions are infrequent[15]).

---

15 See, for example, the story of failed start-up Gear Commons (Brown, 2016).

So, while platform companies could support sufficiency, the jury is still out as to whether we can actually expect fewer objects in the world as a result: the market for peer-to-peer exchange may remain small, and, even when it exists, impacts on resource use are inconclusive. Nonetheless, given their *potential* to increase use intensity, for the right product, the emergence of peer-to-peer platforms for goods and services may be a feature of sustainable production and consumption.(A note: this section has been about the business potential of platform companies in driving resource use reduction; in Chapter 12, we return to peer-to-peer exchange, and prosumption, conducted on a *non-profit-seeking* basis.) Figure 6.2 shows the product and revenue flows for platform companies.

Figure 6.2 **Product and revenue flows for platform companies**

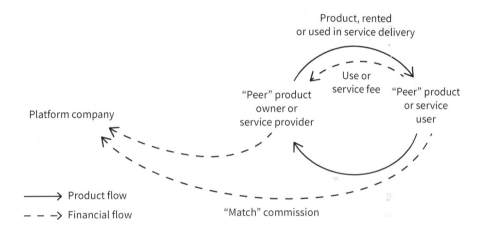

Product-access companies can make a significant contribution to increasing the shareability of artefacts, and support their retrieval for product stewardship

Rental and leasing companies and service providers have the potential to make a significant contribution to resource sufficiency in several ways.

First, while product access only has the potential to support the longevity of items, with careful design its contribution to product shareability is unambiguous. Since revenues are generated from the use of an item, product-access companies are incentivised to *find ways to maximise their use intensity*. For companies that rely on *use fees, service fees or commissions*, the more an object is shared, the greater the revenue. By avoiding a sales-based model, they have successfully aligned their commercial success with the resource reduction imperative. With a caveat again: should the company grow, and wish to serve more customers, it will clearly need *more* items to rent, lease or tools for service provision—requiring more, not fewer, resources. We return the question of company growth in Chapter 9.

Second, product shareability aside, perhaps the most significant contribution of rental, leasing and service provision to resource sufficiency is their ability to solve one of the central conundrums of product stewardship: how to ensure object retrieval at the end of the use phase. In the previous chapter, we considered how manufacturer-stewards could retrieve some user-owned objects from retailer-stewards through buy-back mechanisms, but this mechanism had clear limits. Retrieval of user-accessed items from product-access companies, on the other hand, has far greater potential. With many more user-accessed items compared to user-owned ones, manufacturer-stewards more often deal with product-access companies than with retailer stewards or individual customers. For these manufacturers, this means a shift away from producing objects for resale to end-users, and towards producing objects *for other businesses* for use in their own rental or service provision activities—a considerable departure from what usually happens in the legacy economy. The relationship between manufacturer-steward and product-access company has the potential to make a significant contribution to object longevity and stewardship activities. This is because business-to-business transactions readily support alternatives to sales-based models (as we have seen, for example, with business-to-business leasing of engines, in the legacy economy). Rather than selling items to business customers, *leasing* is often a better alternative for both parties: rental companies and service providers lease items from manufacturer-stewards, and then re-lease them in the delivery of their own product-access activities for customers, before returning them once value can no longer be generated from them. Manufacturer-stewards can then conduct any necessary remanufacture, before re-leasing to a second customer.

A product leasing arrangement between manufacturer-steward and product-access company presents three major advantages. First, since the ownership of objects is retained throughout their life by manufacturer-stewards, incentives are not split in a way that dilutes the case for object longevity (this is the problem of split incentives we encountered in Chapter 5); on the contrary, it is entirely in the manufacturer-steward's best interest

to design durable objects, with all the features that would support longevity—ease of disassembly, remanufacture, replacement of parts and so on. It
is, after all, she who owns the object, derives value from it, and who will be
carrying out "re" activities, so the cheaper and easier the better! But, at the
same time, multiple product-access companies can perform the customer-
facing business of product access, a setup that is likely to make access on
a wide scale much more feasible. Second, while the buy-back mechanism
of the previous chapter encourages the return of items to manufacturer-
steward, a leasing model *guarantees* the retrieval. Retrieval is what makes
the cycle of product stewardship activities possible; and any mechanism
that supports it is therefore making an integral contribution to the slow,
circular motion of artefacts and resources at the heart of the sustainable
economy. Figure 6.3 shows the product and revenue flows for user-access
times between manufacturer-stewards and product-access companies.

Figure 6.3 **Product and revenue flows for user-access items between
manufacturer-stewards and product-access companies**

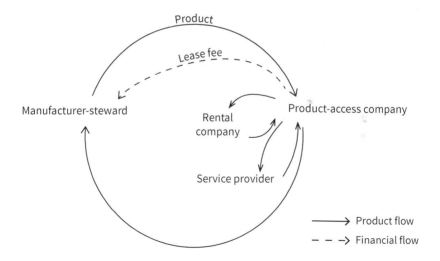

Third, like product stewardship activities, product-access models have
the potential to create product debounds; in their case, by normalising
the experience of product sharing. Not only do product-access companies increase the use intensity of user-access objects, they also support
the necessary cultural change required to increase the number of objects
considered user-accessed (mentioned in Chapter 4). This is significant. For
example, leasing of items usually owned in the legacy economy may help

to attenuate the value of ownership typically assigned to objects by their users (thereby increasing the types of items commonly regarded as user-accessed). Peer-to-peer car ride sharing (through Uber and others) has helped to normalise the idea of "shared use mobility", and users of these services are also more likely to increase their public transport usage (American Public Transportation Association, 2015). By making getting into a car with a stranger acceptable and widespread, something that ten years ago was considered dangerous, the platform companies of car ride sharing may therefore be contributing to the shift to a world where household car ownership is no longer the norm—or when cars are commonly considered user-access items. But, as always, a note of caution: we can expect product-access companies to normalise user access; equally, product-access companies could have unintended effects. For example, holiday peer-to-peer room rentals may help save on hotel costs, both financial and environmental, but, in doing so, they may also help support and normalise frequent travel, with its raft of resource impacts.

Developing financially viable product-access activities and supportive models requires overcoming considerable operational and ethical challenges

Product-access activities share many of the challenges faced by product stewards—but there are more of them, and they're on steroids.

Product-access companies are engaged in activities that are complex and varied. They own (or lease) and maintain objects, deliver items or services to customers, track objects and retrieve them, and begin all over again. These activities, and the logistical and operational complexities involved in them, are similar to some of the activities of product stewards—except product-access companies have to do these much more often, for each rental or service delivered. A first difficulty, then, is to generate sufficient revenue to cover the logistical and managerial expenditure associated with owning, or leasing, and maintaining assets (platform companies sidestep both the logistical difficulties and costs since "peers" own the rented objects or service tools). Service providers face the additional expense of labour costs—which can be considerable for highly skilled work or for product servicing, where ongoing maintenance is part of the offer. The high cost of labour for service delivery, which must often happen where the customer is located (typically in the Global North), in part explains why Product Service Systems have remained largely academic, despite some promising company pilots. In fact, all product-access companies in the legacy economy, whether service providers or not, are hampered by high labour costs in the place of product use, relative to low labour costs in countries that manufacture objects (where resource costs are also low). This has created low barriers to product ownership, which is often more cost-effective, and sometimes easier, than repeated rentals—clearly creating a challenge for rental and platform rental companies. To overcome customer preference for object ownership, and make product-access companies attractive, would require a change in the relative cost of purchase and rental.

As for product stewardship, longer-term leasing and product service models (such as the refrigerator example) require companies that are themselves long-lived, since the ability to offer continued job performance *over time* is part of the offer to customers. If the company goes bust, you may find yourself out of a fridge. Customers would therefore need to have considerable trust in a company's long-term prospects to enter into a leasing and product servicing relationship with it. Again, as for product stewards, this is likely to favour incumbents that have stood the test of time over start-ups. But the incumbent companies of the legacy economy mostly have manufacturing and sales activities, and are ill equipped to transition to product-access activities instead. While there are some examples of legacy companies that have successfully developed a leasing or servicing arm—Xerox, for example, has famously moved from being a printer manufacturer to a provider of printing services (Raval, 2013)—mostly, companies can't really "shift to services". Moving, say, from being a car dealership to a provider of taxi services would require a complete overhaul of company operations. So while we know product-access companies play a central role in the distribution of goods and provision of services in a sustainable economy, the complexities are considerable both for start-ups wishing to set up product-access companies, and incumbents wishing to transition from manufacturing and sales activities to rental or service models.

Finally, uptake of product-access activities, especially at the scale required to support systemic change to consumption and production, poses some significant ethical problems. We could easily imagine a world where a tiny minority of consumers own their products, with the remainder owning nothing. And serious ethical and legal cracks have begun to appear for platform companies. Rather than facilitating access to objects on a mass scale, the most striking feature of peer-to-peer rentals, especially of space, may be its role in exacerbating social inequality. In areas where holiday rentals are particularly lucrative, property is being purchased specifically to rent out on Airbnb—not exactly fulfilling the "sharing economy" promise of spare capacity utilisation, but instead diverting capacity into high-cost, short-term rentals, with a raft of negative effects on the affordability of housing (Woolf, 2016) (and no clear benefits on resource use). In other words, under some conditions "sharing" merely creates further income opportunities for those with existing assets, or for those in a position to acquire them. The relationship between platform companies and the "peers" performing a service through them has also come under scrutiny, with multiple cases brought before the courts in Europe and the United States (Osborne, 2016). "Peers" providing shared taxi rides can often start to look a lot like employees of the platform company, yet do not reap any of the benefits of stable employment. The platform company keeps its costs low—and profits high—while contributing to the casualisation and unreliability of work for many of its "independent contractors". This is far from the founding "peer-to-peer" or "sharing" ethos of many platform companies: in fact, the term "gig economy" is being used with increasing prevalence to reflect platform companies' unwelcome contribution to the precariousness of work. (We return to this issue in Chapter 10.) With a professionalisation of these platforms, the notion that peer providers are "prosumers", imagined as "normal" consumers also engaged in *some* productive activity, falls away, and the platform becomes more of a marketing channel for the providers' livelihood.

But even when peers are more readily identifiable as what we think of as "consumers"—say households occasionally renting out their spare room—we're still not out of the ethical woods. Commercial prosumption leads to consumers taking on a significant amount of work that would usually have been taken on by company employees, essentially for free: be it writing reviews, or for, non-professionalised Airbnb hosts, maintaining a room, changing sheets, making breakfasts and so on. Most of the risk, and most of the work, is transferred to the peer; while the platform company reaps the reward. We return to this problem in Chapter 12.

As I mentioned earlier in this chapter, platform companies (certainly in their profit-seeking incarnation) may remain relatively marginal in overall product access on the economy-in-Planet. But much more prominent object and rental providers also come with their own, serious ethical concerns. To generate the greatest reduction in resource use, all items that could be user-accessed should be. If this approach is taken to its conclusion, we end up with product users and service beneficiaries, businesses and households alike, who own very few objects of their own. An economy in which the majority of goods and services are procured on an access basis through renting or services creates a destitute, vulnerable "consumer" class, with few possessions to their names. Instead, product-access companies, or the product steward if a leasing arrangement is in place, retain both control and formal ownership of objects. This arrangement may help solve the problem of product retrieval, but it creates a much more intractable ethical problem, raising the question of *who owns* the objects we rely on for comfortable lives, across society. We return to this problem in Chapter 10.

With careful design, product-access companies can play a critical role in promoting resource sufficiency by increasing the use intensity of objects (and, to a lesser extent, by supporting their longevity) and a pivotal role in product stewardship through product retrieval. Pioneering companies, then, if not manufacturer- or retailer-stewards, are in the business of product access: rental, leasing, services, platform introductions. But many practical and serious ethical challenges must be overcome to make product-access activities possible at scale, to which we return in Parts 4 and 5.

～

In Part 3, we examined how the pioneering company supports the longevity and shareability of artefacts by aligning its revenue model with carefully designed product stewardship and product-access activities. These models and activities, summarised in Table 6.1, are necessary to make sure long-lived and shareable objects deliver on their resource sufficiency promise. We could in fact say that products must be designed so as to enable them.

While we have identified six alternatives to obsolescence and unshareability driving sales-based models, product stewards and access companies will most likely not have one or the other, but multiple revenue models, reflecting their multiple activities. A retailer-steward, for example, may generate some revenue from slow-sales, some from after-care services—and may even develop some product-access activities, making some objects available on a use-fee basis.

The activities of product stewards and product-access companies paint a picture of the ways in which business activity in the economy-in-Planet differs from activity in the legacy economy. In the economy-in-Planet, manufacturing is a very small part of overall goods and services related activities, largely replaced by the re-activities of product stewardship. The benefits of many different classes of objects are delivered through access rather than ownership, meaning retailers are marginal compared to rental, leasing and service provider companies. Manufacturers and remanufacturers, then, often have product-access companies rather than wholesalers or retailers as their main clients. For some objects and services, there is also some peer-to-peer exchange, supported by platform companies. This exchange comes through a process of prosumption, leading to a greater blurring of the acts of production and consumption compared to the legacy era.

Cumulatively, from a resources perspective, the activities of the pioneering companies create the slow, circular resource flows central to a sustainable economic system. Products remain in use, and in the economic system for as long as possible, used by multiple users at the same time or successively—dramatically reducing resource use. This process is illustrated in Figure 6.4, which shows both the product and financial flows of product stewardship and access companies (illustrated separately in several previous figures).

The role of product stewardship and product access in bringing about the economy-in-Planet makes the uptake of such activities, and supportive business models by pioneering companies (and indeed, by *all* companies), an urgent priority. I am not alone in saying this, and product stewardship and access activities have been called for by business leaders and

Table 6.1 **Product sufficiency business models**

Revenue generation model	What is it?	How the model drives longevity or shareability	Risks/limitations
Slow-sales	Sales of fewer, longer-lasting objects	Minimises the need for future replacement	Does not challenge sales-based model User may discard product prematurely
After-care service fee	Fee for maintenance of user-owned items	Extends the use phase of the product	Customer preference for new rather than repaired items
Secondary sale	Sales of objects to second and subsequent users	Extends the use phase of the product trough multiple successive users Contributes to the social acceptability of pre-owned items	Customer preference for new rather than pre-owned objects
Use fee	Fee for use of rented or leased product	Maximises the intensity of use of an object Contributes to fewer owned items and the acceptability of user access	Mixed evidence regarding leasing and product longevity
Service fee	Fee for service rendered	Tool used across multiple users	Nature of the tool and means of service delivery key to resource impact of service
Commission	Commission for introduction of peers for rental or service provision	Objects used across multiple users for rentals or service delivery Limited planetary impacts of delivery Contributes to fewer owned items and the acceptability of user access	Risk of rebounds No evidence as yet pointing to resource savings

Figure 6.4 **Product stewardship and access activities, products and financial flows**

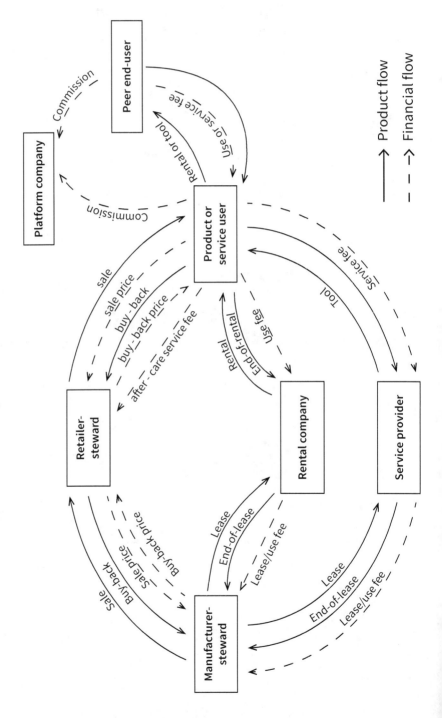

policymakers for several decades—albeit couched in different language, most recently within the framework of the "circular economy".

But the logistical, organisational, ethical and cost barriers to the widespread adoption of product stewardship and access activities continue to prove insurmountable—and there is no reason to believe the situation will change. Observation instead points to fundamental contradictions between the way companies are currently structured and operate, and what would be required for product stewardship and product-access activities to succeed. The high hopes of the circular economy cannot be realised through an attempt to superimpose "circularity" on companies that have taken shape in the era of linear production. Failure to address wider operational and structural changes required in legacy-era companies for product stewardship and access activities is the stumbling block of most circular economy enthusiasts.

Could companies be designed in a way to overcome the current impossibly high barriers to wide and swift implementation of product stewardship and product-access activities? We start tackling this question in Part 4, where we examine how the judiciously designed operations and workplaces of pioneering companies could help make product stewardship and product access possible.

Part 4

Operations and supply chains

Operations are the processes by which supplier inputs are transformed by technology and labour to create goods and services; they are what firms do on a day-to-day basis; they are the mechanism by which value is created.

In Part 3, we examined the type of activities and revenue models that would create durable and shareable products; this part discusses the "how" behind a company's activities. For all companies, minimising operational and supply chain costs is critical in ensuring their goods and services remain competitive. For the pioneering company, operations and supply chains must also be designed to serve two further goals.

First, while the operations and supply chains of many companies in the legacy economy took shape to support product manufacturing and sales, the pioneering company must, naturally, have *operations and supply chains that support product stewardship and access activities*. Operations and supply chains must serve the slow, circular, rather than the fast, linear economy. Second, to improve the resource performance of goods and services, the pioneering company must have *operations and supply chains that are themselves conducive to resource use reduction*. This is because the resources expended in a company's operations and throughout its supply chain for the creation of a good or the delivery of a service are themselves embodied in the object or service. Operations and supply chains, for example, will determine the planetary impacts of a service, including all aspects of its delivery, such as the resources embedded in the tools; storage and transport of the tool; energy expended during tool usage; and so on.

So how should we think about resource efficiency and sufficiency in the context of operations and supply chains, and what would it take for them to be supportive of business activities for resource sufficiency? These are the questions we turn to in Part 4. In Chapter 7, we first examine the importance of operational location and its consequences on the scale of operational units; in Chapter 8, we consider approaches to mixing technologies and labour to support resource reduction goals.

7 The case for proximity and appropriate scale

Significant logistical, ethical and cost hurdles have to date forestalled the uptake of product stewardship and product-access activities. Overcoming these operational hurdles, or, better still, circumventing them altogether— requires designing operations specifically to support activities for product sufficiency. As we'll see in this chapter, such operations must be carefully sited and scaled.

Product stewardship and product-access activities often require proximity between company and customer

The activities of product stewardship and product access require plenty of object to-and-fro: from business to customer and from customer to business and back again. Rental products are hired, used by customers and returned; tools used in service delivery make the same journey, accompanying the service provider. Objects are retrieved for maintenance and remanufacture, before being released or resold. Product stewards and access companies create objects that move around and around. This *particular* pattern of object motion is central to a sustainable economy—it is slow and circular, as opposed to the fast, unidirectional travel of objects in the legacy economy. The change in object trajectory is one of the *defining* changes that heralds the transition from legacy to economy-in-Planet. Crucially, the slow, circular motion of artefacts *cannot happen in an economy of distance.* And, as bad luck would have it, distance is a distinctive feature of the legacy economy. Distance is in fact the underlying cause behind the insurmountable operational barriers that have forestalled progress toward the slow circular economy.

Today, there is much talk of the "global village". Goods for the European market are manufactured in Chinese factories, and services to British customers are provided out of Indian call centres. Distance between company and customers is *seemingly unimportant* to the legacy economy. The "elimination" of distance is the culmination of the process that started in the 19th century, when technologies including the telephone, the telegram and the container ship, and the fossil fuels to power them, massively reduced the cost of transport and communication. The pace of economic globalisation has picked up even more since the 1980s, most recently supported by the Internet. Many would argue that the Internet has also "eliminated" time, by making global communication nearly instantaneous. It's fast, and cheap, for companies to engage with customers on the other side of world. As for oil, it is so plentiful, and such a bargain, that moving goods (and people and services) around the globe is now the norm in our globalised world. So with distance and time "conquered", what matters in siting operations is finding the *cheapest possible option,* often through "outsourcing"; and faraway locations are usually the answer, since the cost of transport and communications are negligible relative to other operational costs, including resource inputs and labour. These faraway locations make sense in the legacy economy; they are at the same time only really feasible for most companies because of the linear motion of travel of objects: from production in the cheapest country possible, to consumption or use in a wealthier market (followed by disposal at the local dump, with some waste exported back to poorer countries from whence it came—usually for landfill. But these later stages of the product's lifecycle tend to fall on municipal authorities to manage, rather than the companies that created, or imported, and sold waste-producing objects.) So, in addition to low cost of transport and cheapness of overseas labour and resources, the linear system of production lends itself to distance—indeed, to a great extent it relies on distance.

But global operations and the distance to markets served by companies pose two serious, even insurmountable, problems for the slow circularity of objects. First, the conquest of distance thanks to cheap haulage may be cheap for *individual* companies, but it is certainly not planetary impact-free. The climate impacts of the huge amounts of fossil fuels required for moving goods around the world are staggering. Transport, both of people and of freight (to which must be added transport infrastructure), relies almost entirely on fossil fuels and represents 15% of global emissions.[1] And this is in a production system where object motion is largely unidirectional! In a system where object motion is circular, the planetary impacts of transport and complex reverse infrastructure required for object retrieval prior to all the re-activities (Chapter 5) would be unacceptably high, if the distances of the legacy economy remained. These would need, for example, to be carefully weighed against the resource efficiency gains of remanufacture. In an *"economy of distance"*, it is likely that the resource benefit rationale of product stewardship would come crashing down. Second, even parking the somewhat major issue of climate-change-inducing haulage, the spatial organisation preferred by fast linearity is completely different to what would best support, or even be required, for slow circularity. Many of the activities of product stewardship and product access are unlike the activities of "traditional" manufacturing and sales in that *they happen in the same location as product use* (Chapter 5). And distance between point of use and a company's operations—and the time it takes to overcome said distance, when travel cannot be replaced by a digital exchange—threatens the viability of the pioneering company's activities. Thinking of product stewardship, if a manufacturer-steward were located on the other side of the world from her customer, chances are any maintenance or repair work would simply be too onerous—in cost, time, difficulty, logistical complexity—to make it worth its while. These complexities in fact add up to the operational barriers hampering legacy companies' transition to more circular models (Chapter 5). While distance and time do not matter for the unidirectional travel of objects from one factory to hundreds of thousands of customers, the same cannot be said for the multidirectional activities of retrieval and return, and remanufacture across continents, countries, jurisdictions. If your appliance breaks down and it's under warranty, chances are the manufacturer will send you a replacement, rather than attempt repair or retrieval (creating yet another dreaded linear product flow!). And unless spares are effortless to procure and repair technicians immediately available, this replacement is likely to be preferable to the customer than the "stewardship activities"

1 United States Environmental Protection Agency, Global Greenhouse Gas Emissions Data: https://www.epa.gov/ghgemissions/global-greenhouse-gas-emissions-data.

of repair. Therefore, a company must often be around the corner to make stewardship an attractive value proposition.[2]

Distance is also a key barrier for the user-access models of product rental or service delivery—or, to say this another way, proximity is a key requirement for these activities: accessing artefacts that way *must* be simpler than purchasing them for these models to work. No one wants to travel hundreds of miles to rent and return, say, an outfit for a special occasion—or wait and incur hefty delivery charges. User-access businesses are simply not a serious proposition for prospective customers if they involve time and hassle. For all the talk of the "global village", the "elimination" of distance and time only really "works" in the legacy economy: for companies engaged in "traditional" manufacture and sales, using one-way trade routes, and benefiting from cheap transport costs. Distance and travel time that cannot be digitalised pose a problem when planetary impacts matter, and are inconsistent with slow circular production and consumption.

To function properly and to reap the resource savings for which they are intended, business activities supportive of product sufficiency often require nearness between product-steward and product-access companies and their customers. Whereas distance travelled by artefacts is not a material issue for the businesses of the legacy economy, pioneering companies *must find ways to minimise the distances travelled by objects* to make its product stewardship or access-based value proposition attractive to customers, and its delivery supportive of resource use reduction.

The minimisation of distance travelled by objects has important implications for the siting of business operations. These distances are smallest, naturally, *when company operations are located in physical proximity to customers, close to the location of the product's use phase.* Not all facets of a company's operations have this nearness requirement: only the customer-facing activities that consist of the motion of artefacts (since we are pursuing the minimisation of distances travelled *by objects* specifically): objects for sales, rental, leasing, or tools used in service delivery. Other business functions can happen from afar—marketing, strategy, support functions, or service delivery that can be digitalised. But the part of the business that deals with "real stuff" that customers touch and feel and that cannot be dematerialised, the artefacts of Part 2, are often best located close to the customer (you can order but not send a fridge over the Internet).

---

2 As we saw in Chapter 4, ease of repair is a key consideration when designing long-lived objects.

Just how close should company and customer be? We can say that a company would be *too far* from its customers when *distance* threatens the viability of product stewardship and access activities; and when the environmental burden of object transport and transport infrastructure would negate any resource saving achieved by these activities, compared to traditional manufacturing and sales. More specifically, the optimal distance will depend on the object "in motion" and the business's activities. Some examples: companies selling user-owned items with little or no maintenance requirements will not need to be as close to their customers as those selling objects that require frequent servicing—think sofas versus computers. The former items may well travel just once from retailer-steward—and ideally, back, for retrieval at the end of its first life or for material recovery. The latter may need to be taken to a retailer-steward frequently for after-care services; or service providers (such as IT consultants), along with their tools, may need to travel to the product end-users to conduct this after-care in situ. Proximity is likely to be far more important for user-accessed items than for user-owned ones. There is *plenty* of object movement in rental and service provision, and, to a lesser-extent, leasing (leased objects "spend" more time with their user than their rented counterparts): to customer and back again, and again, and again. Product-access companies must therefore usually be close to their customers. Note that this does not apply to platform companies at all: the customers themselves, exchanging goods and services, must be close, whereas the platform company can be on the other side of the world. This helps make platform models particularly suitable in areas of low density, where other types of product-access businesses are unlikely to be commercially viable, lacking a critical mass of customers. In general terms, the business activities that thrive within the economy-in-Planet—the re-activities of stewardship, rental, servicing and leasing—are precisely those that are likely to require nearness. (As we saw in Part 3, manufacture "from scratch" and retail have a much smaller role to play in the overall distribution of goods and services, and commercial platform companies will also remain relatively marginal.) The extent to which a company's operations must be located close to its customers depends on its value-creating activities: on the nature of objects exchanged, rented or used in service delivery; and on the frequency of object motion.

The operations of the pioneering company are often dispersed and appropriately scaled

Proximity requirements, when strong, have a significant bearing on the scale of operational units.

When distance simply *does not matter* (as is the case in a linear production system with bargain transport thrown in), commercial imperatives usually drive business activities towards concentration into larger and larger operational units. Why? To be competitive, a business must reduce the unit cost of production of its goods and services. One way to do this is through economies of scale. Economies of scale refer to a common phenomenon in production, where increase of production volume is associated with a decline in the unit cost of production—because the fixed costs of production are spread more widely across units. A factory assembling televisions will require the same machinery (fixed cost), whether it produces 10 or 10,000 televisions (which individually require further inputs, or variable costs). Increasing the volumes of production through economies of scale can enable a business to produce competitive products—a rationale that also holds true for service delivery, since the fixed costs of running a café are the same regardless of how many cups of coffee are sold. Economies of scale usually drive companies to concentrate their operations, with a minimal number of large sites producing as many goods and services as possible. In the legacy economy, few, gigantic operational units are the order of the day—perfectly suited for linear production models, but a high barrier for slow circular ones.

But what of the situation where distance *does* matter—where there is a case for proximity? The delivery of goods and services close to customers requires many more operational units than would be required by concentrated units to perform the same job. Compare a bakery in every village with a centralised bakery serving a number of localities: all villagers still get bread, the difference is how far bread (and people) travel. With a much smaller output than their centralised, concentrated alternative, the village bakeries close to their customers will themselves necessarily be much smaller. They simply do not need to be as large; they would not be viable that way, and some of their productive capacity would remain unused. Nearness to customers, therefore, often requires numerous, "smaller" operational units. I use the term *"dispersed operations"* to describe those that happen close to point of consumption and that are common in an *"economy of proximity"*; in contrast with the *"concentrated operations"* that prevail in the economy of distance. With resource use in mind, dispersed operations have a decisive advantage over their concentrated counterparts: they facilitate product stewardship and product-access activities—that's why they ended up dispersed in the first place! Moreover, while we have so far focused on resource use, there is also a strong argument that dispersed operations, through their number and location, can help build the resilience of local economies—the pioneering company's third challenge (Part 1).

Dispersed operations create risks of resource inefficiency through duplication of operations and supply chains

But these operations are not without their problems. Each dispersed unit may be smaller than its concentrated equivalent, but will require duplicate resource use: each of the nine bakeries requires its own bricks-and-mortar shop, its own equipment, its own ovens and its own supply chains. The legacy economy-of-scale case for concentration also holds true for resource efficiency. The same mechanism that reduces the cost of a unit of production—using the same machinery to produce many products rather than multiple machines for the same output—can also generate resource savings, by limiting the overall number of machines (again, this mechanism also applies to services). By avoiding duplicate machines, the link between economy of scale and resource efficiency is especially strong in capital-intensive sectors. On top of this, economies of scale may generate further efficiencies through the consolidation of supply chains. Concentrated operations require far fewer journeys between suppliers of production inputs and operational sites than their dispersed counterparts: the transport inefficiencies generated by, say, a timber merchant supplying timber to a dozen small operations rather than to one consolidated operation are potentially significant. Having said that, the resource efficiencies and inefficiencies linked to transport in the supply chain may be more relevant in a linear system of production, dominated by manufacturing and sales activities, than in a circular one, which requires a reconfiguration of supply chains for activities close to customers (Chapter 5)—product stewards may not require timber as often, if they are remanufacturing tables rather than building them from scratch. Much like the case for customer proximity, the extent to which an argument in favour of concentration, to avoid the planetary impacts associated with duplicate supply chain journeys, holds true depends on the type of business activities. There are also other factors beyond the control of those seeking to design resource-efficient operations that partly determine operational location and scale—both in the legacy and in the economy-in-Planet. Sometimes, technologies cannot be "dispersed"—a massive chemical plant can't really be replaced with a series of little chemical "ateliers", however well located. Other times, the siting and scale of operations will be determined by the location of energy or material inputs: there isn't much flexibility in the siting of an oil rig or mine, for example, and wind turbines require serious hat-blowing locations.

While in the legacy economy, it's usually "the bigger the better", in the economy-in-Planet company operations are often much smaller. But it's not necessarily the case that "the smaller the better": instead, operations must be appropriately sized, carefully weighing the resource implications both of the operations themselves and supply chains, and of the business activities they support, and factoring any technological or location-specific constraints. Once these factors have been taken into account and balanced, there is such a thing as an *optimal, appropriate* scale for the operations of the pioneering company: the one *beyond or below which scale itself starts to undermine the pioneering company's absolute resource use reduction ambitions.*[3] The scale of a company's operations, then, is no accident: it is designed to achieve this resource-specific goal. Table 7.1 summarises the factors that support smaller scaled and dispersed operations and those that support larger-scaled and concentrated operations.

The operations of the pioneering company are therefore often close to customers but sometimes further away, often smaller but sometimes larger, dispersed or concentrated—whichever location and scale best supports product stewardship and access activities, while paying close attention to the resource inefficiencies that dispersal risks. Since business activities for product sufficiency contribute to absolute resource use reduction, while concentrated (or "less dispersed') operations support resource efficiency only, the pioneering company must, if possible, solve the tension that may arise between "sufficiency-supporting dispersal" and "efficiency-supporting concentration" in favour of dispersal. To do this without creating undue resource inefficiency requires designing operations and supply chains that are themselves low in resource use, and to which we now turn.

3 See Kohr, 1977 for a discussion on critical and appropriate scale.

Table 7.1 **Factors that support smaller-scaled and dispersed operations and those that support larger-scaled and concentrated operations**

Factors that support smaller-scale and dispersed operations	Factors that support larger-scale and concentrated operations
Stewardship activities for objects that require frequent purchase or maintenance activities	Stewardship activities for activities infrequently purchased or that require little maintenance
User- access activities, especially of objects that are frequently rented or services frequently accessed	Platform companies
Companies' activities primarily happen at the product's use phase	Opportunity to generate environmental efficiencies of scale through consolidated sites and avoidance of duplicate supply chains
Infrequent inputs from suppliers into company operations	Inflexibility of location due to natural resources
	Technologies cannot be replicated at a smaller scale

8 The case for worker-centredness

Once operations are optimally sited and appropriately scaled to support activities for product sufficiency—without undue environmental inefficiencies—the pioneering company must focus on the resource footprint of its operations and supply chain. To minimise it, it must choose specific, efficient and sufficient machines, while paying close attention to the nature of the workplaces that these machines create.

Machines exist to create goods and deliver services, and determine the nature of the workplace

A company's operations consist of labour, or workers, and technologies, or machines. Using machines, workers transform production inputs, including materials, energy, and intermediate and finished products procured through supply chains, into the goods and services used in value creation. Operations then, are a process of *transformation*, as shown in Figure 8.1

More about machines. By "machines" I am referring to all the equipment, ranging from laptops, to vehicles, factories and tools, that help workers produce customer-ready goods and services. Machines exist to get a job done: the production of goods and services. Defining machines in this way makes it clear that they are, themselves, artefacts: the human-made objects of Part 2, created to perform a specific task for, and with, their user: specifically, the creation of goods and services with workers. As artefacts, machines embody

Figure 8.1 **Operations as transformation**

Supply chain inputs   **Transformation**

- Materials
- Energy   • Labour/workers
                                        +   Goods and
- Products   • Technologies/machines   services used
                                                            in value creation

resource use and they also often require further resources to perform their function. It is machines, as opposed to workers, that give a company's operations a particular resource profile. To make operations contribute to resource use reduction, then, is to choose to use particular machines supportive of that aim. This choice is complicated somewhat by two features of machines that make them distinctive in the world of artefacts. First, machines are distinctive in that they *exist to produce other artefacts* (and to deliver services, although most of this section is focused on those machines that produce goods). They have a direct bearing on what types of supply chain inputs are required for transformation and on the nature of the transformation process, shaping the resource footprint of the finished product or service. Moreover, their efficacy, or otherwise, in their role as artefact creator determines the volumes of *other* artefacts produced. Machines then determine the *type and the numbers* of objects (and services) in the world. Machines have a second particularity: they *create work, they determine the nature of the workplace*. While all artefacts require interaction with their user to perform their job for them (Chapter 3), the nature of time spent with machines is inherently different to time spent with other artefacts. It's work. Spending eight hours a day operating machinery in a factory is not the same as spending five minutes a day waiting for the kettle to boil. The interaction with the machine is repetitive, lengthy, time-consuming, often occupying most of its user's waking hours: it has a big impact on her quality of life. The nature of the task required by a machine has implications for someone's salary, sense of self-worth, social recognition and life satisfaction. Machines go a long way in determining whether jobs are "good" or "bad". The importance of this second distinctive feature should not be underestimated.

Industrial machines support high levels of labour productivity and output

When reflecting on how certain technologies, particularly machines, can contribute to resource use reduction, it is important not to lose sight of these two features. To see why, let's consider how the role of machines as artefact and workplace creators has played out in the legacy economy—and led to a massive increase in resource use.

The industrial machines of the legacy economy have driven the creation of legacy products; they are "to blame" for unsustainable consumption and production. These machines create the "wrong type" of products. Indeed, the goods (and the services that utilise them) that come from industrial processes embody significant resource use, with associated planetary impacts. This is because industrial machines are themselves born from processes that require substantial material and fossil fuel use; and usually require further considerable fossil fuel use for their operation. Moreover, the inputs transformed by industrial machines also come with a high environmental cost. The primary inputs used in transformation often include non-renewable, extracted resources; the intermediary products will themselves embody resource use; and these inputs will often be well travelled. In fact, the inputs of production in the legacy economy account, as an average across sectors, for some 60% of a company's environmental impact, compared to 40% that can be directly attributed to its own operations: supply chains cannot be thought of as peripheral to a company's operational footprint (Makower, 2013). The machines of the industrial era typically require inputs from ecologically destructive supply chains, often created with labour working in poor conditions; these inputs will be embodied, along with the machines used in transformation, in the final legacy good or service. And while far-sighted companies have taken action to improve their supply chains—for example, by mandating environmental and labour standards among first-tier, and even second- or third-tier suppliers—there are limits to the effectiveness of these approaches in driving standards, in the context of global, anonymous, untraceable supply chains.

In addition to producing the "wrong type" of artefact, industrial machines are, worse still, resulting in *too many* objects. Understanding why this happens requires examining machines as work creators. Machines and workers occupy the same place in the operational process. They are both "trans-formers" (Figure 8.1)—as opposed to the inputs that are "transformed" during that process.[1] In principle, this means that workers and machines are substitutable for each other (Daly, 2013), with operations varying in the extent to which they are *"machine intense"* or *"worker intense"*.

During the industrial era, the worker has been marginalised in the production process, occupying a far smaller share in the transformation process than in previous times. The increase in machine intensity at the expense of labour in transformation—the replacement of worker by machine—is one of the defining stories of the legacy economy.[2] At the early stages of the Industrial Revolution, the Luddites who rebelled against the loss of their jobs due to the textile machines taking over artisanal production were among the first exposed to that process. Unemployment today among the lower-skilled jobs is due largely to technological changes, or newer, better machines (as well as the outsourcing discussed in the previous chapter). Robots are predicted to "steal" 10 million low-skilled jobs in the UK in the next 20 years (*The Week*, 2014). Higher-skilled jobs are also no longer safe: professional services including medicine, accountancy and law are now threatened by their automated equivalents. There may be different explanations for the marginalisation of the worker in her share of the transformation process in the legacy economy, but a strong argument could be made that it simply boils down to cheap oil (and other fossil fuels). As we have seen, industrial machines require oil for their creation and operation. Fossil fuels transform the productive power of human labour: a single barrel of oil has been estimated to be the equivalent of 5,000 hours of human work (Klitgaard and Krall, 2012). While oil is readily available and cheap, often considerably cheaper than labour, it makes sense to substitute fossil-fuel-powered machines for workers, thereby reducing the cost of operations, boosting output, and making products and services more competitive. With far fewer workers required in operations, replaced by cheaper machines and fossil fuels, industrial transformation processes support high labour productivity. Indeed, labour productivity increased massively during the course of the 20th century. And it is these productivity gains of the industrial era that have led to the remarkable production of goods (and services) of the

---

1 Inputs may be physically transformed, and be unrecognisable in the finished output (such as a natural resource or intermediary object); or they may remain in their existing form (a laptop used in operations remains a laptop).

2 In the 1860s, humans and animals did approximately 95% of the work in the economy, and only 5% was done by industrial machines; 100 years later and these figures are reversed: industrial machines do 95% of the work of transformation (Chouinard and Stanley, 2012: 24).

legacy economy—industrial machine and fossil fuels have been astonishingly effective, *too effective*, in their job of artefact creation—leading to our unsustainably large planetary stock of legacy artefacts. At the same time, we shouldn't lose sight of the fact that, while productivity gains have led to planetary boundary-busting resource use, they are also—historically in richer countries, and to this day in poorer, "under-consuming" parts of the world—what have and continue to enable widespread access to goods and services, bringing material comfort and necessities to the many rather than the few. This accomplishment of industrial machines should not be ignored.

With such powerful machines and energy, the marginalisation of the worker in the transformation process makes perfect commercial sense; and work has taken shape around the "needs" of the machines, around technological capacity. For some jobs, industrial machines have led to the de-skilling of what were once skilled professionals (such as replacing seamstresses with factory workers). And, at their very worst, legacy products embody unethical, exploitative work, sometimes made in conditions akin to slavery.[3] But I do not intend to overly bash industrial machines. Many save workers from physical drudgery. The textile industry today, for example, often works with relatively low levels of capital investment and low levels of labour productivity: this is work that could be automated or taken on by machines, but instead relies on cheap, abundant labour, creating the archetypal sweatshops of the legacy economy. Machines also save workers a considerable amount of time; to achieve the same level of output with human labour alone would require far longer hours and often entail more arduous work: compare, for example, the labour requirements of pre-industrial and mechanised agriculture. Whether the marginalisation of the worker in the transformation process is to be mourned clearly depends on the nature of the work machines and oil are taking up on her behalf.

Industrial era operations and supply chains have a significant planetary footprint; and have led to excessive production of legacy artefacts, through transformation processes that are machine and oil intense and which have marginalised the worker. Put this way, it is clear that the pioneering company's "ideal" operations are to have the *opposite* character: a light planetary tread leading to the production of reduced numbers of frugal artefacts, through a reinstatement of the worker in the transformation process.

---

3 The Slavery Footprint project found there are currently 27 million people working in conditions of slavery, many to produce goods and services consumed in the "Global North" (Slavery Footprint: http://slaveryfootprint.org, accessed 30 September 2016).

But, while these "ideal" operations may meet the pioneering company's goal of contributing to absolute resource use reduction, they present some serious ethical concerns. The "ecological overproduction" of goods and services in the legacy economy is what has enabled material comfort; and, in many cases, industrial processes save workers from unacceptably difficult or dangerous work. The resource-reducing pioneering company's operations, then, come with a risk of immiseration to both product owners, or consumers, and workers—the two groups that have benefited from industrial machines' tremendous success at creating goods and services, and, in many instances, lightening workloads. In a way, the activities of pioneering companies as described in the previous part can be seen as a way to stave off the risk of consumer immiseration: product stewardship and access are mechanisms to retain the material comfort and benefits derived from artefacts, with far fewer of them in the world. The "right number" of artefacts in the economy-in-Planet is that which supports decent material comfort within planetary boundaries—achieved via goods and services that are brought through product stewardship and access models (and others, as we'll see in Chapter 12). This leaves us the risk of worker immiseration: to stave it off, the pioneering company must carefully consider the nature of the workplaces in its operations, balancing both its resource use reduction goals and its potential to create "good" over "bad" work.

The pioneering company's machines are efficient and sufficient

To think through what resource-use-reducing operations would look like, while countering the risk to workers associated with a greater share in the transformation process, it is useful to examine machines as artefacts—no less because we have, conveniently, already identified the properties that would make them *frugal* (Chapter 4). These machines are *resource-sparing* and *nature-inspired*: they embody minimal amounts of resource use and are, ideally, made of renewable materials, harvested at sustainable rate. They also require minimal energy use for their operation. Ideally, they are "fully" nature-inspired, using energy that is clean and renewable and generating no waste. With the larger share of a company's planetary impacts attributable to its supply chain, efficiency should also be sought in primary resources, and in intermediary or finished products used in transformation, by "pushing" resource efficiency down the supply chain, among first-, second- and subsequent-tier suppliers, through good procurement choices. Regarding sufficiency attributes, the pioneering company's machines must clearly be *durable*—a new tool for each new good or service is clearly a silly proposition, and would, besides, come with an unacceptably high resource cost. At the same time, the role of machines as artefact creators means that their durability can be a double-edged sword—they can sometimes "lock" companies into inefficient processes or products, which we return to later in this chapter (the nature of today's capital investment is what determines tomorrow's consumption). Countering the path dependency risk of long-lived artefacts (Chapter 4) is therefore particularly salient for machines. The *sharing* of machines among multiple different companies would reap significant resource benefits, avoiding duplicate, idle machines. But, with operations at the heart of a how a company creates a distinct and competitive offer, the sharing of machines may be commercially difficult, especially for those that would result in the creation of an identical good or service.

User-centredness, best described in the context of machines as *"worker-centredness"*, is a defining quality of the pioneering company's machines. The resource efficiency of the machine, as an artefact, can be improved by increasing the worker intensity required for its use (Chapter 4): the relative share of machine and worker in the transformation process is mutable. Clearly, this is not always possible—it's hard to imagine the flight of a plane or digital data management achieved through less-machine-intense processes. But, when it is possible, the job still gets done, using fewer resources and greater human input. Since this is the opposite to the legacy economy process of boosting labour productivity through greater machine and resource use, it also reduces the rate of output—thus reducing the number of artefacts (for machines engaged in the production of goods rather than services). With a legacy-era hat on, we would think of this outcome as a failure; but, since we're now after *fewer* artefacts, it is clear that we must rethink what constitutes an effective machine.

Increasing worker intensity, and therefore helping to meet its resource use reduction ambitions, the pioneering company must at the same time pay close attention to the *nature of the work* created by machines, both countering the risks, and seizing the opportunities, presented by the reinstatement of the worker at the heart of the transformation process. It must focus on the creation of "good" work—both in its own operations, and, as for environmental performance, throughout the supply chain. The nature of "good' work, the quality taken on by worker-centredness, will depend on the operations, and will vary in scope and potential depending on the technologies used. Worker-centredness, at its most basic, is about creating occupations that are safe, and pay a secure wage, enough to meet living expenses, while respecting labour rights.[4] At their best, these occupations also offer fulfilment by allowing the application and development of skills and autonomous working. These are the types of jobs that make use of the "appropriate technology" envisaged by E.F. Schumacher, or the "convivial" tools imagined by Ivan Illich: the former enable their users to "perfect their gifts and skills" and to collaborate with others; the latter stress the importance of enabling workers their "right to work with independent efficiency" (Schumacher, 1979; Illich, 2001).

It is worth noting that this focus on "good" work is not simply "a nice-to-have", a "perk" of the pioneering company. The Natural Step, pioneered by Karl-Henrik Robèrt, has constructed an authoritative science-based approach to sustainability. It identifies four system conditions required for a sustainable society: while the first three refer to environmental conditions, the fourth is a social condition: namely, a sustainable society requires that there be "no structural obstacles to people's health, influence, competence, impartiality and meaning".[5] In other words, "bad" jobs, those that pose a risk to the health and safety of their workers, and deny their workers a living wage, are a problem beyond the (already unacceptable) exploitation of the worker: they are also a threat to achieving sustainability. The meeting of human need is both the goal and a requirement of sustainability—and it can, in part, be supported by the worker-centred operations of the pioneering company.

So far, the operations of the pioneering company, its frugal machines and their worker-centredness, have been all rather theoretical: we spend the remainder of this chapter looking at what they could mean in practice, in the concentrated and diffuse settings of the economy-in-Planet.

---

4 The International Labour Organization sets global baseline labour standards (see Labour Standards: http://www.ilo.org/global/standards/lang--en/index.htm). The UK Living Wage Foundation sets a voluntary minimal hourly rate required for work to pay for living expenses (see What is the Living Wage? http://www. livingwage.org.uk).

5 The Natural Step, The Four Systems Conditions of a Sustainable Society: http:// www.thenaturalstep.org/sustainability/the-system-conditions/

The pioneering company aims to maximise the resource efficiency and flexibility of its concentrated operations

When the operations of the pioneering company are best concentrated (Chapter 7), these operations resemble in some ways those of companies in the legacy economy—but concentration can also be reinvented to serve the economy-in-Planet.

Like their legacy economy predecessors, the machines of concentrated operations often embody and utilise significant resource use—but the pioneering company seeks to reduce the resource footprint of its operations as much as possible. For example, its machines should be powered by renewable energy, with many areas generating their own energy requirements onsite. "Industrial ecology" approaches are used to minimise, or even to neutralise, the negative environmental impacts of operational processes (Duchin and Hertwich, 2003). Processes aim to "close the loop" by reusing materials and avoiding process waste. Particular attention is paid to sound sourcing of materials, with strict environmental and social criteria applied in supply chain management. These measures are sometimes improvements on existing processes, and can therefore be "retrofitted" to existing company operations: far-sighted companies of the legacy economy are in fact already aiming for zero waste generation, and implementing closed-loop manufacturing.[6] Lenzing, for example, an Austrian viscose manufacturer, has pioneered a close loop system for viscose production, generating minimal amounts of chemical wastes compared to "conventional" viscose.[7] In addition to process improvements, new technologies, such as industrial photonics, digital technologies and additive manufacturing (3D printing) are helping to make concentrated technologies more ecologically sound. For example, in additive manufacturing, digitally designed objects are printed straight into their desired finish form, avoiding waste that may be created in subtractive manufacturing techniques. These techniques are already being used in industries as diverse as medicine, construction, automobile and pharmaceuticals, either to print parts or finished items—including printing whole wings for planes, and limbs for surgery patients. With these new approaches, the pioneering company improves the resource efficiency of

6 See examples in Elkington, J. (2012). *The Zeronauts, Breaking the Sustainability Barrier.* London and New York: Routledge
7 Lenzing Fibres: http://www.lenzing-fibers.com/en/tencel, accessed 2 April 2016.

operations and furthers any resource benefits that may already have been generated thanks to their concentration (Chapter 7).

Sound sourcing and efficient operations lead to improved efficiency of the products created. Moreover, these mass-produced objects are often durable and identical, rendering them particularly apt for stewardship and access activities. But, while measures can support the "right" type of artefacts, concentration poses an artefact volume problem—all the more since resource sufficiency requires fewer objects overall. As concentrated machines require a significant initial financial outlay, a firm can find itself bound to produce a high volume of products (or deliver a high number of services) to recoup this capital investment—subordinating all other considerations to the logic of production volumes. (Furthermore, these machines can become environmental and financial liabilities as technologies improve and they fail to keep up with improvements.) These machines have trapped even the most far-sighted companies of the legacy economy in a manufacturing and sales model—their concentrated operations have made any meaningful shift to product stewardship or access nigh on impossible; it was simply not what they were built to deliver (they are also, of course, often too far from the markets they serve).

The risk of becoming locked in to inefficient and "unsufficient" products comes from concentrated machines' high resource and capital intensity—which renders them particularly *durable*. It is therefore particularly important for the pioneering company with concentrated operations to plan for *path independency*, prioritising "flexible" machines where possible (Chapter 4). For example, additive manufacturing supports the printing of multiple different digitally designed objects—whereas object shapes are limited in subtractive manufacturing by the machines designed to create them. But there is a further sufficiency shortcoming of concentrated machines: they cannot readily be shared. Commercial consideration aside, from a purely practical perspective, it would be hard for multiple companies to share machines that are few and far between, immobile and specialised. Concentration may result in efficiency economies of scale, but it also leads to sufficiency "diseconomies of scales".

A possible approach to reduce production volume would be through a reduction in working hours, possibly as low as the 21-hour working week, or through longer holidays.[8] Fewer hours of machinery operation would

---

8 See New Economics Foundation, 2010 for environmental and social benefits of the reduced working week.

clearly result in fewer resource inputs, and rein in production volumes. Moreover, the benefits to workers could be considerable, especially when concentrated machines are highly automated (as is the case with, for example, refineries or chemical plants), and when workplaces therefore provide more tedium than opportunity for skill development and autonomous working. Worker-centredness in that context may be more about creating the time and opportunity for fulfilment *outside* the workplace. But reducing working hours is not entirely straightforward either: it either means both environmentally and commercially inefficient idle machines; or more operators working shifts—creating high worker costs (and unsociable hours for the worker), and, besides, negating the resource benefits promised by shorter hours, if production output remains unchanged. And while both these problems could be solved through machine sharing, as we have seen, the sharing of concentrated machines can be impractical.

Dispersed operations may be the opportunity of our time for the pioneering company

Dispersal may help solve the problems of concentration—with more machines in more locations, they could more readily be shared than their concentrated counterparts. And, when shared, they weaken the resource efficiency argument in favour of concentration, which rests on the avoidance of duplicates (Chapter 7). Moreover, the machines of dispersed operations are less prone to the multiple lock-ins that come from the high cost and rigidity of their concentrated counterparts—simply because they are smaller and cheaper. And, of course, operational dispersal has the decisive advantage of enabling product stewardship or access activities more readily than concentration (Chapter 7). We can identify two types of dispersed operations: those where workers take on the bulk of the work of transformation at the expense of machines, and those where they do not: *dispersed, worker-intense* operations, and *dispersed, less-worker-intense* operations.

Dispersed, worker-intense operations rely on artisanal tools, many of which existed in some shape or form in the pre-industrial era: the hammer, the chisel and the spinning wheel. Inputs—timber, iron and the like—are also pre-industrial; energy requirements for transformation may be low. Supply chains may be relatively straightforward, with fewer inputs than required for more complex objects; and often prioritising regional materials—thus solving some of the challenges associated with complex, global sourcing. Together with their supply chains, these machines, low in embodied and use-phase resources, create products and services that are themselves resource-efficient, with small planetary impacts. Moreover, dispersed worker-intense operations result in low volumes of objects and services—and the rate of output cannot readily be sped up. These operations have the additional benefit that they lend themselves well to the creation of worker-centred workplaces, as envisaged by E.F. Schumacher or Ivan Illich: artisanal tools often require skilled, creative labour, and artisans may find their work fulfilling.

Contributing to resource use reduction, and with the potential to support worker-centredness, there is a strong case that goods and services that do not require industrial machines for production *ought* to be delivered through dispersed, worker-intense operations. With one very important caveat: unless the driver for increasing the machine intensity of the transformation process during the legacy economy was to save workers from intolerable toil. But assuming "good" workplaces can be created, and worker-centredness can be realised, it seems imprudent to "waste" resources, and planetary sinks and regulation, on machine-intense processes for goods and services that could be produced in a less automated way. These artisanal operations could provide us with many objects used in day-to-day activity, such as crockery, clothing or household furniture; or be used as tools by many providers of everyday services—restaurants, cafes, hairdressers, cleaners. We are in fact already witnessing something of a renaissance of artisanal production in the legacy economy—often in protest at industrialised production of identical goods and services. Vida Verde, for example, is a cleaners' cooperative in Boston, MA, which uses handmade cleaning products in its services;[9] the Oakland Makers is an organisation supporting businesses engaged in artisanal production and custom manufacturing in California.[10] The revival of artisanal production has also been supported through digital marketing channels, such as Etsy, which enables small artisanal producers to easily access global markets[11] (in that sense the production is not "dispersed" as described in this section, as it is not close to the market it serves, even if the technologies used are worker intense). But this

---

9 http://vidaverdethestory.blogspot.co.uk, accessed 30 September 2016.
10 http://oaklandmakers.org/mission-statement, accessed 30 September 2016.
11 https://www.etsy.com/uk, accessed 4 September 2016.

is all good and well for craft cider: what about goods and services that are not quite so "old-timey"?

Dispersed, worker-intense operations are as old as the economy itself; concentrated operations, through their scale and capital-intensity, share some commonalities with those of the legacy economy; but *dispersed, less-worker-intense* operations are currently emerging. These operations retain the dispersed nature of artisanal production, often yielding the same resource benefits—but with the potential to produce and deliver a much wider array of goods and designs. They have the potential to replace products and services hitherto delivered in concentrated setting, or complement them—without the resource risks that come from concentration. Dispersed, less-worker-intense operations may be the opportunity of our time for the pioneering company.

Machines in these operations are high-tech—digital technologies, robotics, additive manufacturing—but, unlike their concentrated counterparts, are suitable for small or medium-sized operational units. Decentralised, onsite power generation, using renewable energy sources, creates "clean" operations. For additive manufacturing, resource efficiency is further supported by the massive simplification of supply chains afforded by this technology: printers and energy aside, the only input required is printing material (ranging from plastic to metals, and from concrete to seaweed). The argument *against* dispersal based on the fact that resource efficiencies could be generated from consolidated supply chains no longer holds; in fact, the near-absence of supply chains has the significant advantage of precluding the numerous environmental and labour issues associated with them. Moreover, less prone to lock-ins than their concentrated counterparts, the machines of dispersed less-worker-intense operations may be the answer to both the practical and commercial challenges associated with the sharing of machines: with digital technologies, different companies could conceivably design their own products, but print them on machines held in common with other firms. They can also support "optimal" siting of operations: with decentralised energy and virtually eliminated supply chains, digital technologies enable most business functions to happen from afar, with *material* production only sited so as to best deliver product stewardship or access.[12] Further, these operations support worker-centredness—high-tech

---

12 This flexibility on location contributes to the blurring of production and consumption of the economy-in-Planet mentioned in the previous part, now that these activities do not necessarily happen in distinct locations, with consumption

machines may require specialist, creative skills for their operation. Start-up Lyf Shoes bills itself as a "digital cobbler": the company is hoping to revolutionise the shoe industry by enabling customers to choose digital shoe designs, or make up their own, to be printed in dispersed ateliers and shop floors, merging design, manufacturing and retail.[13] This consumer participation in the artefact production process is another example of the prosumption discussed in Chapter 6. While this customer co-creation creates a product rebound risk, opening the possibility of "mass customisation" of "conspicuously produced" items, these dispersed ateliers may also make a significant contribution to product stewardship. They could be ideally suited to the printing of replacement or spare parts, for example—supporting re-activities, and blurring of boundaries between manufacture, repair and remanufacture.

Table 8.1 summarises the suitability, characteristics and resource benefits and risks of three potential operations "archetypes" for the pioneering company.

The pioneering company's operations reposition the worker at the heart of value-creating activities

A few final thoughts on the operations of pioneering companies.

As we have seen, the operations of pioneering companies may be concentrated or dispersed, and more or less automated—the worker may occupy a lesser or greater share in the transformation process. A company's contribution to resource efficiency and sufficiency can be directly linked to the worker intensity of its transformation process. But running such operations, today, competitively, is a significant challenge. Artisanal production of goods and services (dispersed, worker intense) has long existed and continues to exist today. But, in the legacy economy, artisanal creation can only remain niche, since considerably cheaper industrial production methods exist: industrial machines pretty much monopolise our economic activity.[14] As we saw in Part 3, the current mismatch between labour and resource

traditionally imagined to happen in the home, and production in the factory or office.

13 http://lyfshoes.com, accessed 29 September 2016.

14 The monopoly of one technology over another is the situation Ivan Illich calls "radical monopoly" (Illich, 2001).

Table 8.1 **Pioneering company operations archetypes**

Name	Concentrated	Dispersed, worker-intense	Dispersed, less worker-intense
Suitability	When case for dispersal is weak Suited for the manufacturing of user-access goods or infrequently accessed services	Suited to many everyday goods and services that preceded the industrial era	Suited to products that cannot be produced artisanally Suited to many stewardship activities Suited to services, including those requiring high-tech equipment
Machines and energy	"Traditional" industrial machines New technologies Energy-intense	Pre-industrial, artisan's tools Low resource intensity Low energy input	New technologies: digital, robotics, additive manufacturing Low energy inputs
Supply chains	Potentially complex, global	Simplified supply chains Often, local and regional sourcing prioritised over global sourcing	Ranging from complex to potentially virtually eliminated (for additive manufacturing)
Work	Skilled, technical Operator, automated	Ranging from unskilled to highly skilled	Skilled, creative, technical, automated Customer co-creation
Resource benefits	Could generate environmental efficiencies of scale Scope to minimise impact through industrial ecology approaches	Low-impact operations, supply chains create resource-efficient products Low production volumes	Resource-efficient compared to concentrated setting Supports stewardship activities
Resource risks	Resource-intense machinery Supply chain impacts Risks of lock-in to high production volumes	Likely to be better suited to user-owned items, weakening the rationale for dispersal	Additive manufacturing risks "unnecessary" production of objects

costs in the locations of stewardship and access activities and those of man-ufacturing presents a near insurmountable barrier for the uptake of prod-uct sufficiency activities. This cost differential constitutes the same barrier in the design of operations, affecting choice of technologies and the extent of their worker-centredness. There is no easy way to overcome this cost bar-rier: for the most far-sighted companies of the legacy economy, the choice is usually between remaining in a higher-priced, niche market, or moving toward cheaper industrial production, eroding environmental and social commitments, but reaching a much wider market.[15] Nonetheless, the pio-neering company must seek to develop the operations that will prevail in the economy-in-Planet, contributing to resource use reduction with frugal machines and worker-centredness—increasing worker share in the trans-formation process at the expense of machines.

Consequently, the pioneering companies could be seen as deliberately reversing the process of cost reduction achieved through increasing the capital intensity of operations and the productivity of labour. This strat-egy has prevailed in the legacy economy, and is therefore counterintuitive. But cost savings can only be achieved this way when materials and energy, especially fossil fuels, are available, and cheaper, than labour. In the econ-omy-in-Planet, on the other hand, conditions will be different: We will face availability constraints for some materials; we will be obliged to minimise and mitigate the environmental impacts of extraction and harvesting; and we will leave the vast majority of remaining fossil fuels un-burnt in the ground to avert dangerous climate change (Part 1). Worker productivity gains afforded by fossil-fuel-reliant industrial machines, then, are neither feasible, nor are they an unquestioned "good" to be pursued by business executives (and policymakers), in the transition to sustainability. Instead, we can expect a significant decline in the machine and fossil fuel inten-sity of the transformation process (as resource-hungry machines and fos-sil fuels become more scarce) and in the productivity of labour (as they become more expensive). This does not mean productivity gains will be lost across all sectors—and large-scale renewable energy, robotics and digital technologies may help counter the decline of fossil fuel energy and indus-trial machines. Nonetheless, the unprecedented labour productivity gains

15 Alternatively, larger players move into the market space of what were once niche products, but large scale may result in the loss of some of the original benefits. The organic food market is a case in point here: while organic foods were introduced to the market by small cooperatives, the bulk of organic food sales now happen in supermarkets.

of the industrial era cannot be sustained in the economy-in-Planet.[16] The operations of the pioneering company described in this chapter can be seen as pre-empting this decline in labour productivity: rather than designing operations that seek to maximise it, marginalising the worker in the transformation process, the pioneering company instead makes the nature of the work required in transformation central to the value proposition, be it taken on by artisans, operators or skilled technicians. Products and services are sold, in part, on the nature of the work used in their delivery (this is consistent with the service models to replace ownership that we described in Part 3). Operations are designed *to support worker-centredness*; goods and services are offered to customers, in part, on the basis that they come from worker-centred operations—making, for example, handcrafting, customised services, "good work", or even a reduced working week, a selling point. We already have examples in the legacy economy of such goods: fairtrade products are often not qualitatively different to their non-fairtrade alternative, but are sold to customers on the basis of enhanced worker conditions.[17]

To conclude, to contribute to absolute resource use reduction, the operations of the pioneering company must consist of worker-centred machines that lead to the "right" production volumes. But the challenge of prioritising frugal machines and worker-centredness in a way that is commercially viable, while industrial production is the order of the day, should not be understated.

$$\sim$$

16 It is interesting to note a paradox: while *individual* industrial machines have taken up the largest share of work in the transformation process (i.e. have replaced human labour), the *overall* productivity gains afforded during the industrial age have not, as predicted by many, freed the worker from work. Industrial-era productivity gains have, to date, supported the increasing production of artefacts and services, rather than increasing leisure time.

17 This strategy may be more effective during the transitional phase toward the economy-in-Planet rather than during its sustaining in that, in the latter period, all firms will be worker-centred. Nonetheless, how worker-centredness manifests itself from firm to firm will vary.

Company operations in the legacy economy serve fast linear models of production and consumption. Any consideration of the planetary impacts of these operations, including the material and energy intensity of the transformation process and the impacts of transport, tends to be an after-thought. Company operations in the economy-in-Planet must serve the slow circular economy, by making product stewardship and access activities possible and attractive. This often requires smaller-scale operational units located close to customers, or dispersed operations. To ensure the operations themselves contribute to resource use reduction also requires paying careful attention to the mix of machines and workers required in the transformation process. Machines are resource-efficient and, where possible, path-independent, and shared. Where technically feasible, and when the nature of the work required in the transformation process lends itself to the creation of a "good" workplace, workers are reinstated at the heart of the artefact production process or in the delivery of services.

Optimal operational arrangements vary from pioneering company to pioneering company, depending on how each firm weighs and reconciles manifold considerations, including the nature of their activities, the strength of the case for dispersal or concentration, available technologies, and the scope to create good workplaces. So, whereas in the legacy economy the vast majority of goods and services are produced and delivered in similar ways—through industrial processes that are material- and energy-intense—operations are far more diverse in the economy-in-Planet. Some are concentrated and gigantic, others are dispersed and smaller-scaled; processes are artisanal, industrial or near fully automated through robotics or digital technologies. Together, they add up to a system of production that is neither the robot techno-utopia imagined by those who have forgotten about planetary boundaries, nor the neo-artisanal world envisaged by those who too easily romanticise the pre-industrial era.

The diverse operations of the economy-in-Planet are designed to enable product stewardship and access activities. But, as we saw in Part 4, these activities come with challenges beyond the operational— that is to say, challenges that cannot be solved through refashioning operations. To solve these requires structural changes to companies, which we turn to in Part 5.

Part 5

Ownership structure, financing and legal form

The sustainable business literature is quiet on the issue of company owner-ship. Ownership is considered immutable; and, as such, not an aspect of a company that needs to be considered for sustainability. But this is a mistake. A business wouldn't exist without its owners; clearly, then, their identity matters. In fact, ownership has a decisive bearing on whether a company is likely to, or in a position to, adopt a sustainable course. Different own-ers have different priorities, seek different rewards from their business, set their company in different directions and put in place different governance arrangements to reflect these commitments. A company's ownership also determines the range of capital-raising options open to it, which may itself impact the feasibility of adopting environmental initiatives. The situation is the same with a company's legal structure: it is taken as a given, despite the fact that owners *chose* it among other possible legal forms for their venture.

If there are different types of owners and legal forms out there, with their particular financing opportunities, it is conceivable that some types are, for reasons that we explore in Part 5, more likely to be supportive of the activities and operations described in this book than others. It is also conceivable that the prevailing ownership and legal structures of companies in the legacy economy, and their financing arrangements, have had a hand in our current ecological predicament. If that were the case, we would need to think creatively about alternative structures that could instead support the work of the pioneering company.

While we identified three challenges for the pioneering company in Part 1, we have primarily focused on resource use in product and services, activities and operations. In Part 5, we broaden this to include the other challenges. And, while all the preceding chapters have focused on solutions, exploring pioneering companies, fit for the economy-in-Planet, Chapter 9 is an exception: in this chapter, we examine the role of today's shareholders, in particular those of the publicly traded corporation, in creating the legacy economy's unsustainability. But dwelling briefly on what's gone wrong is instructive. It helps us identify in Chapter 10 how other types of owners—*workers, beneficiaries, investors*—and alternative legal structures could be well suited to support the work of the pioneering company.

9 The problem with shareholdership in the legacy economy

[handwritten annotation: are they really owners?]

Although owners are not usually classified according to their relationship with the firms that they own, that is precisely where we will start. We can identify three types of owners in the legacy economy: *workers*, who are actively involved in the running of the companies they own; *beneficiaries*, who stand to benefit from the company's good or service; and *external shareholders*, who own a stake in private companies or in those traded on the public markets, public corporations. In Chapter 9, we first survey the legacy economy's three types of owners, before examining the unusual owners and structure of the public corporation, and its role in creating the unsustainable legacy economy.

Despite the fact the majority of firms are worker-owned, companies owned by external shareholders, especially the public corporation, dominate the global economy

Company owners who perform *the actual job* of product creation and service delivery, and all the associated activities that they require, I call *worker-owners*, and their businesses, *worker-owned* companies. Rather than simply showing up at an annual meeting (if that), worker-owners *are* the people designing, marketing and producing and delivering *their* products or services. The term "worker" here refers to anyone *directly participating in the work or running of the firm*, wherever the person may be in the company hierarchy, from forklift operator to director, or whether this person is a solo entrepreneur.[1] In the legacy economy, the overwhelming majority of businesses are at least partly, if not fully, owned by workers—the worker-owned company is by far the most prevalent type of enterprise by numbers; in fact, the owners of *nearly all* companies are involved in running them. At the smallest level, business owners can be self-employed, sole proprietors or in small partnerships. These enterprises often remain on a micro scale, often a one-person show—and owners therefore do all the work of their business as *entrepreneur-owners*. Many sectors are well represented by these micro-enterprises, including the building and other specialist trades, as well as professional occupations.[2] If business is good, those working alone may form small businesses and take on staff, therefore becoming *manager-owners*. Manager-owners continue to work alongside their staff. Such businesses can remain sole proprietorships, but more often will be limited companies, which create a legal distinction between company owners and their firms, and reduces owners' liability in case of losses. A far less common type of worker-owned company is that owned by its employees. *Employee-owners* either fully or partly own their company directly, as shareholders of their company, or indirectly, with their shares held in a trust. There are a few thousand such companies in the US, and a few hundred in the UK (Millstone, 2015) ; famous examples include Bob's Red Mill (Koopman, 2012) or the Scot Bader Commonwealth (Scott Bader, 1973). Worker cooperatives are a specific type of employee-owned company; they are fully owned by their workers, and run on democratic principles. There are many high ideals associated with worker cooperatives, but working examples are few and far between, numbering a few hundred in both the UK and the US (Co-operatives UK Ltd, 2012).

Another form of company owner, much rarer in the legacy economy, is what I call the *beneficiary-owner*. As its name suggests, this type of owner

---

1 Worker-ownership usually refers to ownership by employees; here, I expand the definition to include anyone with a hands-on engagement in the activities of the company.

2 Self-employment is at an all-time high in the UK, now representing 15% of the workforce. Office for National Statistics, Trends in self-employment in the UK. https://www.ons.gov.uk/employmentandlabourmarket/peopleinwork/employmentandemployeetypes/articles/trendsinselfemploymentintheuk/2001to2015.

is also the direct beneficiary of the company's product or service. Companies owned by their customers are often called "consumer cooperatives", and have a long history stretching back to the middle of the 19th century. Consumer cooperatives were founded to enable poorer customers to collectively bulk-buy goods and services that they could not procure individually. Like worker cooperatives, they are run on democratic principles. Such *customer-owned* companies are well established, and, although they have been in significant decline since their heyday 50 years ago, there are still over 30,000 consumer cooperatives in the US, and close to 3,500 in the UK, the most famous and largest being The Co-operative Group (Millstone, 2015). In addition to customer-owned businesses, a handful of companies are owned by a specific geographical community, with community members as sole or primary customers. These *community-owned* companies may be structured as companies limited by shares, or may wish to enshrine their service to community through another structure, such as the Community Interest Company (CIC) in the UK. Often, businesses come into such ownership when a venture performing a community service is set to close—such as a pub, café or bookshop—and local residents come together to avoid the loss of the amenity, issuing shares sold to community members. Other sectors suited to community ownership include utilities and energy. Community-owned businesses are very rare, but there are many initiatives to promote and support their development.[3]

While firms owned by their workers (as defined here) constitute the overwhelming majority of companies by number (and beneficiary-owned companies also exist, albeit in far fewer numbers), as they grow many of these companies become, at least in part, externally owned. This process of transferring ownership to external shareholders begins when a company seeks outside investment for the first time. In exchange for investment, the company issues shares that usually entitle their holder to participate in the governance of the company, and, more importantly, to a share of the profits. I call these equity holders *"external shareholders"* to emphasise that *they are neither workers nor beneficiaries*, are not directly involved in the work of the company, nor directly benefit from its products or services. Shareholders are, of course, often workers or beneficiaries; but here I seek to examine those shareholders whose relationship to the firm is solely investment. In most cases, external shareholders are at first friends and family—and for

---

3 See for example the Power to Change project in the UK. http://www. thepowertochange.org.uk, accessed 3 March 2016.

many companies, these will remain the only shareholders. But if a company seems to be on the road to success, it may start to attract professional investors, such as wealthy individuals (so-called "angel investors"). All going well, and as the company continues to grow and require financing, private equity firms or institutional investors may purchase a stake. What was originally a worker-owned company has become owned externally.

External shareholder ownership of firms is often considered the paradigmatic form of ownership in the legacy economy. This is in part because, despite the overwhelming majority of existing companies being largely or wholly worker-owned, most economic value is presently generated by the minority of companies largely or wholly owned by external shareholders (if workers or beneficiaries own shares, it is accidental rather than by design). These include firms owned by private equity groups, or, representing a greater share of economic activity still, publicly traded or public corporations, structured in the UK as a public limited company, whose shares are traded on stock exchange floors. In the UK, for example, 42 of the largest hundred firms are owned by private equity groups, while the few thousand firms traded on the London Stock Exchange contribute half of national GDP. (Hutton, 2012). Internationally, there are about 50,000 listed companies,[4] although their numbers are shrinking all the time as they consolidate; and the revenues of some of the largest are comparable to national economies (Dietz *et al.*, 2013).[5]

With such overwhelming sway in global economic activity, the publicly traded corporation is usually taken for granted, and its form (if not its practice) is largely unexamined and unchallenged by sustainable business advocates and environmentalists. Somehow, the public corporation, and some of its "iconic" companies and brands, seems part of the natural order of things. It's hard to even imagine a world without Coke. But looking at the corporation more closely reveals a number of peculiarities—seven to be precise—about its owners and their relationship to the firm that they own. These are worth examining as they have a direct bearing on the unsustainability of such companies, and of the economic system as a whole.

---

4 Econ Stats: http://www.econstats.com/wdi/wdiv___76.htm, accessed 30 March 2016.

5 While comparing company revenue to GDP gives an idea of the scale of companies, it is also somewhat misleading in that it is comparing company income to national value added. A more accurate comparison would be comparing company value added (i.e. company revenue minus cost paid to suppliers) to national value added (Roach, 2007).

First, a public corporation has *plenty* of owners. A corporation can easily have tens, if not hundreds of thousands of shareholders, spread around the world, remote from the operations or markets of their firm.

Second, whereas the overwhelming majority of businesses are directly managed by their owners, public corporations are not run in this way—not least because it would be impossible to have thousands of owners all having their say in day-to-day company activities. Instead, the public corporation separates owners and managers, with a professional managerial class running the show. While this model is often left unquestioned, it is, nonetheless, an anomaly: most business owners run, and want to run, their organisations to ensure they are run in their best interest.

But, thirdly, owners of public corporations don't actually need to be involved at all to be sure their businesses are being run for their benefit: the public corporation operates according to the doctrine of "shareholder primacy", which gives managers a fiduciary duty to run the firm in the interest of shareholders, which is understood to mean maximising the return on their investment (Stout, 2012). The public corporation is, then, legally structured to create shareholder wealth. FedEx Corporation, for example, has turned its mission statement into a direct statement of its managers' responsibility to: "produce superior financial returns for its shareowners by providing high value-added logistics, transportation and related business services".[6] What FedEx actually does, logistics and transportation, is a means to the end of shareholder value, rather than the other way round! So, safe in the knowledge of this fiduciary duty, why be involved in the running of the firm at all, when you can simply sit back and wait for dividends to appear? In fact, much thinking has been expended on figuring out how management-run firms should operate to best promote the interests of owners, in a context of separation of ownership and management (for example, often high-level managers are given small ownership stakes in an effort to align their interests with shareholders); arguably, this is why the discipline of "corporate governance" exists at all.

With so many shareholders, all with no real need to be involved in the firm, it is not surprising that external shareholders of public corporations have scant commitment to the companies they own. In fact, fourthly, shares in public companies are readily alienable, and are bought and sold on public markets—a defining feature of the public corporation. Holding stock in

---

6 http://investors.fedex.com/company-overview/mission-and-goals/default. aspx, accessed 5 July 2014.

a public company is often a purely speculative exercise, to be sold at the earliest opportunity, be it in the next few months or, worse, through high-frequency trading.[7] Most owners of public corporations are therefore best thought of as speculators rather than investors.

The situation is, fifthly, further complicated in that many owners of public corporations are indirect: the shares are held by institutions such as investment or pension funds rather than directly by individual, "beneficial" owners. In the UK, institutions, rather than households, own two-thirds of the shares traded on public markets.[8] Beneficial owners of the public corporation are unusually distant, removed from their company.

This distance, this institutional layer, leads us to the sixth particularity of owners of public corporations: many (or even most?) beneficial owners are likely to be unaware of their ownership stake.[9] These are owners who don't even know that they are owners, and yet "their" companies are managed on their behalf! They stand to benefit when times are good, and are not responsible when disaster strikes—it is managers rather than owners that take the hit when there's a catastrophic oil spill or industrial accident.

That beneficial owners are neither legally nor morally responsible for the actions of their companies is the seventh feature of the public corporation. Unaware of their ownership stake, lacking responsibility for their firm, the link between shareholder and public corporation is very tenuous indeed. In fact, in 2003, the UK's House of Lords upheld a 1948 Court of Appeal ruling which found that "shareholders are not, in the eyes of the law, part owners of the company" (Kay, 2015). So who owns public corporations? The answer, it turns out, is no one—legally, public corporations are a vehicle for the generation of financial returns to legal non-owners . . . a truly odd arrangement.

7 Two-thirds of trades in US stock markets are now high-frequency, as are 35% of trades in European markets (Hutton, 2012).

8 In comparison, the majority of shares were household-owned in the 1960s (Hutton, 2012).

9 Or, worse, these beneficial owners could be using the anonymity afforded by public corporations to mask criminal activity.

Public corporations' legal form and the character of their ownership create companies that have driven the unsustainability of the legacy economy

These seven traits of external shareholders of publicly traded corporations and of their relationship with the firms that they don't "own" after all, create companies that have distinctive features—and, as misfortune would have it for those of us interested in the economy-in-Planet, these features make it difficult, perhaps impossible, to support the activities and operations described in earlier parts of this book.

The amorphous mass of external shareholders scattered around the world in locations unknown creates companies that are un-anchored, with no relation to place. Lacking this commitment to any particular locality, these are precisely the type of companies whose operations are ripe for outsourcing to cheap, faraway locations—creating local economies that are vulnerable to "delocalisation" and making operations more or less incompatible with product stewardship and access activities (Chapter 7). Distant from the work of the firm, it is easy for owners, especially the furthest-removed beneficial owners, to not have environmental or social issues linked to "their" company on their radar at all. Ownership of a few shares traded in London seems unrelated to poor practices of factories in distant lands. In this context, the odds of, say, workplaces being worker-centred, or of manufacturing being resource-efficient, are very slim indeed. The lack of commitment to place extends to lack of commitment to the company itself; as we have seen, ownership stakes are short, shares traded frequently, accounting periods quarterly. This fosters a short-term outlook on firm strategy, both for shareholders and management. Sustainability, on the other hand, requires taking the longer view, and effectively integrating a time dimension into one's approach (see Introduction)—something a frequent turnaround of external shareholders simply cannot do. The lack of legal or moral responsibility attached to the shareholders of public corporations creates a further difficulty for sustainability, since they are not held to be directly responsible for any negative environmental or social impacts of business operations (at worst, for them, these impacts could affect business performance, with disappointing dividends).

But perhaps the most intractable problem caused by the external shareholders of public corporations, for the economy-in-Planet, is the imperative for company growth necessarily created by this ownership structure and by the public trading of shares. Right from the beginning, on flotation, the seeds of growth are sown. A public corporation is valued on the expectation of future profit, rather than the worth of its assets. Both individual and institutional shareholders (who have a fiduciary responsibility to their members for the value of their portfolios) are interested in, and expect management to deliver, growth for increased profitability and higher share price. "Shareholder primacy" and speculation on share prices ensures this pursuit of growth is sustained well after flotation: the public corporation, as we saw earlier, exists in law to maximise shareholder returns. And significant growth in financial value is a problem for the economy-in-Planet.

Instead, such an economy requires global steadiness in resource use, once current resource use has been sufficiently "shrunk" and the economy "resized" to fit within its planetary boundaries (Chapter 2). Company growth, while usually referring to financial growth, also requires growth in resource use: new tools, further materials and energy use for the production of objects and services. This is true regardless of the company's business model: even product sufficiency activities require more products to steward or lease if they are growing. Now this wouldn't be too much of a problem if only one company were growing. But the global economy is composed of millions of businesses all over the world: if they all, or many of them, or perhaps even just some of them grow, the global economy grows. And chances are this growth will happen (and, indeed, it's what has happened in the legacy economy), since the global economy is dominated by the public corporation, whose ownership and legal structure require it to grow. We are in fact in a situation of ecological overshoot in part because of the collective growth of companies—especially of public corporations.[10] In the transition to the economy-in-Planet, some companies may still grow while others shrink, but as a *group* will need to degrow until the economy has been "resized", after which, the same group will need to be "collectively steady" in their resource use. At the moment, while in global ecological overshoot, for owners of a pioneering company confronting their ecological responsibilities, the only "reliable" course of action is to opt out of their company's "share" of collective growth. This may all be a bit abstract but, in fact, we already have an idea of what kind of scale companies should be aiming for: as we saw in Chapter 7, there is such a thing as an appropriate, optimal scale for a company's operations, the one at which resource use is minimised both in activities and operations. Rather than an ownership structure

---

10 In addition to publicly traded corporations, privately held companies and state-owned companies, are all contributors to growth.

that drives growth, the pioneering company instead needs a structure that makes it viable at appropriate scale. And this is something that the public corporation cannot do—but is one of the key challenges for the pioneering company.

That the public corporation leads to such unsustainable outcomes should not really surprise us: with roots reaching back to the 17th century with public trading of shares but coming of age in the 19th with limited liability for investors, the public corporation as we know it today was created in the industrial era. A product of its time, it is a structure apt for raising the necessary capital for the resource-intense, concentrated, gigantic companies that suited the era of "unlimited" Planet, and the fast, linear business models that prevailed.[11]As a form, it also, during this time, came to dominate the economy, by extending its reach beyond the capital-intense, riskier sectors for which it is uniquely suited, with public corporations dominating all sectors, regardless of whether other forms of ownership could be equally, or better, suited for the delivery of goods and services (it is hard to see a rationale for publicly traded care home operators, for example). But times have changed. A company's ownership structure must now be a vehicle for resource use reduction, and support resilience and the viability of steadiness. It must support business models for product sufficiency, which have cost and revenue structures quite different to their fast, linear predecessors. Capital must be raised and risk shared in a way conducive to these new models (ING Economics Department, 2015). There is no evidence to suggest that flotation on the stock market is the way to support the pioneering company—quite the opposite.

There is, then, an *inherent* tension between the ownership model of the public corporation and the requirements of the economy-in-Planet. But what about the other owners of the legacy economy—workers, beneficiaries or shareholders of private firms—who, in fact, together own the overwhelming majority of companies? We turn to these different owners, and their effects on their firms' potential contribution to sustainability, in the next chapter.

---

11 Some would argue that the publicly traded corporation is, in practice, more about the generation of financial value than a vehicle to raise capital for investment.

10 Ownership by workers, beneficiaries and investors

To avoid the unsustainable outcomes described in the previous chapter requires moving to a system in which economic activity would be conducted by firms other than the public corporation. For reasons that we explore in this chapter, workers and beneficiaries, and, in some specific circumstances, external shareholders of private, non-listed companies, have the potential, as company owners, to support the background conditions required for activities and operations for resource use reduction, resilience and viability at a steady scale. This is no guarantee they will do so; this chapter is about the *possibilities* created by different types of company ownership.

Ownership by workers or beneficiaries can foster companies with activities and operations for product sufficiency

Ownership of firms by their workers or beneficiaries presents some significant advantages for the economy-in-Planet that stem from the direct, hands-on participation that comes through working in the firm, and, to a lesser extent, the direct enjoyment of the benefits of the work of the firm; as well as from the way owner-worker and owner-beneficiary companies are financed.

Ownership by workers or beneficiaries often creates companies that are *rooted in place*—the opposite of what is created by the owners of the public corporation. While an owner-worker may choose to move her business to another location, if she does this, she will need to move herself. Worker-owned companies are not "outsourced" or "delocalised", even when labour costs are cheaper elsewhere (no less because these owner-workers don't really think of themselves as "labour costs"!). When times are tough, and the operations of companies not owned by their workers may be re-sited overseas, worker-owned companies would rather explore other options to retain jobs in their current location, such as reducing working hours. Location matters to worker-owners, and companies remain sited where they, the workers, are.[1] Location also matters to beneficiary-owners. Since beneficiary-owned companies exist to serve a specific group, they are also often located close by.[2] These sorts of companies' *anchor to place* creates positive benefits. First, an anchor to place helps build the resilience of local economies and communities—crucial in the Anthropocene epoch. In fact, committed to place, many of these businesses engage in community service activities, such as construction, care, transport, or maintaining restaurants, grocery stores and laundry services. The Evergreen Cooperatives in Cleveland, Ohio, engaged in solar energy, laundry services and food production, are a well-known example of how employee ownership can help support the building of resilient local economies.[3] The anchor to place can also help foster resource-efficient operations. Companies anchored in their locality, or, more precisely, where *owners* live in the same place as their *operations*, are less likely to engage in poor environmental practices, which would threaten the integrity of the local environment—it's where they work and live, after all (personalities, of course, also come into play). Finally, the ongoing proximity to customers for product stewardship and access activities also requires a company commitment to a particular locality. Ownership by workers or beneficiaries, through their anchor to place, opens the possibility of proximate siting of operations—whether locations were chosen with activities for product sufficiency in mind or not.

Besides location, there are other ways in which ownership by workers or beneficiaries may support activities and operations for sufficiency. The

---

1 Thank you to Gar Alperovitz for pointing this benefit of worker-ownership out to me.

2 Note that this anchor to place does not exist for platform companies, which can essentially serve their customers from anywhere in the world.

3 http://www.evgoh.com/about-us, accessed 31 August 2016.

operations of firms owned by their workers are more likely to be worker-centred (Chapter 8)—good jobs are a priority. When owners are workers, they are less likely to think of themselves in abstract or financial terms, as "human resources" or as "labour costs" (as external shareholders might), but rather as people, with aspirations that can, in part at least, be fulfilled through their livelihoods. The employee-owned John Lewis Partnership famously exists to promote "the happiness of all [its] members, through their worthwhile, satisfying employment in a successful business".[4] Worker-owners are more likely to be more invested, and more productive, in their work compared to non-owning employees (Levin, 2006). They may bring more of themselves to their workplaces, and may pride themselves in their distinct contribution. This could support a certain service ethos, which would make them well suited to the service tasks at the heart of product stewardship and access activities. Companies owned by their beneficiaries may also sustain the service culture required for these activities: such companies already exist to serve their beneficiaries. Many existing consumer cooperatives are in the services industry, and perhaps already exhibit the right ethos for supporting business activities for product sufficiency. This is especially relevant as the absence of a culture of service is identified as one of the key organisational barriers in shifting away from manufacturing to the servicing activities of product stewardship (Chapter 5).

Finally, one of the most striking advantages of ownership by workers or beneficiaries is that it could help solve some of the seemingly insurmountable ethical barriers to the uptake of certain product-access activities. As we saw in Chapter 6, the sufficiency benefits of product access often derive from the incentives for rental and leasing companies to retain products as assets. But this model also has potential downsides, from the perspective of both the customer and society as a whole. While the customer does benefit from the product she borrows, not owning her objects leaves her vulnerable. Should the company fold, should prices rise, or should firm owners no longer be interested in her custom, she loses access to product benefits. These risks are clearly a key barrier to widespread household (and business) implementation of Product Service Systems—who wants to suddenly lose their fridge or flooring? Their vulnerability makes product-access offers often, understandably, unattractive to customers. On a societal level, the retained ownership of products by firms poses ethical issues by creating a

---

4 http://www.johnlewispartnership.co.uk/resources/faqs.html, accessed 31 August 2016.

particularly vulnerable class of customers. Companies, the traditional owners of the means of production, would also become owners of the means of consumption, potentially leaving customers at the mercy of the market in every area of their life. But lack of customer acceptance, and ethical hurdles, could be overcome if *customers also owned the product-access companies*—in other words, if product-access activities were delivered by companies *owned by their beneficiaries*. In this case, customers' continued access to products is no longer contingent on the interest of faraway, amorphous investors, as it would be for the public corporation: instead, customer and owner interest are aligned (being one and the same), leaving customers much less vulnerable in their continued access to products. Ownership of product-access companies by beneficiaries could also help solve the question of the longevity of the firm required to sustain these models over time: the firm will continue to exist so long as it is worth the while of customer-owners.

Another significant way that an adjustment of ownership structure could make product-access models more attractive involves platform companies. As we saw in Chapter 6, while the attraction of a "peer" providing a service is notionally central to the "peer-to-peer economy", in reality many of the most successful platform companies have seen widespread professionalisation of "peer" service providers: taxi drivers for "ride-share" services, property managers for "guest stays", and so on. Many providers rely on participating in these platform models as an important, or indeed as a primary, source of income, but do not benefit from a secure, guaranteed wage, nor from the other advantages provided by employment. Abandoning any pretence that the services are provided by "peers", the "gig economy" could be turned into something else if *platform companies were worker-owned*—that is to say, if they were owned by the "peer" service providers themselves. This would help solve the ethical concerns associated with these companies, by alleviating the work insecurity they often create. New York-based start-up Juno, for example, intends to rival other car-sharing services, but with a strong focus on driver work satisfaction—and with drivers owning half of the founding shares (Kessler, 2016). Such ownership would help solve the ethical problem of prosumption, whereby, at their worst, peers or prosumers of platform companies take on work that would traditionally have been carried out by employees, with minimal reward.

Ownership by workers or beneficiaries can foster companies with the potential to be viable at optimal scale

But perhaps the most significant strength of worker-owners or beneficiary-owners for the economy-in-Planet is that they do *not necessarily seek to grow their firms.* Instead, such companies tend to remain relatively small over time, viable at whichever scale they're at. This is a key difference from the public corporation—and makes ownership by workers or beneficiaries far better suited to the global steadiness of resource use required for the economy-in-Planet.

In the legacy economy, we already know that ownership by workers or beneficiaries creates companies that seldom grow and rarely become gigantic. The overwhelming majority of businesses owned and run by managers range from micro to small (from one to 20); while employee-owned businesses are themselves small to medium-sized, especially when fully owned by their workers. Exceptions to this rule (such as the John Lewis Partnership mentioned earlier) exist, but they are famous for being unusually large.[5] In general, ownership by those who do the work tends to push firms toward remaining at a smaller scale. Why? First, if you're a worker-owner, expansion to your business may simply be too risky, or too much of a hassle; the potential benefits of growth past a micro, small or medium size may not be worth the additional effort or threat of insecurity. If you're a solo entrepreneur, there are just so many hours in the day. For a manager-owner, opening a second site can create logistical complexities that outweigh the benefit of staying a more manageable size. For employee-owned companies, especially firms fully owned by their workers, the case for expansion is even weaker: it may generate economies of scale, but presumably would require new employee-owners to manage the expanded operations—weakening any growth incentive. While an external owner of a café might double her profit by opening a second identical location, employee-owners might decline the same opportunity since it would keep profit-per-worker the same (the pie would be twice as big, but split among twice as many workers).

The factors that tend to result in a smaller, manageable size for companies owned by their workers do not apply to beneficiary-owned firms. But many of these firms also remain relatively small. These companies exist to

---

5 Nearly all the larger worker-owned firms were originally family-owned businesses, with a visionary founder, or heir to the founder, who gave the company over to his employees.

ir beneficiaries: sometimes needs are best served on a larger scale,
a smaller scale will suffice. For a retailer owned by beneficiaries, a
firm sized for sufficient buying power will be large enough; this may require
a national scale, but a smaller shop may also do the trick. For beneficiary-
owners, company growth is not a goal to pursue for its own sake, but only to
pursue if it helps to further meet their needs (Millstone, 2015). While growth
denotes success for a public corporation—it is the mechanism through
which external shareholders are rewarded—growth is not the yardstick
through which to measure the success of firms owned by their workers or
beneficiaries. The case for growth is simply not a given for them. If they do
grow, that growth is considered and serves specific goals. Unlike the public
corporation, they are not legally structured to be vehicles of growth; this
opens the possibility for a wider reflection on the part of business owners
on the desirability of growth and appropriate scale.

By only pursuing growth in certain "conscious" circumstances, companies owned by workers or beneficiaries often remain steady and are viable
and successful at a limited scale. And, as we have seen, there is such a thing
as an optimal scale for the pioneering company (Chapter 7)—the scale at
which resource use is minimised through operations and business models. While there is no *a priori* reason why the company scale at which beneficiary needs are best met, or worker livelihoods best secured, should be
aligned with optimal scale, the fact that worker- and beneficiary-owned
companies tend to operate and remain at a *particular* scale makes them
more suited, potentially, to operating at *optimal scale* than public corporations structured to grow. For optimal scale to be achieved and maintained,
worker-owners or beneficiary-owners would need to consider how to meet
the challenge of resource use reduction, alongside their other company
goals. If they do so, the legacy experience of worker and beneficiary ownership suggests that these companies could be well suited to contribute to the
global steadiness of resource use of the economy-in-Planet.

The fact that company growth is not necessarily an attractive proposition to worker-owners and worker-beneficiaries makes companies with
these types of ownership advantageous for the economy-in-Planet. But
there are instances, for the owners, where bigger would be better: when a
larger company would deliver better, more secure livelihoods or improve
the meeting of beneficiary need. There are also instances where, from a
resource use perspective, concentrated, larger, capital-intense operations
may be preferable (Chapter 7). Moreover, we need to make the distinction
between the economy-in-Planet and the journey to it: while in the former,

ownership structures conducive to steadiness and optimal scale are desirable, in the latter we may first want a pioneering company to expand its market share at the expense of unsustainable competitors (while making sure not to grow the market overall). For this potential growth phase, ownership forms conducive to steadiness may be a hindrance. There are two ways around this problem: the first would be to find ways to support the replication of optimally scaled companies rather than the upscaling of the individual pioneering company—but replication clearly does not hold the same promise of reward as expansion for the successful business owner. The second would be to design flexibility in ownership structure, recognising that different ownership forms may, at different moments in the life of the firm and in the transition to the economy-in-Planet, support growth or viability at scale. There are precedents of companies changing hands in the legacy economy: from unknown shareholders to private hands, from management to workers. Dell Computers, for example, used to be a listed company, but became private in 2013; the John Lewis Partnership was owned by its founding family before being given over to its employees in 1950. Changes in ownership are, then, not unheard of: for the pioneering company, viewing ownership as mutable can help support its response to the challenge of resource use reduction and steadiness. But mutable ownership is not the panacea either: as we saw earlier in this chapter, some product sufficiency activities are best supported by particular ownership structures. The challenge for the pioneering company is to reconcile the sufficiency benefits of some activities and the viability at scale advantage of some ownership forms—while making enough of a dent in the market to drive the change toward the economy-in-Planet.

While a case for growth may exist, these companies are limited in their expansion ambitions by their financing arrangements. When *fully* owned by workers or beneficiaries, these firms have no access to outside equity; they must instead finance their company through internal funds, debt, or equity from workers or beneficiaries only. These options come with their own challenges. Funding a business through internal funds, sometimes known as bootstrapping, consists of committing a share of the profit to finance future activities. Thinking of considered growth, bootstrapping has the advantages that it supports unhurried, organic company growth, on its own timetable (rather than on a creditor's timetable, for example) (Bamburg, 2006).[6] Its distinctive disadvantage is that retaining income for future

---

6 See Bamburg, 2006 for the advantage and disadvantages of boostrapping.

activities requires income in the first place; in practice, the generation of future income may well require up-front expenditure: say, for new machinery or market research.[7] Some of these expenses may be, in part, paid out of membership dues (say, for consumer cooperatives), but up-front expenditure often requires taking on debt, in the form of loans from personal contacts, banks or potentially, the "crowd" through "crowdfunding". Taking on debt has advantages over bootstrapping alone: it can help with cash flow or be used to purchase fixed assets, and can be paid back over a number of years. On the downside, whoever they are from, loans need to be repaid: the firm must generate enough profit to pay back interest on an agreed timetable, on terms set by the creditors. The parameters set by creditors may be constraining; and, thinking about the challenge of viability at scale, may drive a company to grow in order to keep up with interest repayments, rather than in the more deliberate manner mentioned in the earlier section. Avoiding these constraints requires equity capital to be sought from worker-owners or beneficiary-owners (for firms wholly owned by these types of owners, which is what we are discussing here). And, unless the owners are fabulously wealthy and willing to risk their wealth, *not* seeking outside equity becomes a de facto decision to remain small, un-innovative, engaged in low-risk activities, or in those not requiring significant start-up capital investment. In fact, legacy companies wholly worker- or beneficiary-owned are in the business of providing everyday goods and services, and are absent from activities such as pharmaceuticals and new technologies.

Lack of external equity, then, presents some serious challenges for the firm. It means exclusion from certain sectors and from innovative, risky activities. To overcome these difficulties, and secure access to the finance that they need to launch, run and grow their business, many owners seek outside investment. While even today the majority of firms are owned by workers, many are not wholly owned that way. Instead, they are part or even majority-owned by external shareholders, most often by friends and families. In the previous chapter, we examined how such external ownership of firms has been a driving force in causing unsustainability; but we have not yet mentioned the numerous advantages to the *individual* company in seeking external shareholders in the first place. Issuing shares for external ownership is first and foremost a mechanism to secure long-term, flexible

---

7 This may be more of a problem for start-up organisations: Doug Henwood claims that the overwhelming proportion of capital expenditure of mid-sized manufacturing firms comes from retained earnings (Henwood, 1998: 72-75).

finance. Investment in exchange for equity does not require interest payments or repayments on a given timetable. For shareholders, if the business is a success, they can expect to share in that success; if it's not much to write home about, dividends will be small; if it is an abject failure, they will simply lose their original investment (since their liability is limited to this initial outlay). This helps new ventures and activities get off the ground. In addition, having external shareholders can help firms obtain credit. Lenders are more likely to offer credit, especially larger sums, when their risk is spread with shareholders willing to risk their equity stake (Jensen and Meckling, 1976). Finally, the argument is often made that external shareholders can help bolster boards and professionalise organisations. External shareholders usually take part in governance by voting at shareholder meetings, and, as the last in line for repayment in case of bankruptcy, they have a clear stake in the success of the business, and an attendant strong interest in effective strategy and governance.[8] External shareholders, then, are essential to raise flexible capital, to help spread risk and obtain credit, and can also help contribute to successful company governance.

The necessity or advantages to individual worker- or beneficiary-owned firms of seeking outside equity in the legacy economy also hold true in the economy-in-Planet. Thanks to external shareholders, these companies can grow, could potentially be present in a larger range of sectors, and ultimately occupy a greater share of economic activity—with all the planetary benefits that these types of companies provide. But here's the rub. What I have been describing in this chapter are beneficial attributes of firms for the economy-in-Planet that come from the fact they are owned by their workers or beneficiaries. The likelihood and potential of these benefits would clearly be diminished as the ownership share of external owners grows and that of workers and beneficiaries shrinks. This is particularly true for the effect on growth and scale, which comes not so much from the nature of workers or beneficiaries as owners, but from the particular incentives facing a company that is *not* externally owned. In fact, in a situation of ecological overshoot, the viability at scale of companies owned by workers or beneficiaries is such an advantage that operations ought to be designed, as much as possible, in a way as to make them suitable for worker or beneficiary ownership

---

8 While equity shareholders are usually involved in management, not all shareholders have voting rights: equity known as "common" equity is involved in management, whereas "preferred" equity has no voting rights and fixed dividends. Common equity is the money that is truly at risk and last in line for repayment should the business fail.

and to reduce the need for external shareholders. In light of this, the fact that the dispersed, appropriately scaled operations of Chapter 7 have low financing requirements and could therefore, potentially, be viable without external ownership may be a greater benefit for the economy-in-Planet, in terms of supporting a steady company scale, than the low resource use of such operations. This would militate in favour of a series of independently owned operational units close to customers, rather than, say, a large centralised company or franchise licensor operating multiple dispersed units.

There are ways to select outside equity holders to minimise the risks to sustainability posed by external ownership

But in instances where outside equity is required, could companies owned by workers or beneficiaries reap the benefits that come from external shareholders, thus becoming in part, or even majority externally owned, without losing their attributes propitious for the economy-in-Planet? With difficulty, since these attributes come from lack of external ownership—but there may be ways to maximise their retention. The "extreme" shareholders of the public corporation share some peculiarities: their large numbers, geographical remoteness, lack of engagement, commitment and responsibility (Chapter 9). Shareholders with these characteristics lead to companies that are incompatible with the economy-in-Planet. But shareholders of private companies are different to those of public companies in many ways. Most companies owned by external shareholders do not have hundreds of thousands of shareholders but dozens at most; shares are held for a while rather than used speculatively and traded in private transactions; and shareholders are often active participants in the governance of their firms. If there were a way to create external owners with opposite characteristics to the shareholders of the public corporations—*few in numbers, close to the firm, engaged, committed, responsible*—we could, conceivably, end up with companies that are compatible, or, more precisely, not incompatible, with the sustainable economy. This new type of owner, which I call the *"investor-owner"*, would enable companies to reap the benefits of access to external equity while lessening the likelihood of a move away from activities and operations supportive of the economy-in-Planet. In this section, I consider how this could be done.

A company seeking access to outside equity first ought to seek the smallest number of investor-owners required to raise the requisite capital and spread risk.[9] In other words, it should, as much as possible, seek to remain "closely held" or owned by a small number of people.[10] Of course, this works better in principle than in practice: it is hard to find buyers for shares in the first place, especially for start-ups where failure rates are high, and equity holders will not expect to see dividends any time soon (as any profit will probably be retained for future growth). Despite these difficulties, relying on the smallest possible number of external investors must be the goal for the pioneering company, as many of the desirable characteristics that we are seeking to create in investor-owners supportive of the economy-in-Planet flow from their small number.

Why? First, low numbers allow entrepreneurs to hand-pick friendly, skilled investors. This is especially important if seeking to create a pioneering company: many an "ethical" company in the legacy economy has suffered from "mission drift" once the founder has lost ownership and control of their business (Ben & Jerry's sale to Unilever is often given as an example of this process). Second, in addition to selecting for alignment in aims, low numbers allow selection for location. In the same way as the legacy economy is characterised by distance between sites of production and those of consumption, it is also characterised by distance between firm owners and firm operations (and workplaces). Just as the economy-in-Planet often requires shrinking distances between companies and customers (Chapter 7), it also often requires shrinking distances between owners and the companies they own. Like the manager-owners mentioned earlier in this chapter, investors are far less likely to take decisions detrimental to communities and the environment if they live in the place affected by those impacts.

---

9 Since any number of shares can be issued at any price on company formation, to be sold at market rate at a later time, a company seeking to minimise shareholder numbers could in theory simply issue fewer, more expensive shares, or require a minimal number of shares per owner.

10 A "closely held" company is one that is owned and controlled by a small number of owners, usually management or family members. The US's Internal Revenue Service defines a closely held company as a corporation that has more than 50% of the value of its outstanding stock directly or indirectly owned by five or fewer individuals at any time during the last half of the tax year. See https://www.irs.gov/help-resources/tools-faqs/faqs-for-individuals/frequently-asked-tax-questions-answers/small-business-self-employed-other-business/entities/entities-5. Closely held does not necessarily mean "small": some of the world's largest companies are closely held.

Investor-owners should therefore, as much as possible, be physically close to the work of the companies they own. Third, with a low number of investors, the pioneering company can ensure the company's controlling stake is retained by workers or beneficiaries. A low number of outside investors who could still be outvoted is one way to do this; other firms, including some worker-owned cooperatives of the legacy economy, have issued different classes of shares for external owners. Workers have retained the common, voting equity stake; while preferred equity, which comes with fixed dividends and no voting rights, has been offered externally.[11] In both these approaches, the benefits for the economy-in-Planet of owner or beneficiary ownership are less likely to be eroded, despite some external ownership.

But, when external owners are few, the question of how to raise sufficient finance for company goals remains. One way worker-owner and worker-beneficiary firms have done this is through "crowd equity", using platforms such as Crowdcube.[12] But the pioneering company should tread carefully here: clearly, ownership by the crowd goes against the principle of having the smallest possible number of committed investors. While crowd investors have a direct relationship with the companies they invest in, they are unlikely to be committed owners, if only because their large numbers foster disengagement, as they do for the public corporation (whether they have voting rights or not). Low numbers, on the other hand, foster commitment to the firm. They also foster active engagement in governance: with fewer owners, the weight of opinion, and the voting rights, of individual owners matters a lot more than when there are dozens, or even hundreds of other owners to contend with. Commitment and engagement can be further secured with mechanisms for making trade in shares more onerous: one of the ways in which lack of "owner" commitment in the public corporation expresses itself is the ease with which she can dispose of her shares on the public market; in a closely held firm, by contrast, trading of shares often requires private negotiations, or a relational rather than purely transactional exchange.

Finally, a small number of engaged, committed owners have the decisive advantage that they will remain responsible for their firm. A "closely held" company, unlike the public corporation, and, indeed, unlike the crowd-owned firm, has the distinct advantage of having clearly identifiable *persons*

11 See the example of Equal Exchange and Organic Valley Family of Farms in Bamburg, 2006.

12 http://www.crowdcube.com, accessed 15 May 2015.

as owners: that is to say, identifiable *moral agents*. Clear identification of owners, which is absent for public corporations, confers certain moral (and legal) rights and responsibilities on them. This was affirmed by a 2014 US Supreme Court case, *Burwell v Hobby Lobby*, where the justices ruled that firm owners could conduct their business according to their religious beliefs (in this instance, refusing to include birth control in employee health insurance plans). Tellingly, the ruling only applied to closely held companies, not to public corporations: indeed, since we cannot identify the owners of public corporations (they have none!), we cannot identify persons whose religious or moral beliefs may be in conflict with particular regulatory requirements. While moral agency does not by any stretch mean that owners of closely held firms will necessarily consider sustainability in their decision-making process—what they do will surely depend on their own moral outlook—having moral agents as owners is a *precondition* for decisions supportive of the economy-in-Planet. This is because the case for sustainability rests on a moral rather than a business case (as we saw in the Introduction), and therefore requires business owners who accept the moral responsibility to steer their firms in a sustainable direction. The small number of owners in a closely held company makes them morally responsible for the company they own; this moral responsibility is diluted, and therefore the potential for sustainable action eroded, as the number of owners increases—until shares are traded on public markets and moral responsibility is lost altogether.

If the pioneering company requires external investment, it should therefore seek a small number of engaged, committed, morally responsible investors, located in close proximity to the work of the firm. That way, it can hope to minimise the risk of the company being steered toward an unsustainable course, and instead stay true to its environmental and social ambitions. All these are "soft" measures to foster investor engagement in the firm for the benefit of sustainability, but there are "harder" measures too. A firm's articles of association can set a social or environmental mission, creating a "mission-driven business". These companies already abound in the legacy economy; in the UK, for example, 70,000 businesses claim to exist primarily for social or environmental goals.[13] While some of these companies do not have atypical legal structures and are simply company limited by shares, others structurally enshrine their social or environmental mission in their legal form. Existing forms include the Benefit Corporation, the

13 Social Enterprise FAQ. Social Enterprise UK: http://www.socialenterprise.org.uk/about/about-social-enterprise

Flexible Purpose Corporation or the Low-profit Limited Liability Company (L3C) in the US; or the Community Interest Company (CIC) in the UK. In companies with these legal forms, the mission is prioritised over owners' financial reward. This prioritisation can be operationalised through asset locks, which prevent the assets of a company from being used for private gain instead of the stated purpose of the organisation, or dividend caps, which limit how much profit can be allocated to individual owners. These legal forms de facto result in investor-owners committed to what the business is seeking to achieve—or, presumably, they would not have invested in the organisation in the first place. These forms often, then, appeal to so called "impact investors" who are seeking to generate positive social and environmental benefits through their investments. But these legal forms only really work when owners are imbued with a sense of the wider benefit of their venture—whereas the "social" mission of the majority of enterprises tends to not go beyond meeting customer satisfaction. For all these other firms, the majority of companies incorporated simply as companies limited by shares, we must fall back on the "softer" measures described earlier in this section to seek to create investor-owners fit for the economy-in-Planet.

Ownership by workers or beneficiaries gives firms the background characteristics of the pioneering company, the *potential* to adopt activities for product sufficiency, to contribute to resilience building and to be viable at a certain, steady scale. These characteristics can also be fostered in companies owned by external investors, through particular legal structures for mission-driven businesses, or softer measures for all other companies. All this is good news. There is nothing inherently amiss in the ownership and legal structure of companies that, in terms of numbers, already dominate the economy today to suggest that these same companies could not exist in the economy-in-Planet, provided they adopted the products and services, activities and models, and operations described in this book.

～

The ways in which a company is legally incorporated and owned, and how it goes about raising capital, has implications that go far beyond providing a structure for activities or securing the financial future of the company. Legal and ownership structures have a direct bearing on whether a company's operations and activities are likely to be supportive of resource use reduction and resilience building, and crucially, the extent to which a company will grow or be viable at a steady scale. Legal structure, ownership and financing options are therefore an integral part of the design of the pioneering company. Table 10.1 summarises the benefits and risks for sustainability of different types of owners, and the legal structures and financing options open to them.

If there is no place for the public corporations, which so dominate economic activity today, in a sustainable economy it is clear that the transition to, and the sustaining of, the economy-in-Planet will require a much greater share of economic activity to be undertaken by other sorts of companies, owned instead by workers and beneficiaries, or investors close and committed to the work of the firm, and backed with a supportive legal structure. The typical pioneering company, then, will be owned by workers, beneficiaries or investors (as described in Part 5); such ownership is a prerequisite to the successful uptake of the interventions described in this book's earlier parts.

In Parts 1 through 4, we've covered the products and services, activities and models, operations and supply chains, ownership, financing and legal structure of pioneering companies: do we now, finally, have a "truly" sustainable business? To be able to answer an unequivocal "yes" to this question requires exploring one final topic: the business form itself. For if there is an intrinsic incompatibility between the business form and sustainability, the private sector, as we know it today, could not exist in the economy-in-Planet—regardless of the leadership of pioneering companies. This topic, then, certainly merits our attention: in the final part of this book we turn to the essence of business.

Table 10.1 Company ownership structure, legal form, financing options and sustainability benefits and risks

Owners	External shareholders	Worker-owner	Beneficiary-owner	Investor-owner
Who are they?	• The "paradigmatic" shareholders of the legacy economy • Individuals • Institutions • Private equity groups	• Owners who are directly involved in the running of their company • Entrepreneurs • Managers • Employees	• Owners who are direct beneficiaries of the good or service produced by the company • "Consumers" • Communities	• The "new" "external shareholders" of the economy-in-Planet • Individuals with attributes that make them committed to the work of the firm
Firm legal form	• Private company limited by shares • Corporation (US) • Public Limited Company (UK)	• Private company limited by shares • Community Interest Company (UK) • Mission-focused structures (US): Benefit Corporation, Flexible Purpose Corporation, Low-profit Limited Liability Company		
Main financing options	• Private finance • Equity markets if public	• Bootstrapping • Debt • Member equity • Membership dues		• Bootstrapping • Debt • Outside equity
Sustainability benefits		• Fosters socio-economic resilience • Fosters operation with sound environmental and social practices • Fosters firms supportive of product sufficiency business activities • Not necessarily growth-seeking • Viable at a steady scale		• Could help overcome some of the financing limitations of worker and beneficiary ownership
Sustainability risks	• Subordination of sustainability issues to financial bottom line • Growth seeking structures • A driving factor of unsustainability in the legacy economy	• Cannot readily scale up even when larger scale preferable for sustainability • Absent from certain sectors • Financing limitation precludes these companies occupying a greater share of economic activity in the legacy economy		• "Dilutes" some of the benefits of worker and beneficiary ownership • Risks mitigated by limited numbers and choice of investors or by the company's legal structure

Part 6

The purpose, scope and limits of business

What is a business? In *The Personal MBA*, Josh Kaufman (2010) sets out to come up with an answer to this question by distilling business down to the core elements all firms have in common. A business is "a repeatable process that 1. Creates and delivers something of value; 2. That other people want or need; 3. At a price they're willing to pay; 4. In a way that satisfies the customers' needs and expectations; 5. So that the business brings in enough profit to make it worthwhile for the owners to continue operations" (Kaufman, 2010: 38). This definition effectively captures what business is all about. But many of the elements captured by Kaufman are equally applicable to individuals and organisations other than businesses. An artist or a home-maker can "create something of value" for the benefit of art appreciators or her household; needs-satisfying services can be provided by public bodies; goods sold on the market can also be provided on a charitable basis.

What is unique to business is the fifth part of Kaufman's definition: the fact that the whole enterprise, points 1 through 4, take place *in view of generating a profit for its owners*. All other endeavours described above, while they share some of companies' defining characteristics, are "non-profit" (if they are seeking to generate a surplus through the trading of goods, this profit accrues to a charitable cause rather than to owners). To be a business, as opposed to something else, a company must be run on a for-profit basis for its owners; or, more accurately, it must *seek* to generate said profit. Ideally, profit is actually generated; if not, business owners must have a strong confidence that their pursuit of profit will indeed pay off at some stage in the future, and will be content to break even for the time being. To simplify Kaufman's definition further still, at its very bare bones, a business is *a profit-seeking entity*.

In the legacy economy, a business's orientation towards profit-seeking is unquestioned. But given the role of some companies, entities *defined* by their profit orientation, in creating our dire ecological predicament, the specific role of *profit-seeking* in unsustainability warrants closer examination. How has profit-seeking manifested itself in the legacy economy, and what role can it play in the economy-in-Planet? We turn to this question in this book's final part.

In Chapter 11, we review profit-seeking in the legacy economy to ascertain its place in the economy-in-Planet. In Chapter 12, we examine the links between profit-seeking and the meeting of customer need, in both these economies. By examining what is unique and essential to business, we can establish the role, scope and limits of business, in light of the challenges of our time.

11 Profit, financial and worthwhile

Profit is captured in the same way for all firms: a single financial metric, a bit of good news in a profit and loss account. A number and a dollar sign lend themselves to comparing the financial success of companies, but clearly cannot tell the full story for our purposes. Indeed, as we saw in Part 5, while some companies will create unsustainable outcomes in their pursuit of profit, others will not. We must therefore make a distinction between profit that precludes sustainability, and profit that may support it.

In this chapter, we first take a closer look at profit in the legacy economy to establish how, and the instances in which, profit itself could have the qualities that make it conducive to the transition to, and the sustaining of, the economy-in-Planet.

Profit in the legacy economy usually relies on negative externality generation and company growth

A profit is generated when a firm's revenue exceeds its running costs, including investments in maintenance or new productive capacity. As the difference between revenue and cost, the generation of a profit is therefore the generation of a financial surplus or gain. Before profit can be pursued, the entrepreneur must spot a good opportunity: one where there is potential to meet the needs of would-be customers through a good or service, which could be charged for more than it would cost to deliver. Subsequently, in a competitive market, there are more or less two ways to generate, and hopefully increase, profit: cost minimisation and company growth.

First, in a competitive market, profit can be increased by minimising costs, or, more precisely, by widening the gap between revenue and cost. Good business strategy and management can perhaps be distilled to the simple goal of widening this gap: finding ways to attract and retain customers on the one hand, while keeping costs low on the other. There are in theory two ways to go about this: by increasing revenue through higher prices, or by lowering costs, by achieving savings on operational and supplier expenditure. In practice, though, high prices would mean losing customers to competitors—there is only so much marketing can do.[1] So the route to profit generally relies on delivering customer satisfaction at the lowest possible cost to the business.

Improvements in operational processes may help to achieve cost reduction, but, for companies in the legacy economy, there are far more effective opportunities to lower cost than through internal change. Once all supplier and operational costs have been minimised, costs can be further shrunk through externalisation. The term "externality" refers to a business's environmental and social impacts that affect parties other than the business itself or its customers (while externalities are sometimes positive, here I use the term "externality" to refer to "negative" externalities, which hurt people who are not directly involved in the business). Examples abound, but look no further than the polluted environments and diminished health and wellbeing of many populations living close to mines and factories. Costs are externalised, in that the cost of creating or delivering the good or service doesn't include the costs of any remedial action needed to mitigate, manage and eliminate the harms caused to neighbouring people. Those costs are often borne by victims (who might see housing prices depressed, or health ruined and lives shortened), or by taxpayers (when governments intervene to clean up the mess); business gets a free pass.

This free pass has its roots in a dominant world-view, with all its ramifications for how our society is organised, which sees the natural environment as limitless "resources", there for the taking at the right price (as illustrated in Figure 1.2 of Chapter 1). If this world-view were true, rather than entirely wrong, businesses could externalise away, since waste and pollution would

---

1 This is the scenario in a competitive market: companies that are monopolies or oligopolies achieve profit not so much as described but by benefiting from high barriers to entry into their market, enabling them to charge high prices.

not constitute an environmental problem (although their consequences for human health would still need to be addressed). More subtly, the free pass is supported by the fossil fuel bounty, which enables the economy of distance (Part 4). This is because externality generation often *requires* distance. Without distance, businesses would find it harder to get away with polluting their customers' local environment; and customers might not be so willing to put up with products and services created and delivered by slave labourers, if the slaves lived on their doorstep (or were their children). But in the legacy economy, out of the sight and out of the minds of both customers and business executives, exploiting low labour costs and lax environmental legislation, or creating negative externalities of unmet human need and ecosystem destruction, is perfectly feasible, cost-effective and, worse, "good strategy". We know about the polluted rivers of China, the worker deaths of the factories of Bangladesh, but all this is very, very far away.

Despite businesses' free pass to generate externalities, business executives tend not to congratulate themselves on their good fortune. Instead, externalities are usually understood to be the unfortunate, inadvertent, regrettable, but ultimately unavoidable by-product of business. Some legacy economy businesses do spend time and effort trying to manage their impacts, sometimes compensating affected parties. But "internalising" externalities is complex and there's only so much "internalising" an individual company can do in a global context of "externality permissiveness" without rendering its products uncompetitive—since all its competitors are operating in the same permissive legal framework. In fact, in the legacy economy, generating profits by minimising costs usually *requires* generating externalities. We could say, for example, that large parts of the global supply chain exist *precisely* to take advantage of labour and resource cost differentials.[2] One way in which some companies have brought their reliance on externalities for profit creation to light, albeit inadvertently, is through the keeping of so-called "environmental profit and loss accounts". Apparel giant Kering, for example, has experimented with keeping such accounts, which purport to report on "environmental performance" (Kering, 2013). These "accounts" take the form of a financial valuation of environmental impacts generated in the supply chain (with no "environmental profit" to show). While these "accounts" are presumably an attempt to acknowledge impact and demonstrate Kering's credentials as a "responsible" company, financialised, they

---

2 Other parts of the supply chain are more "natural" due to uneven geographic distribution of resources.

are in fact indicative of the environmental externalities that Kering relies on in its value creation. These impacts may be identified, but cannot really be mitigated without seriously affecting Kering's bottom line. In fact, the generation of externalities has become so central and essential to the way companies operate that, in a particularly revealing study, the charity Trucost has shown that the remedial cost of externalities generated worldwide by businesses, especially those in the primary and agriculture sectors, tends to exceed their revenue (Trucost, 2013). It turns out that many companies in the legacy economy cannot "internalise" their costs without going out of business.

Once costs cannot be minimised further, when no additional externalities can be exploited, profits will plateau. At that stage, the only way to generate further profit is to grow the company. And financial growth requires growth in productive capacity, as we saw in Chapter 9. Company growth is in fact doubly attractive to business owners. Even without changing the revenue–cost gap, growing the company to new markets and new customers can add to profit, building profit through volume of transactions rather than higher margins. Growth can also support further cost saving through economies of scale (Chapter 7)—indirectly shifting the gap between cost and revenue; but, in any case, company owners grow their firms to grow their profits (increasing capacity does not always result in increased financial value—but since that was presumably the aim, such outcomes are merely a failure).[3]

Profit generation in the legacy economy largely rests on two pillars: environmental and social cost externalisation and company growth. Both of these pose significant challenges for the pioneering company.

Since all business activity requires resource use, there is arguably always some externality generated through business activity: the environmental impact associated with the use of the resource. Having said that, this resource could be well managed (in the case of certification schemes such as the Forest Stewardship Council); and some companies are even aiming to become "net positive", an ambitious and to date unimplemented idea that companies could "give more than they take" to society and the environment. Perhaps a distinction must therefore be made between the generation of minor, occasional, mitigated-as-much-as-possible externalities; and

---

3 Again, this is the case in a competitive market but not in a monopoly or oligopoly, where profits could be higher if production levels are lower, by charging a higher price per item.

major, ongoing, unresolved ones. The far-sighted companies of the legacy economy claim to conduct their business while seeking to minimise environmental impact. But doing so should severely limit their access to externality generation as a cost minimisation measure—thus making the profit that comes from externality generation rather meagre.

For the pioneering company, going by the book (this one!), read skeletal. *Externality-created profit* undermines what a truly responsible, pioneering, company should be trying to do. The products and services, the business models, the operations and supply chains described throughout this book could in fact be read specifically as ways to think about how to avoid negative externalities. The cost savings that can be reaped through irresponsible sourcing and cheap labour overseas are not available to companies that create, for example, artisanal products, close to their markets (and this holds true for all companies seeking to deliver frugal products and services, whichever activities, operations and ownership structure support this goal). More generally, the ability to reap profit from the generation of externalities rests on specific conditions of the legacy economy, which will no longer exist in the economy-in-Planet when distance is replaced by proximity (Chapter 7); when the majority of economic activity is driven by companies owned by their workers or beneficiaries, or "redefined" investors (Chapter 10); and when, in time, a more accurate understanding of the place of economic activity in the planetary system comes to replace the current, erroneous dominant world-view (Chapter 1). With the features of the economy-in-Planet in mind, the problem with the generation of *growth-created profit* is more straightforward still. One of the economy-in-Planet's defining features, after all, is steadiness at an ecologically sustainable scale, following degrowth of the legacy economy (Part 1). And, since company growth requires resource growth, it is clear that growth-created profit is contrary to these goals. Moreover, to contribute to resource-use steadiness, the pioneering company must be viable at optimal scale—again, requiring a steady rather than growing company size (Chapter 10).

If the profit of the pioneering company can rest neither on systematic externality generation nor on growth, it could be argued that it cannot really be a profit-seeking enterprise at all—that pioneering companies are not so much businesses as non-profit organisations. If this were the case, the shift toward the economy-in-Planet would represent a shift toward a non-profit world.[4] To think what might be "lost" in such a world is to identify the role profit plays in the business enterprise—or could companies simply do away with their profit-seeking?

For many ventures, in the legacy economy at least, profit, or more exactly its expectation, helps motivate the entrepreneur. Profit in fact is often spoken of as *the* motivator for business, without which enterprise would not exist. Businesswomen are only in business to generate as much cold hard cash as possible. In reality, profit is usually one motivator *among* others; in fact most small business owners claim they are not primarily motivated by profit but rather by "lifestyle" (Ivanko, 2008). But, even if the profit motive tends to be overstated (and plenty of low- or non-profit ventures are doing just fine), it is still the case that profit *is* a motivator, and that many businesses would not exist without the expectation that some profit could be made: aspiring entrepreneurs do not usually set out to break even, but to make a surplus. Perhaps more important than acting as a motivator for the entrepreneur, would-be investors must have an expectation that a venture will be profitable to make it an attractive prospect. Without this expectation, and potentially high returns, investors would have no reason to put their money in private ventures that could readily fail (their cash would be far safer in government bonds, for example). Profit is perhaps, then, a necessary inducement for risk-taking by would-be investors. So, while the expectation of profit as a motivator for the entrepreneur may be overstated, the expectation of profit is required for investment. The fact that a venture is seeking to generate a profit helps it bring in external capital, gets it off the ground, and helps it become established. For customers as well there may be a benefit to profit. One of the further features of business as identified by Kaufman is market agency: a company brings its goods and services to customers through market exchange. The fact that customers are willing to pay for a good or service provided by a profit-seeking organisation suggests that they may see a benefit in profit-seeking itself—perhaps it could help reassure them of the quality of the product or service they are purchasing. Customers may have a certain expectation of for-profit companies, which they may not have of non-profit organisations, *because* they are profit-seeking: the possibility of repeat purchase, consistent quality and accountability should expectations fall short. So for the millions of customers engaged in their daily transactions with businesses, it seems that the generation of a

---

4 Thank you to Donnie Maclurcan for raising in conversation the possibility that sustainability will require a not-for-profit world.

profit is a "fair" reward for a good product or effective service (or the fact that their transactional counterpart is profit-seeking is simply irrelevant).

So while externality- and growth-reliant profit is clearly at odds with sustainability, the utility of profit-seeking for the firm in the legacy economy—as an important motivator for enterprise, as a means to attract investment and custom—still stands for the pioneering company.[5]

On the economy-in-Planet, profit cannot be understood as exclusively financial and must instead be "worthwhile" in different ways

What attitude must the pioneering company adopt towards profit? How can a pioneering company seek to generate profit that does not rely on the creation of negative externalities and planetary boundary-busting growth?

To think through these questions, it is useful to return to the question of ownership. Recalling Kaufman's definition, businesses are distinctive not only in being profit-seeking, but more specifically in trying to bring in "enough profit to make (them) worthwhile for (their) owners". Profit is sought by owners, for owners. What makes profit "worthwhile" goes to the heart of owners' motivations for being in business in the first place, the very purpose they see in their firm.[6] We can think of a range of owner motivation: from an understanding of profit as exclusively financial, to a broader understanding, which encompasses a larger realm of motivations, including non-financial goals—what I call *"worthwhile profit"*. The importance of financial profit in that larger realm of motivations varies from business to business and even from owner to owner within the same company: for some owners, financial profit may represent the sole motivation for engagement with a

---

5 It is also worth noting that, even if we were to wish away profit-seeking, we couldn't wish away profit in the economy-in-Planet. As a surplus, as the difference between business revenue and cost, it is highly unlikely that all companies could simply break even, even if that's what they set out to do. In a competitive economy, successful companies will generate a profit, and unsuccessful ones will go out of business. Even when profit is not a motivator for the altruistically minded businesswoman but a happy consequence of success, it has still been generated.

6 Jensen and Meckling (1976) posit that everyone involved in a firm has a contractual relationship with it, from which it seeks to derive maximum utility. This notion is close to the motivation discussed here.

firm; for others, financial profit may represent an important but not overwhelming factor; while other owners may be sufficiently content for their businesses to break even. (Owners may even choose to enshrine their motivation through a specific legal form for their company.) Even if individual motivation may vary, we know that some types of owners are less likely to be primarily motivated by financial returns than others. Owners of family businesses, for example, have been shown to assign emotional, and not only financial value to firm ownership (Zellweger and Astrachan, 2008). If we think back to some of the owners of Part 5: worker-owners are motivated by the possibility of secure, enjoyable work created by their enterprise, in addition to financial returns;[7] investor-owners of mission-driven businesses are both interested in financial gain and the furtherance of the company's mission; while external shareholders, as described in Chapter 9, are only in it for the money.

Distinguishing between financial and worthwhile profit is useful because, while the pursuit of financial profit subordinates all environmental and social considerations to that goal, the pursuit of worthwhile profit does not—since other, non-financial goals come into play. Importantly, while it is always in the interest of owners seeking financial profit to *maximise* it, it is not always the case for owners generating worthwhile profit, who may be content with the generation of some, rather than maximal financial profit, if this is conducive to fulfilling their other goals. And, whereas a drive to maximise profit creates further pressure to maximise the cost minimisation and revenue potential that comes from externality creation and growth, mere profit-seeking does not automatically create the same impulse. Profit-seeking businesses may create *some* negative externalities certainly, but these may be mitigated and managed rather than used to reduce cost as much as possible. Thinking of firms as profit-seeking rather than profit-maximising opens the possibility of profit that is "steady", as businesses forgo the opportunities for profit maximisation that would come through company growth.[8]

Profit-seeking, rather than its maximisation, lessens what is so problematic for the economy-in-Planet about the way profit has been pursued in

---

7 When owners are beneficiaries, they seek both financial profit but also wish to reap the benefits of the goods and services produced by the firm.

8 It is interesting to note that all the companies reviewed in a German study of long-lived, successful, non-growing companies shared the commonality that they were manager- and family-owned and -run, rather than owned by external shareholders (Liesen *et al.*, 2015).

the legacy economy. It is then perhaps not profit-seeking per se that has driven unsustainability, but the fact that the owners of the companies that dominate the legacy economy, the shareholders of the public corporation, have financial returns as their sole motivation for company "ownership". Such owners exclusively pursue financial rather than worthwhile profit, and consequently seek to maximise it, irrespective of environmental and social impacts. This is why it is so hard to see a role for public corporations, and, to a lesser extent, for private equity firms, which exist as vehicles for financial profit generation—in the case of the public corporation, through its mandate to maximise shareholder value, in the case of private equity firms, through the expectation of a lucrative future sale—in the economy-in-Planet. The profit-seeking of firms with other types of owners, especially those owned by their workers, is considerably less environmentally and socially destructive—in part because owners seek to generate worthwhile profit. In fact, we can understand Chapter 10 as an exploration of the conditions and forms that would limit the likelihood and extend to which owners see their stake as purely financial—in the case of investor-owners, for example, the soft measures described aim to foster a particular attitude towards a business, as a substitute for simply placing legal constraints on financial reward. And if such worthwhile profit was generated specifically on the back of products and services, activities, operations and business structures as described in this book, its pursuit can be seen to be creating the *positive* externalities of resource use reduction, stabilisation and the building of resilience. Under these *specific* circumstances, the profit-seeking of the pioneering company serves the needs of the economy-in-Planet.[9]

Beyond the key difference between financial and worthwhile profit—one drives unsustainability, the other doesn't—lie others. While financial value is entirely captured by a monetised metric, worthwhile profit can only be partly captured that way: a number with a dollar sign tells us nothing about the extent to which an enterprise is fulfilling its owners' motivations, or the benefit she derives from her company. In fact, while most companies in the legacy economy are already generating worthwhile profit, since the promise of financial returns is one motivator among others, accounting and reporting procedures do not reflect this broader understanding of profit; left uncounted, it is all too easily forgotten. Moreover, because it reflects the fulfilment of motivations, worthwhile profit cannot be allocated

---

9 See the work of Johanisova, Crabtree and Franková on social enterprises and positive externality generation (Johanisova *et al.*, 2013).

among owners in the same way as financial profit, which are easily divisible and distributable. These features of worthwhile profit mean that it has largely been ignored in the legacy economy, despite its central role in business enterprise.[10] Acknowledging it, and distinguishing it from profit that is purely financial, is important in understanding the role of profit in the economy-in-Planet.

In the legacy economy, profit-seeking, the core attribute that makes a business a business, has often been mistakenly understood as profit maximisation. This is not surprising, since the economy is dominated by firms mandated to maximise financial returns for their shareholders. Since the main routes to financial profit are harnessing of negative externalities and growth, the pursuit of financial profit alone cannot play a large part in the economy-in-Planet. On the other hand, we can identify a second type of profit, which makes an enterprise "worthwhile" to business owners, for whom financial gain is one motivation among others. The pursuit of worthwhile profit offers the possibility of firms that do not drive major cost externalisation and do not necessarily seek to grow. And, when generated by companies in the ways described in this book, we can say that the pursuit of such profit by pioneering companies is supportive of the requirements of the economy-in-Planet and the shift toward it—or, at least, that there is no intrinsic tension between worthwhile profit-seeking and sustainability.

Whereas profit maximisation has given business a particular role in the legacy economy, companies that are instead *profit-seeking* redefine that role, as we will see in the next chapter.

---

10 See, for example, the working paper of Vroom and McCann (2009), which suggests that owner-managed firms are less likely to seek profit maximisation compared to professionally managed firms.

12 Lifestyle creation, through business or otherwise

The preponderance of financial profit-seeking, and the drive towards its maximisation, has had far-reaching implications for the way legacy firms respond to their customers' needs—and far-reaching implications for the place occupied by business in the provision of goods and services in the legacy economy, and in society as a whole.

In Chapter 12, we examine the implications of meeting of human needs (the "things that other people want or need" in point 2 of Kaufman's definition), specifically through the vehicle of financial profit-maximising entities in the legacy economy, before examining how the role of business may change in a system where worthwhile profit-seeking prevails.

In the legacy economy, profit-maximising businesses have gone far beyond meeting their customers' need to shaping our way of life

Driven by the pursuit of maximum profit, businesses of the legacy economy have assumed a social importance that goes far beyond "meeting customer needs". Today's profit-maximising firms play a major role in creating our way of life. As we saw in Chapter 3, identify formation, as well as our daily experiences, are shaped by the consumption of goods and services—and these are, by and large, presently provided by business.

How has business made itself so central to our everyday life? This process begins in competitive market exchange. For its goods and services to stand out, a business must meet its customers' needs and wants in a new way. Without novelty, there is no distinctiveness in the business's offer to set it apart from competitors; there would be no reasons for customers to prefer the products and services offered by a particular company over another. Most often, the novelty is very subtle, or even imperceptible to the customer—it may be, for example, an incremental change of process, generating cost savings that are passed on to customers through a lower price; or a slight improvement on the functionality of an existing item. Whatever its form, novelty is what creates a company's unique selling point and helps it find success in the marketplace; this investment in commercial success is what makes businesses agents of innovation.[1]

How does this innovation work? To begin with, the legacy economy was, and continues to be, a time of significant technological breakthroughs. While these breakthroughs often happen in universities or within government, for inventions to leave the ivory tower or military base and become products and services traded on the market requires commercialisation. This means refinement, prototyping, cost reduction, marketing—everything necessary to make it "saleable". This is the role that businesses, as market agents, excel at. Business's role in innovation, especially when they offer altogether new products and services (the first smartphone rather than the new, improved one) can therefore more precisely be described as commercialising invention.[2] By bringing invention to market, companies offer new, distinct products and services to their customers. New technologies alone do not create new goods and services, and we must not underrate the role played by business in, for example, converting the technology for military aircraft into commercial jets.

When commercialisation is conducted by firms that are structured to maximise their profits, new products and services are rapidly diffused. This has led to radical changes in lifestyle. In the last 70 years, businesses have transformed the homes, work and leisure of their customers, through

1 Ashford describes how innovation may result in three different types of changes to the way customer needs are met: "where the customer perceives no difference in the product or service; where the customer does perceive a quality difference in what is essentially the same kind of product or service; or where the customer's needs are met in a completely different way" (Ashford and Hall, 2011: 306).

2 Some authors describe innovation purely in commercial terms, considering innovation as the preserve of business. See e.g. Drucker, 2002.

televisions, washing machines, computers and digital gadgets. The firms of the legacy economy have enabled their customers to live lives of unprecedented material comfort; but the lifestyles they created have also come with a high resource price tag. Profit-maximising companies have shaped our modern, *"resource-intense lifestyles"* in three principal ways. First and most obviously, the mass production and diffusion of technologies, driven by commercialisation, has involved increasing resource use: quite simply, we own and use many more artefacts in our daily lives now compared to the pre-industrial era. Second, in seeking to maximise their profits, companies have become adept at using advertising and marketing to create new wants, and therefore new markets—an activity that far exceeds simply "responding" to customer needs. Companies, for example, have spent enormous sums warning consumers of the dangers of germs to spur the sales of antibacterial hand washes, which, it now transpires, may present a greater risk to health than the use of water alone. They have also expanded their markets by loading products with "undue" cultural significance—that is to say, accentuating their symbolic role over their "real" one (Chapter 3) and thus normalising arguably unnecessary product ownership. Third, and most subtly, as products and services become more widely used, they often become what Leopold Khor (1977) has called "technological necessities"—that is, artefacts that we require, not for the meeting of basic need, but to participate fully in socio-economic life. Once these technological necessities have reached a critical mass among consumers, they are suddenly required by all but the most committed hermits: we could say that technological necessities lead to product rebounds, as one such artefact is likely to drive the creation of many others (Chapter 3). This is great news for the profit-maximising companies that sell them. Objects such as cars and smartphones have become so ubiquitous, and have such substantial infrastructures built around them, that someone who lacks access to these objects might find themselves shut out of substantial parts of contemporary society. Moreover, such "technological necessities" often have ambiguous, or even detrimental, impacts on quality of life: widespread car ownership, for example, made public transport less viable, leading to massive traffic congestion. Profit-maximising companies have thus put us on a "consumption treadmill", a process by which we are led to consume more and more goods and services, not so much to meet our needs, but simply to retain a decent standard of living. Profit-maximising companies have created the consumer society. In fact, business's dominant role in shaping and driving our consumption of artefacts—and of resources—may well come to be seen as a further defining feature of the legacy era.

On the economy-in-Planet, companies contribute to a resource-light way of life

It is important to give this history serious consideration because, while there is broad consensus on the need for business to shift towards sustainable *production*, we must also recognise business as the key social actor for the shift towards sustainable *consumption*; it is business, after all, that is largely responsible for our current unsustainable, resource-intense consumption patterns. Sometimes, it is suggested that "consumers" are best placed to lead the way to sustainable consumption, through "ethical" or "green" consumerism, which reflects a "latent" demand for less socially and ecologically harmful items.[3] This thinking rests on the belief that, were all consumers to embrace "green" values, their consumption practices would change, and, in time, business production patterns would change as well. However, evidence suggests that, even for "eco-conscious" consumers, a concern for ecological issues does not translate into lifestyle-altering consumption patterns, which would result in meaningfully reduced environmental impact. This is the so-called "behaviour gap" between professed values and observed lifestyles. People who worry about climate change might save energy by living in apartments, using green energy and ditching their car—but, at the same time, may have higher-than-average emissions due to air travel. The belief that "green" values among consumers would lead seamlessly to sustainable consumption, pulling sustainable production behind it, badly underestimates the extent to which consumption choices are framed by the availability, accessibility and price of goods and services (as well as social factors, such as consumption preferences of peer groups).[4] In essence, consumption is largely shaped by what is offered

3 See, for an example on the role of the consumer in achieving sustainable consumption, World Economic Forum, 2011.

4 Jackson (2005) makes the case that it is not "consumerist values" that lead to unsustainable consumption but habit, social norm, identity and peer groups. To move to sustainable consumption requires three conditions: a person must want to change her consumption habits, change must be possible within a person's social context, and change needs to be possible. Businesses can support all three

by businesses, in markets constructed by them: they are so-called "choice architects", delineating the parameters of consumption choices.[5] In the legacy economy, profit maximisation has driven a significant expansion of consumption, through more and more product and service "choices", usually with scant attention to ecological impacts.

Our current crisis means we now need to see an opposite trend: the onus is on companies, using their particular expertise in commercialisation, to lead the change towards sustainable consumption. The challenge for the pioneering company is to create *"resource-light"* responses to their customers' needs, and support the creation of a way of life that is low in resource intensity. How could the pioneer company radically change our lifestyles? It should be comforting to remember that the private sector has done this before: legacy companies were incredibly successful at enabling the fast and broad uptake of new goods and services. Through a similar process, companies could conceivably support the broad uptake of better, efficient goods and services. Our best hope of moving from, say, diesel to electric cars, fast, may rest more with firms than with policy directives or community initiatives. And, of course, through their product stewardship and access activities, pioneering companies normalise the idea of second-hand goods and product sharing (Part 3), and expand the type of goods considered user-accessed (Chapter 4)—significantly lowering the resource impact of our consumption habits. The capacity of the firm to deliver rapid, large-scale change in the way we own and access the artefacts we use in our daily lives may be the most obvious way business can lead the transition to sustainability.

Not so fast. The companies that delivered the fast, widespread changes to our lives in the last century were driven by profit maximisation: the pioneering company, on the other hand, is merely a profit-seeker (Chapter 11). It does not search for new markets with the same gusto as the dominant legacy-economy companies. This is both a good and a bad thing. A good thing, because the drive for expansion is a problem even when companies have adopted product stewardship or access activities: a greater number

---

of these changes, through the products and services it offers, and how these are marketed.

5 Holt (2012) argues that sustainable consumption will not come from a shift away from "consumerist values" but through the construction of sustainable markets, one sector at a time. Private sector businesses are best placed to lead on these sectoral initiatives, because they have such an intimate knowledge of their industry.

of exchanges means more rented products, and more tools used in service delivery—that is to say, more resource used. A bad thing, because, being less inclined to seek out new markets than its profit-maximising counterpart, the pioneer's products and services may not be taken up at the scale and speed required to make a meaningful contribution to resource use reduction. So there are problems related to the pioneering company's profit-seeking both in the transition to the economy-in-Planet and within it: during the transition, profit-seeking may not drive an increase in market share significant enough to support the shift to resource-light lifestyles; while, within the economy-in-Planet, an ongoing pursuit of profit, even worthwhile profit, may support an increase in the size of the market overall, thereby increasing the resource footprint of consumption. These problems are hard to solve: imperfect options may be the mutability of ownership structure or the replication of successful models that we encountered in Chapter 10, enabling respectively the shift from growth-seeking to "steady" companies, or an increased reach of individual pioneering companies.

Non-profit mechanisms play an important part in the provision of goods and services in the economy-in-Planet

As a mechanism to give a sustainable shape to our consumption patterns, the profit-seeking company has its drawbacks. In that sense, the legacy assumption that the private sector is best placed to produce and distribute goods and services across society must be revisited; and its alternative, *non-profit* provision, explored, now that our system of production and consumption must serve the goals of resource use reduction, stabilisation and resilience building. While, as we saw in Chapter 11, many of the advantages of profit-seeking *for the individual firm* in the legacy economy remain in the economy-in-Planet, *non-profit* provision may have *systemic* advantages—and technologies may be ripe to support such provision.

To consider the potential of non-profit provision of goods and services, we can first turn to the experience of the legacy economy. There are many organisations in the legacy economy that have flourished *because* they are not seeking to generate a profit. Wikipedia contributors, for example, are willing to share their expertise for free, no doubt in part because no one is lining their pockets on the back of their generosity. This non-profit approach has met a collective need for knowledge far more effectively than a for-profit encyclopaedia could. Sometimes, then, a product or service itself can be devalued when something that could be delivered for free is instead delivered commercially, at a price. Compare renting and lending a tool to a neighbour. While some of the end results are the same—the same person uses the tool, the same resource savings are earned—socially, the exchange is clearly different. In our culture, familial, friendly and neighbourly relations are partly defined by being non-commercial; while we often do business with friends, it would strike us as bizarre to pay a friend for her company or conversation. The notion that things can be traded, lent or given away on a non-commercial basis is both longstanding—public libraries are a well-known non-commercial product-access model—and expanding: examples include well-established schemes such as Freecycle, or non-monetised community trading schemes such as Local Exchange Trading Systems (LETS); London-based start up The Library of Things is currently developing a community lending model, similar to the municipality-run Berkeley Tool Lending Library.[6] As well as clear resource benefits, these approaches also have the distinct advantage that they help to build local socio-economic resilience—both by building social ties or social capital, and by contributing to the diversity of mechanisms by which goods and services can be procured: by "consumers" themselves, through social or community mechanisms, or through market mechanisms.[7]

Many of these object-sharing schemes are effectively the non-commercial version of the product-access companies of Chapter 6, and constitute a direct challenge to these same businesses. I earlier suggested that the peer-to-peer product-access model of the platform company may remain marginal in the overall provision of good and services on the economy-in-Planet; here I would like to suggest that its non-commercial version may, instead, occupy an important space in sustainable consumption. Why is that? In the "sharing economy", prosumers often carry out work that would normally be done by employees, with neither the remuneration nor the benefits of employment (Chapter 6). While the ethical problems this poses can sometimes be solved through worker ownership of platform companies

6 The Library of Things: http://libraryofthings.lend-engine-app.com, accessed 3 September 2016; Berkeley Tool Lending Library: https://www.berkeleypubliclibrary.org/locations/tool-lending-library, accessed 3 September 2016.

7 Wealthier neighbourhoods, where many goods and services are accessed on a commercial rather than "neighbourly" basis, have often be found to be among the lowest in social capital.

when "peers" are actually professionalised (Chapter 10), this structure would be inappropriate when "peers" remain genuine "peers": your neighbours, the people you may want to borrow a stepladder from, and say hi to. In those instances, the "sharing economy" can live up to its name by being non-profit—especially since there is no clear added value to commercial exchange, only disbenefits. As well as building community resilience, non-commercial platform exchange also solves the ethical issue of prosumers working for free to line someone else's pockets. In the sustainable economy, we are not so much prosumers as co-creators of social, community value.[8]

There is one final, significant, advantage to non-profit provision over its commercial alternative: non-commercial entities can be construed entirely as a *response* to need, rather than creators of *new* needs and wants, thus avoiding the risk of unnecessary consumption. Non-commercial provision of services, in response to need rather than the opportunity for profit, is in fact already well established in certain areas of life (think of public healthcare provision). But the opportunity now exists for the widespread uptake of non-commercial production of goods as well.

In Chapter 8, we examined the new technologies that could support a pioneering company's dispersed operations: digital technologies and additive manufacturing. Importantly, these technologies lend themselves equally well—and perhaps better—to non-profit production.[9] Through digital design processes, ideas can be crowdsourced and developed collectively by an unlimited number of contributors—arguably resulting in far better design than what we could expect from a small number of employees in a company setting, constrained moreover in designing only products (and services) that have commercial potential. And, while contributors may be sharing their expertise for free, this does not give rise to the same ethical issues as prosumption for commercial purposes, since they are working for a non-profit endeavour, for the public good. For example, following a crowdsourced design process involving thousands of volunteers, Open Source Ecology is making the design and additive manufacturing production plans of 50 machines required for modern living, such as tractors and

---

8 At the same time, it could be argued that commercial "sharing" could be a first step toward "real" sharing in areas where social capital is currently weak.

9 See the work of Rifkin (2015) for the potential of these types of technologies to supersede commercial models. See also Michel Bauwens's work on the peer-to-peer economy (e.g. Bauwens, 2006) for benefits of this type of networked, distributed peer production.

ovens, available for free online.[10] In these sorts of projects, design specifications are developed and held in common, accessible to all—the opposite of intellectual property rights, which commercial organisations rely on to develop new goods. In this context, innovation is no longer the preserve of business—another legacy economy assumption—and for-profit endeavours cannot be easily generated on the back of this shared knowledge. And, while the knowledge is global, additive manufacturing can support local, community-level production of artefacts, in a way that is needs-based and dispersed. Operations reliant on digital and additive manufacturing might, therefore, be best run on a community, non-profit basis, with global design input. Significantly, such a provision would support resource use reduction, as the commercial drivers of consumption would no longer exist—a major advantage as we seek to create and eventually sustain the economy-in-Planet.

Given the systemic benefits of non-profit provision of goods and services, where does this leave the pioneering company? Since the pioneer is seeking to be a force for good in society, it must first ascertain whether non-profit provision may be preferable than its for-profit counterpart. Is there a risk, for example, that a for-profit product-access business might lure customers away from informal, non-monetised exchange, thereby commercialising, and potentially weakening, existing social relations, with no resource savings to speak of? Or could a case be made that a profit-seeking product-access company is better placed than its non-profit counterpart to challenge product ownership, fast? More broadly, does profit-seeking promote individual provision of goods and services that could otherwise be delivered in common, or their "artificial" obsolescence? These are the types of question the pioneering company must answer. It may be that, in the same way as the pioneering company must be open to changes in ownership structure at different stages in its maturity and in the transition to the economy-in-Planet, it could consider moving away from its profit orientation once it is well established (and especially if it relies heavily on prosumption in its activities). Sometimes it may well be that organisations that do not seek to generate a profit are undoubtedly a more effective way to deliver goods or services that support resource-light lifestyles than their commercial counterparts—and that the pioneering company ought to opt out of that potential business opportunity.

---

10 http://opensourceecology.org/about-overview, accessed 14 December 2015.

The legacy economy orthodoxy that tends to rate the private sector as the best producer and distributor of goods across society does not necessarily hold true in the economy-in-Planet. For-profit, market exchange of goods and services is not always the best way to deliver the greatest satisfaction of need overall, within planetary boundaries.

The economy-in-Planet is, therefore, characterised by diversity and pluralism: not the false diversity of consumer choice all created through identical industrial processes by a handful of public corporations, but the true diversity of business structures, forms, scales and orientations towards profit. Such pluralism and diversity create the flexibility and the redundancies characteristics of a resilient system (Chapter 2). And, with a greater diversity of organisations, concentrated and dispersed, for-profit and non-profit, all engaged in the production and distribution of goods and services, the private sector is smaller and less dominant on the economy-in-Planet than it has been in the legacy economy; an inconvenient fact often ignored by sustainable business advocates. Business on the economy-in-Planet plays a far smaller role in the creation of our way of life than it does in the legacy economy: it contributes to our way of life, rather than shaping it.

~

The companies that dominate the legacy economy are owned for, and structured around, profit maximisation, relying on cost externalisation and growth. This relentless focus on financial profit, associated with the special role of business as a commercialiser of technological innovation, has given legacy firms a major role in driving not only unsustainable production, but also unsustainable consumption. They have created our resource-intense lifestyles.

The pioneering company has the opposite task at hand. It must seek to create resource-light lifestyles. One important way it does this is through profit-seeking rather than profit maximising, as business owners seek both financial and non-financial goals. This limits business owners' interest in pushing "unnecessary" consumption—but, importantly, does not necessarily do away with it altogether. Moreover, profit-seeking runs the further risk of crowding out non-profit, community or public provision of goods and services, which may be more apt at building resilience and contributing to a steady economy.

Before launching its enterprise, the pioneering entrepreneur must therefore first carefully assess opportunities for value creation, scrutinising the suitability of *commercial* provision for her proposed good or service, in light of the challenges of our time. She must then design companies that are sustainable in their production processes—but also directly support sustainable consumption among their customers. We could in fact say that sustainable production must *serve* sustainable consumption; on the economy-in-Planet, and in the transition towards it, its contribution to a resource-light, but comfortable, way of life is what delineates the social role of the firm.

To fulfil this role, the pioneering business leader must reflect on, and remain cognisant of, the way her business shapes its customers' lifestyles through its goods and services. Its innovation must go beyond technological improvements in processes and products, to encompass innovation in its own organisation and wider "social innovation" among its customers[11]—through innovation in business activities, models and structure, as described throughout this book. Considering these interventions through a consumption lens, we can see how they help support new forms of consumption, conduct and even norms among customers, all in service of resource use reduction. Through its customers' lived experiences, the pioneering company plays a crucial societal role in making the transition to

---

11 See Ashford and Hall, 2011 for a typology of different types of innovation.

resource-light lifestyles desirable, and degrowth socially and politically acceptable.

In this book, I have described the new type of multifaceted innovation taken on by companies seeking to address the resource use reduction and stabilisation, and resilience-building, imperatives. This innovation, which we can describe as "frugal",[12] supports both the sustainability of production and consumption. Rooting its commercial success in such innovation, the pioneering company creates a new type of "good" value, one that rises to the challenges of our Crowded Planet, and which I call *"frugal value"*.

---

12 Frugal innovation is a term often used to describe innovation aiming to use resources more efficiently, especially in the Global South. Here, as elsewhere in this book, I use the term "frugal" to refer both to resource efficiency and sufficiency in the Global North.

Conclusion: what would it take to make frugal value possible?

This book has been about a new type of business value creation. The frugal value created by pioneering companies delivers customer satisfaction while creating a successful, worthwhile business. The pioneering company contributes to absolute resource use reduction, develops models that support steadiness of resource use, and helps to build socio-economic resilience. In doing so, it addresses the great challenges of our time and plays a positive role in the transition to a sustainable society. The creation of frugal value is what today's "genuinely" sustainable business is all about; to fulfil its promise, the discipline and practice of sustainable business must take the challenges of our age seriously, and strive to adopt the sort of interventions described throughout this book.

And now for the bad news: for even the most far-sighted company, the creation of frugal value, within the legacy economy, is more aspirational than feasible. As we have seen repeatedly throughout this book, the barriers to adopting the proposed approaches are high and manifold, nearly insurmountable. Within the context of an economic system dominated by growth-driven companies, with global reach, which disregard the planetary impacts of resource use in business activities, developing a customer offer on the basis of opposite conditions—steadiness, proximity, low and stable resource use—is a challenge. Doing so competitively, and on the scale required to steer the legacy economy into a sustainable trajectory, fast, may be impossible—at least without significant changes to national and international regulatory and policy contexts. These changes would merit their own book, but, as a conclusion, I would like to suggest briefly the three key system-level changes that would enable pioneering companies to flourish, and make frugal value possible.

The first change is the *move away from an economy of distance to an economy of proximity*. As we have seen throughout this book, the shift from unsustainability to sustainability is partly about establishing nearness in space, and in relationships. Distance in the legacy economy takes many forms: it is the distance between operations and customers, between companies and their suppliers, business owners and workers, owners and their firms. Distance serves many of the legacy economy's undesirable, unsustainable features, and hinders the creation of frugal value, which instead requires proximity. Distance lends itself well to fast, linear production models, but makes slower, circular activities considerably more difficult; distance creates the opportunity for cost minimisation through environmental and social cost externalisation (with the added benefit that businesses can plead ignorance if need be) but makes companies that are unable and unwilling to reap the cost savings of externalisation uncompetitive. With nearness, costs cannot be saved through cheap, or, worse, slave-like labour, and poorly managed resources. Seeking to operate on the basis of nearness rather than distance is simply too costly in the legacy economy for many companies to develop a competitive offer. But move towards an economy of proximity we must if we are interested in launching firms that would create, and thrive within, the economy-in-Planet: companies must cease to be itinerant, following cost-saving opportunities, and must instead become anchored in their locality.

To succeed fully this change requires a reversal of what had until very recently seemed like an unstoppable trend towards globalisation, and a shift towards a process of de-globalisation and re-localisation. Part of this change is a matter of policy; and the old policy consensus of the economic (and developmental) benefits of international, free trade is already under substantial pressure. A re-localisation, pro-environmental policy agenda would demand a more considered approach to trade, focusing on those goods and services, supply chain inputs, and foods that cannot be produced close to their markets, and would concentrate on revitalising regional and local economies. But this process of de-globalisation should not lead to parochialism, and we must not abandon the gains of the global village. Rather, de-globalisation applies specifically to economic activity, to the production and distribution of goods and services. It is essential that knowledge sharing, creative and cultural exchange, design and invention continues to thrive in this system through global networks, since these could provide key support to re-localised productive activity.

The second set of changes involves a *move away from a growth-reliant economy dominated by one form of organisation, the external shareholder-owned for-profit company, to a plural economy, where multiple organisational forms co-exist, flourish and support degrowth.* In the legacy economy, for-profit companies are considered the most effective organisations for the production and distribution of goods across society, and external ownership through shares is taken to be the paradigmatic form of ownership. But, as we saw in the later parts of this book, the shareholder ownership model and profit maximisation cannot be reconciled with the resource use reduction and stabilisation imperatives. Compared to the legacy economy, the economy-in-Planet features many more different types of organisations playing a role in the production and distribution of goods and services: from informal community networks, to non-profit organisations, and profit-seeking companies, some investor-owned, many others owned by workers or beneficiaries: whichever channel is most apt at meeting needs and wants, in a way that supports resource-light, resilient lifestyles.

For the organisational pluralism of the economy-in-Planet to take shape requires a move away from the current stranglehold of for-profit, shareholder-owned companies, especially the public corporation, on global economic activity. This shift demands considerable changes in the way companies are legally incorporated, owned and financed. While the legacy regulatory framework supports the generation of financial value and economic growth, a regulatory framework designed for the economy-in-Planet would support the viability of, and create a level playing field for, organisations that support degrowth and steadiness. Nothing short of a complete volte-face in the regulations that shape how businesses, and other organisations, operate is required in the transition from unsustainability to sustainability. This might mean making limited liability incorporation more difficult to get—for example, by requiring new enterprises to demonstrate to a public body that their proposed offer, approach and structure would contribute to resilience and a way of life low in resource use, much as new entrants in the charitable sector today are obliged to demonstrate how they generate public benefit. This would recognise that the ability to generate transactions at profit does not guarantee "good" value creation, and would restrict the benefits of incorporation to those firms committed to a social and environmental purpose. The regulatory and policy context must also be conducive to plural ownership structures; this can be achieved by facilitating and incentivising other arrangements, and helping different ownership structures occupy a much larger share of economic activity at the expense of the shareholder model. Soft interventions could include education on the benefits of alternative structures, and how to move from one structure to another, at different stages of an organisation's maturity, or constructing networks to facilitate experience sharing and replication; slightly harder measures could include preferential access to public procurement contracts for firms under specific ownership, or tax incentives designed to increase their competitiveness, much in the same way as non-profit companies currently benefit from tax breaks.

Firms owned by their workers or beneficiaries could also be supported through public banking: as we have seen, limited access to finance is often a key barrier faced by these firms. Public banking could promote these companies through preferential, low interest rates. Supporting "non-traditionally" owned firms through public banking would have several benefits. First, these firms would access financing without having to seek external shareholders, which we know present a threat to sustainability. This could be particularly useful in supporting, say, worker-owned or community-owned platform companies or indeed, their non-profit equivalent. Second, such public finance could lead to a more discerning approach to funding compared to what we have seen in the legacy economy: private funders are better placed at identifying the profit potential of ventures, rather than their social utility. Third, public banking could also be instrumental in supporting the replication of successful worker- or beneficiary-owned enterprises, bearing in mind that, in many instances, it may not be a single company scaling up that is required—many resource-reducing companies will be relatively small—but widespread reproduction of proven, tried-and-tested models. For this to happen would require incentives for the successful entrepreneur to help set up new independent businesses, rather than expand her own, perhaps in a licensing-type like arrangement, with similar business models, activities and operations, but separate, localised supply chains, serving geographically defined markets.

In addition to all these approaches to supporting different types of ownership, significantly reducing the share of global economic activity conducted by legacy companies owned by external shareholders would also require interventions to limit these types of firms. These could include the public benefit test discussed above, or changes to the fiduciary responsibility those firms legally owe to shareholders. Further, structural interventions are needed to address the purpose and practice of externally owned firms, especially the public corporation, interventions so substantial that such firms may well become unrecognisable: this scale of change is needed, since it is today's public corporation that most dangerously drives unsustainability, among all business forms. Potential interventions could include a limit to the maximum number of shareholders; a minimal time period for holding ownership stakes to limit the use of share trading as a speculative tool; a requirement for complete transparency of ownership, including of beneficial owners; or geographic requirements requiring owners to maintain a domicile near the firms they own. All these interventions would aim to limit the exclusively financial approach to profit, and dethrone profit maximisation from its current position at the top of all corporate priorities: a crucial change for achieving a sustainable economy.

Lastly, in parallel to interventions supporting pluralism of company legal and ownership forms, further regulatory interventions are required to resolve what can be seen as a major market failure for sustainability. As we saw in the latter parts of this book, while profit-seeking enterprises play a major role in a sustainable economy, their very nature, their commercial interest, makes them prone to driving consumption, and therefore resource use. While this risk can partly be managed through ownership, legal form and capital-raising arrangements, these company-level design interventions nonetheless remain imperfect and must be supplemented by systemic, economy-wide approaches, which limit the generation of profit and growth. These interventions could include maximum profit levels or firm sizes; further, alternatives to the current pension system, which requires ongoing growth of the financial markets, must be found. For all the regulatory and policy interventions described in this section, and many potential others, the measure of success is the extent to which they create the economic degrowth that the transition to the economy-in-Planet requires.

The final, and most critical, set of changes concern the relationship between the socio-economic system and the planetary system on which it depends—or, more precisely, *changes to how the resources used in economic activity, and their associated planetary impacts, are determined, allocated and valued.* In the legacy economy, scant attention is paid to resource use and its associated impacts; while there are many, laudable initiatives to protect the natural world, these are consistently subordinated to the imperative of economic growth. The economy-in-Planet, on the other hand, requires mechanisms to ensure resource use for economic activity is congruent with sustainability. As we saw in the Introduction, there are two distinct moments in the "life" of a resource: its point of entry from the planetary system into the socio-economic system; and its journey within that system. These two moments require two different mechanisms.

At point of entry, the process must regulate the inflow rate of resources into the economy at replenishment rate for renewable resources, and, for non-renewable resources, at the rate of generation of renewable alternatives, with present and future need in mind. Certainly, the legacy economy's mechanisms for regulating resource inflow rate have been woefully inadequate—resting pretty much solely on whether a buyer and seller could agree on a price. But what should replace it? The legacy era's catastrophic failure to establish sustainable resource inflow rates should make us deeply suspicious of any market-based approach for the "primary sector" (willingness to pay for a barrel of oil tells us nothing about the sustainability or ethics of its burning). The alternative to commercial interests selling resources to whomever will buy them must start with an attitude adjustment. Our generation is not just here to cash in on planetary resources, but is the Earth's custodian for the next generation. This is the ethical basis of sustainability. Non-market-based mechanisms for allocating global planetary resources such as the oceans, climate and biodiversity, often referred to as the "global commons", must therefore take place in the context of an ethical and science-based system, reached on the basis of iterative, cooperative deliberation.[1] This would include the scientific consensus on resource renewability, and the ethical consensus on the use of the resource and on the opportunity cost of using a non-renewable resource now rather than in the future: taking of course both resource use itself, and the impact of its use and pollution generated on the integrity of planetary systems, into account. We are already seeing the contours of how such a system to govern global resources, sinks and regulation may work, with the progress achieved on climate through the UN, most recently, with the Paris Agreement. Detractors may, with good reason, call the Agreement too little, too late; nonetheless, the notion of a global "carbon budget"—that there is a finite share of the planet's climate regulation capacity that can be used now, which must be allocated "fairly" among different parties, and that global economic activity must urgently be reoriented to reflect this reality—may provide the outline of an effective, non-market-based approach to the governance of all planetary systems. This same global approach could be replicated at different, nested levels of governance, at a local or bioregional level as most appropriate for the

---

1 See the work of Nobel prize-winner Elinor Ostrom (1991) for alternative, non-market, cooperative-based approaches to the management of common resources.

management of the resource at hand: for example, in determining rates of abstraction of freshwater at watershed level. Such a management approach would require a similar approach to the "carbon budget", involving the scientific and geographic communities of the watershed, in a process of collective management of the resource for the common good. This management approach, replicated for resources held in common is considerably more likely to result in their sustainable management than a simple market-based approach, since these communities are not simply driven by the mercantile possibility of the day. And it is quite different from the current turn toward the disastrous notion of "ecosystem services", whereby a dollar sign is assigned to planetary systems' contribution to economic activity to establish its "value". This approach could have dire effects if widely adopted, since the financial value of planetary sinks and regulations has nothing to do with preserving their integrity (not to mention the fact that trying to accurately put a financial value on, for example, the pollination "work" carried out by bees is an entirely futile exercise); assigning a value to them suggests that the natural world should be yet again subordinated to economic potential. A mechanism based on scientific and ethical consensus would better regulate the introduction of resources into the economic system.

Once within the economy, the second moment in the "life" of the resource, the question of allocation remains. Again, in this second moment of the life of the resource, non-market allocation is appropriate—as is the case for global emissions, allocated not on a global market but among UN member states, according to their contributions to reduction targets. National allocations are imperfect, especially when expanded to other resources: the "natural" level of governance—say a bioregion—is unlikely to reflect political boundaries, a complication already experienced today in the management of cross-border resources, such as freshwater rivers. Nonetheless, countries are a useful unit of resource use allocation, inasmuch as we understand resource endowment and use within jurisdictions. National allocations according to development needs, reflecting the principle of equity in resource use and share of impact on planetary systems to be reached through the process of contraction and convergence (Chapter 2) is likely to be the most practical mechanism for allocation (even if significant differences of need and resource use exist within national borders).

National allocation has the further significant advantage that it is within states that policies and industrial strategies are formulated, and therefore where the potential exists to have regulations and strategies conducive to the slow, circular economy. Within jurisdictions, resource allocations must be used deliberately to support such an economy. Resources might be allocated, for example, on a sectoral basis, depending on the importance of a particular sector in securing decent livelihoods. Particular attention must be paid to the resource use requirements of different technologies, to enable a broad range of technologies, from the artisanal to the high-tech to coexist; as well as to the feasibility of product sufficiency business activities, in different sectors, and their resource and labour requirements. This second, intra-border process of allocation must also come from a non-market, political process since it must be reflective of society-wide environmental and economic priorities, rather than the resource requirements and commercial potential of individual firms. Only then, after a rate of inflow and national allocation mechanism based on scientific and ethical consensus, and intra-border allocations to support the slow, circular economy, may market allocation of resources between firms be appropriate. But unlike the resource market allocation of the legacy economy, it will pose no threat to sustainability, since we have, hopefully, "covered" both questions of inflow rates and allocation, taking both scientific and ethical considerations into account.

Under such a mechanism set, highly polluting resources will be costly, as their rate of inflow will be limited (and presumably, they will be best allocated to socially crucial sectors whose technologies require such resource use); whereas well-managed, renewable resources, the use of which has benign effects on planetary systems, will be considerably more affordable (and widespread across the economy), since their rate of inflow will be higher (and within replenishment rate). In that sense, this approach has some similarities with calls for the "internalisation" of environmental costs, whereby prices would reflect planetary impacts, often put forward as the panacea for all our environmental ills (even when its advocates fail to explain how it would work in practice, as they overestimate what can be captured in a financial metric, which would both need to be a mediation of supply and demand and a true indication of ecological impact). But it is also different in a major way: namely, cost internalisation alone tells us nothing about the overall sustainability of the use of a particular resource; it can only tell us that an expensive product is likely to be more environmentally destructive than its cheaper counterpart. On the other hand, a high cost in the system described in this section reflects planetary impact, but one that has been effectively managed inasmuch as the rate of inflow of the resource has been sustainably determined, as well as ethically allocated to that particular country and politically allocated to that sphere of economic activity.

With resource inflows into the economy and their allocation constrained on a scientific and ethical basis, we should expect fewer resources in the economic system—the goal of such mechanisms, in fact—and higher costs across the board. A slow circular system should function effectively with fewer resources, and should help resolve the currently unfavourable relative cost of labour and resources, which lead to high labour productivity and the fast, linear production models at the heart of unsustainability. Whereas resources in the legacy economy are "under-priced"—the externalities created by their use is not captured in their exchange value, and they preclude many worker-intense activities required for product sufficiency business activities—in the economy-in-Planet, they are accurately priced. They reflect at once the real scarcity of resources and planetary sink and regulation capacity, determined by: input rates; a fair allocation among parts of the world; and, lastly, the resource's ability to generate commercial value in the slow, circular economy.

In the economy-in-Planet, then, a host of competent authorities, at different levels of governance, are involved in determining appropriate extraction and harvesting rates of resources, based on a scientific, ethical and cooperative basis; as well as exerting influence over allocation, based on strategies for supporting an economy that delivers a resource-light, resilient way of life, achieved through slow, circular artefact and resource flows. This approach is, of course, considerably more complex than resource exploitation and allocation on a transactional basis—but is absolutely essential for sustainable management of our global commons.

The breadth and depth of the systemic changes required to move from the legacy economy to the economy-in-Planet are awesome: we're talking reversing globalisation, the establishment of regulations to frame markets and organisations around a degrowth paradigm, and the institution of a new relationship to the resources that power our economy, which should instead be understood as a global commons to be managed on the principles of sustainability. While these systemic changes will only happen through policy and regulatory interventions at all levels of governance, from the local, to the national and global, I believe these changes could be driven by the leadership of pioneering companies. For new ways of creating and distributing goods and services across society to be found, for a sustainable economy to take shape—one that delivers lives of decent material comfort but low resource use, through the slow, circular motion of artefacts—will require an openness to risk-taking, the trialling of new models, the willingness to learn and pick up again from failure. Legislators, rightfully accountable to their constituents, are poorly suited to this kind of experimentation. Businesses, with their capacity for innovation, are in a position to play just that role. Pioneering companies could provide the on-the-ground exemplars of success that policymakers and regulators need to make the case, and put in place the measures for systemic change that will enable the transition to the economy-in-Planet. Surely, even with all the challenges ahead, this is enough of a reason for pioneering companies to get going straight away.

Bibliography

Alcott, B. (2005). Jevon's Paradox, *Ecological Economics*, 54: 9-21.

American Public Transportation Association (2015, March 3). Uber and Lyft users more likely to use public transit frequently, own fewer cars and spend less on transportation. Retrieved from http://www.apta.com/mediacenter/pressreleases/2016/Pages/160315_Shared-Use-Mobility.aspx

Ashford, N.A., & Hall, R.P. (2011). *Technology, Globalization and Sustainable Development: Transforming the Industrial State*. New Haven, CT/London: Yale University Press.

Atkins, P. (2010). *The Laws of Thermodynamics: A Very Short Introduction*. Oxford, UK: Oxford University Press.

Ayres, R.U. (2007). On the practical limits to substitution. *Ecological Economics*, 61: 115-128.

Bakker, C., den Hollander, M., van Hinte, E., & Zijlstra, Y. (2014). *Products That Last: Product Design for Circular Business Models*. TU Delft Library.

Bamburg, J. (2006). *Getting to Scale: Growing your Business without Selling Out*. San Francisco: Berrett-Koehler Publishers.

Bansal, P., & DesJardine, M.R. (2014). Business sustainability: It is about time. *Strategic Organization*, 12(1): 70-78.

Bauwens, M. (2006). The political economy of peer production. *Post Autistic Economics Review*, 37(3): 33-44.

Benyus, J.M. (2002). *Biomimicry: Innovation Inspired by Nature*. New York: HarperCollins.

Bocken, N.M.P., & Short, S.W. (2016). Towards a sufficiency-driven business model: Experiences and opportunities. *Environmental Innovation and Societal Transitions*, 18: 41-61.

Botsman, R., & Rogers, R. (2010). *What's Mine Is Yours: The Rise of Collaborative Consumption*. New York: Harper Paperbacks.

BP (2012, June). *Statistical Review of World Energy*. Retrieved from www.bp.com/statisticalreview

Brown, H.J., Cheek, K.A., & Lewis, K. (2012). *Naked Value: Six Things Every Business Leader Needs to Know about Resources, Innovation and Competition*. USA: dMASS Media.

Brown, M. (2016). Sharing in the outdoors: Lessons learnt from a failed sharing economy start-up. Medium.com. Retrieved from https://medium.com/@MichaelBrown22000/sharing-in-the-outdoors-558534adb50e#.49ys2icvh

Chouinard, Y., & Stanley, V. (2012). *The Responsible Company: What We've Learned from Patagonia's First 40 Years*. USA: Patagonia Books.

Clark, D. (2013, November 20). Which companies caused global warming? *The Guardian*. Retrieved from http://www.theguardian.com/environment/interactive/2013/nov/20/which-fossil-fuel-companies-responsible-climate-change-interactive

Co-operatives UK Ltd (2012). *The UK Co-operative Economy 2012: Alternatives to Austerity*. Retrieved from http://www.uk.coop

Cooper, T. (2005). Slower consumption reflections on product life spans and the "Throwaway Society". *Journal of Industrial Ecology*, 9(1–2): 51-67.

Cooper, T. (Ed). (2010). *Longer Lasting Products: Alternatives to the Throwaway Society*. London/New York: Routledge.

Da Silva, J. (2014) *City Resilience Index: Understanding and Measuring City Resilience*. The Rockefeller Foundation and ARUP.

Daly, H.E. (1990). Toward some operational principles of sustainable development. *Ecological Economics*, 2: 1-6.

Daly, H.E. (1991) *Steady-State Economics* (2nd ed.). Washington, DC: Island Press.

Daly, H.E. (2013). A further critique of growth economics. *Ecological Economics*, 88: 20-24.

Defra (Department for Food, Environment and Rural Affairs, UK) (2011a). Extending product lifetimes. Retrieved from http://sciencesearch.defra.gov.uk/Default.aspx?Menu=Menu&Module=More&Location=None&Completed=0&ProjectID=17047

Defra (Department for Food, Environment and Rural Affairs, UK) (2011b). Public understanding of product lifetimes and durability. Retrieved from: http://randd.defra.gov.uk/Default.aspx?Menu=Menu&Module=More&Location=None&Completed=0&ProjectID=17254

Desvaux, M. (2011, August). The sustainability of human populations: How many people can live on Earth? *Population Matters*. Retrieved from https://www.populationmatters.org/documents/HowManyPeople.Summary.pdf.

Diamond, J. (2003, June). The Last Americans, environmental collapse and the end of civilization. *Harper's Magazine*: 44.

Dietz, R., & O'Neill, D. (2013). *Enough is Enough: Building a Sustainable Economy in a World of Finite Resources*. London: Earthscan.

Dittrich, M., Giljum, S., Lutter, S., & Polzin, C. (2012). *Green Economies around the World? Implications of Resource Use for Development and the Environment*. Retrieved from: https://www.boell.de/sites/default/files/201207_green_economies_around_the_world.pdf

Drucker, P.F. (2002, August) The discipline of innovation. *Harvard Business Review*.

Duchin, F., & Hertwich, E. (2003). Industrial ecology. International Society for Ecological Economics, *Online Encyclopaedia of Ecological Economics*. Retrieved from http://isecoeco.org/pdf/duchin.pdf

Engage Spark Blog (2013, May 2). Which legal structure is right for my social enterprise? A guide to establishing a social enterprise in the United States. Engage Spark Blog. Retrieved from http://engagespark.com/blog/incorporating-social-enterprise-simple-legal-guide/

Environment Agency, The (2005). *Life Cycle Assessment of Disposable and Reusable Nappies in the UK*. Bristol, UK: The Environment Agency.

ETC Group (2011). Who will control the Green Economy? Corporate concentration in the life industries? ETC Group Communiqué, 107.

European Commission, DG Environment (2014). Development of guidance on Extended Producer Responsibility. Retrieved from http://ec.europa.eu/environment/waste/pdf/target_review/Guidance%20on%20EPR%20-%20Final%20Report.pdf

European Commission (2015). Closing the loop: An EU action plan for the circular economy. Retrieved from http://eur-lex.europa.eu/resource.html?uri=cellar:8a8ef5e8-99a0-11e5-b3b701aa75ed71a1.0012.02/DOC_1&format=PDF

Friedman, L. (2015, May 7) Little chance to restrain global warming to two degrees, critic argue. *Scientific American*. Retrieved from https://www.scientificamerican.com/article/little-chance-to-restrain-global-warming-to-2-degrees-critic-argues

Gansky, L. (2010). *The Mesh: Why the Future of Business is Sharing*. New York: Portfolio/Penguin.

Georgescu-Roegen, N. (1975). Energy and economic myths. *Southern Economic Journal*, 41(3): 347-381.

Green Alliance (2013). Resource resilient UK: A report from the circular economy taskforce. Retrieved from: http://www.green-alliance.org.uk/resources/Resource%20resilient%20UK.pdf

Henwood, D. (1998). *Wall Street: How it Works and for Whom*. London: Verso Books.

Holt, D.B. (2012). Constructing sustainable consumption: From ethical values to the cultural transformation of unsustainable markets. *Annals of the American Academy of Political and Social Science*, 644(1): 236-255.

Hubbert, M.K. (1956) *Nuclear Energy and the Fossil Fuels* (Publication No 95). Houston, TX: Shell Development Company. Retrieved from: http://www.hubbertpeak.com/hubbert/1956/1956.pdf

Hutton, W. (2012) Plurality, stewardship and engagement: The Report of the Ownership Commission. The London Stock Exchange. Retrieved from http://www.londonstockexchange.com/statistics/companies-and.../list-of-all-companies.xls; on 31 August 2016.

IEA (International Energy Agency) (2012). *Key World Energy Statistics*. Retrieved from http://www.iea.org

Illich, I. (1974). *Energy and Equity*. New York: Harper & Row.

Illich, I. (2001). *Tools for Conviviality*. London: Marion Boyars Publishers.

ING Economics Department (2015). Rethinking finance in the circular economy. Retrieved from https://www.ing.nl/media/ING_EZB_Financing-the-Circular-Economy_tcm162-84762.pdf

IPCC (Intergovernmental Panel on Climate Change) (2007). *Climate Change 2007: Synthesis Report. Summary for Policymakers*. Retrieved from http://www.ipcc.ch/pdf/assessment-report/ar4/syr/ar4_syr_spm.pdf

IPCC (Intergovernmental Panel on Climate Change) (2014) *Climate Change 2014: Synthesis Report. Summary for Policymakers*. Retrieved from https://www.ipcc.ch/pdf/assessment-report/ar5/syr/AR5_SYR_FINAL_SPM.pdf

Ivanko, J. (2008). Operating a small, sustainable business: Resources for ecopreneurs. *Ecopreneurist*. Retrieved from http://ecopreneurist.com/2008/08/14/operating-a-small-sustainable-business-resources-for-ecopreneurs

Jackson, T. (2005). *Motivating Sustainable Consumption: A Review of Evidence on Consumer Behaviour and Behavioural Change*. Sustainable Development Research Network. Retrieved from: http://www.sustainablelifestyles.ac.uk/sites/default/files/motivating_sc_final.pdf

Jensen, M.C., & Meckling, W.H. (1976). Theory of the firm: Managerial behavior, agency costs and ownership structure. *Journal of Financial Economics*, 3(4): 305-360.

Jevons, W.S. (1866). *The Coal Question* (2nd ed.). London: Macmillan & Co. Retrieved from http://oilcrash.net/media/pdf/The_Coal_Question.pdf

Johanisova, N., Crabtree, T., & Franková, E. (2013). Social enterprises and non-market capitals: A path to degrowth? *Journal of Cleaner Production*, 38: 7-16.

Kaufman, J. (2010). *The Personal MBA: Master the Art of Business*. New York: Portfolio/Penguin.

Kay, J. (2015, November 10). Shareholders think they own the company: They are wrong. *Financial Times*. Retrieved from https://www.ft.com/content/7bd1b20a-879b-11e5-90de-f44762bf9896

Kering (2013) Environmental profit and loss: Methodology and 2013 result. Retrieved from http://www.kering.com/sites/default/files/document/kering_epl_methodology_and_2013_group_results_0.pdf#page=24

Kessler, S. (2016, February 29). Inside Juno: The company that wants to beat Uber by wooing its drivers. Retrieved from https://www.fastcompany.com/3057182/inside-juno-the-company-that-wants-to-beat-uber-by-wooing-its-drivers

Kiron, D., Kruschwitz, N., Rubel, H., Reeves, M., & Fuisz-Kehrbach, S. (2013, December 16). Sustainability's next frontier: Walking the talk on the sustainability issues that matter the most. *The MIT Sloan Management Review.* Retrieved from http://sloanreview.mit.edu/projects/sustainabilitys-next-frontier

Klitgaard, K.A., & Krall, L. (2012). Ecological economics, degrowth, and institutional change. *Ecological Economics,* 84: 247-253.

Kohr, L. (1977). *The Overdeveloped Nations: The Diseconomies of Scale.* Swansea, UK: Christopher Davies.

Koopman, K. (2012). *People before Profit: The Inspiring Story of the Founder of Bob's Red Mill.* Portland, OR: Inkwater Press.

Krajewski, M. (2014, September 24). The great lightbulb conspiracy. *IEEE Spectrum.* Retrieved from http://spectrum.ieee.org/geek-life/history/the-great-lightbulb-conspiracy

Krausmann, F., *et al.* (2009). Growth in global materials use, GDP and population during the 20th century. *Ecological Economics,* 68: 2,696-2,705.

Levin, H.M. (2006). Worker democracy and worker productivity. *Social Justice Research,* 19(1): 1-14.

Liesen, A., Dietsche, C., & Gebauer, J. (2015). Successful non-growing companies. Humanistic Management Network, Research Paper No. 25/15.

Liptak, A. (2014, June 30). Supreme Court rejects contraceptive mandate for some corporations. *New York Times.* Retrieved from https://www.nytimes.com/2014/07/01/us/hobby-lobby-case-supreme-court-contraception.html?_r=1

Lovelock, J.E. (2000). *Gaia: A New Look at Life on Earth.* New York: Oxford University Press.

Makower, J. (2013). *State of Green Business 2013.* GreenBiz Group. Retrieved from http://info.greenbiz.com/rs/greenbizgroup/images/state-green-business-2013.pdf

Martinez, V., Bastl, M., Kingston, J., & Evans, S. (2010). Challenges in transforming manufacturing organisations into product-service providers. *Journal of Manufacturing Technology Management,* 21(4): 449-469.

McDonough, W., & Braungart, M. (2009). *Cradle to Cradle: Remaking the Way we Make Things.* London: Vintage.

Meadows, D., Randers, J., & Meadows, D. (2004). *The Limits to Growth: The 30-Year Update.* London: Earthscan.

Meadows, D.H. (2008). *Thinking in Systems: A Primer* (Diana Wright, Ed.). College Station, TX: Chelsea Green Publishing Co.

Millstone, C. (2015). Can social and solidarity economy organizations complement or replace publicly traded companies? In P. Utting, Ed., *Social and Solidarity Economy: Beyond the Fringe?* (pp. 86-99). London: Zed Books.

Mollison, B.C. (1988). *Permaculture: A Designer's Manual.* Tyalgum, Australia: Permaculture Resources.

Mont, O.K. (2002). Clarifying the concept of product-service system. *Journal of Cleaner Production,* 10(3): 237-245.

Mont, O., Dalhammar, C., & Jacobsson, N. (2006). A new business model for baby prams based on leasing and product remanufacturing. *Journal of Cleaner Production*, 14(17): 1,509-1,518.

New Economics Foundation (2005). *Behavioural Economics: Seven Principles for Policy-makers*. Retrieved from http://www.i-r-e.org/docs/a005_behavioural-economics-7-principles-for-policy-makers.pdf

New Economics Foundation (2010, February 13). 21 hours: The case for a shorter working week. Retrieved from http://neweconomics.org/2010/02/21-hours

Osborne, H. (2016, July 19). Uber faces court battle with drivers over employment status. *The Guardian*. Retrieved from https://www.theguardian.com/technology/2016/jul/19/uber-drivers-court-tribunal-self-employed-uk-employment-law

Ostrom, E. (1991). *Governing the Commons: The Evolution of Institutions for Collective Action*. Cambridge, UK: Cambridge University Press.

Prindle, D. (2015, March 3). New French law tells consumers how long appliances will last. Retrieved from http://www.digitaltrends.com/home/france-planned-obsolescence-law/

Raval, A. (2013, January 4). Xerox says shift to services is paying off. *Financial Times*. Retrieved from https://www.ft.com/content/bac264c8-662e-11e2-bb67-00144feab49a

Rees, W.E. (2011, April). Toward a sustainable world economy. Paper presented at the Institute for New Economic Thinking (INET) Annual Conference, Crisis and Renewal: International Political Economy at the Crossroads, Bretton Woods, NH, USA.

Reisch, L.A. (2001). The internet and sustainable consumption: Perspectives on a Janus face. *Journal of Consumer Policy*, 24: 251-286.

Rifkin, J. (2015). *The Zero Marginal Cost Society: The Internet of Things, the Collaborative Commons, and the Eclipse of Capitalism*. London: Palgrave Macmillan.

Ritzer, G., & Jurgenson, N. (2010). Production, consumption, prosumption: The nature of capitalism in the age of the digital "prosumer". *Journal of Consumer Culture*, 10(1): 1,336.

Roach, B. (2007). Corporate power in the global economy. Global Development and Environment Institute, Tufts University. Retrieved from http://www.ase.tufts.edu/gdae/education_materials/modules/Corporate_Power_in_a_Global_Economy.pdf

Rockström, J., Steffen, W., Noone, K., Persson, Å., Chapin, F.S., Lambin, E.F., Lenton, T.M., Scheffer, M., Folke, C., Schellnhuber, H.J., Nykvist, B., de Wit, C.A., Hughes, T., van der Leeuw, S., Rodhe, H., Sörlin, S., Snyder, P.K., Costanza, R., Svedin, U., Falkenmark, M., Karlberg, L., Corell, R.W., Fabry, V.J., Hansen, J., Walker, B., Liverman, D., Richardson, K., Crutzen, P., & Foley, J.A. (2009). A safe operating space for humanity. *Nature*, 461(7263): 472-475.

Sample, I. (2014, October 16). Anthropocene: Is this the new epoch of humans? *The Guardian*. Retrieved from https://www.theguardian.com/science/2014/oct/16/-sp-scientists-gather-talks-rename-human-age-anthropocene-holocene

Schneider, F. (2012, May) What shall degrow? Proposals of bottom-up degrowth of capacity to produce and consume. Paper presented at the International Conference on Degrowth in the Americas, Montreal, Canada.

Schneider, F., Kallis, G., & Martinez-Alier, J. (2010). Crisis or opportunity? Economic degrowth for social equity and ecological sustainability. *Journal of Cleaner Production*, 18(6): 511-518.

Schumacher, E.F. (1973). *Small is Beautiful: A Study of Economics as if People Mattered*. New York: Vintage.

Schumacher, E.F. (1979). *Good Work*. New York: Harper & Row.

Scott Bader (1973). *A Kind of Alchemy*. UK: Scott Bader Company Ltd.

Spangenberg, J.H. (2012, September). Sustainability impact assessment of major public infrastructure projects. Paper presented at the 5th Concept Symposium on Project Governance. Retrieved from https://www.ntnu.edu/documents/1261865083/1263461278/1_4_Spangenberg.pdf

Spangenberg, J.H., Fuad-Luke, A., & Blincoe, K. (2010). Design for sustainability (DfS): The interface of sustainable production and consumption. *Journal of Cleaner Production,* 18(15): 1,485-1,493.

Stockholm Resilience Institute (n.d.). What is resilience? An introduction to a popular concept. Retrieved from http://www.stockholmresilience.org/research/research-news/2015-02-19-what-is-resilience.html

Stout, L. (2012). The problem of corporate purpose. *Issues in Governance Studies,* 48: 1-14.

UNEP (United Nations Environment Programme) (2010). *Clarifying Concepts on Sustainable Consumption and Production.* Retrieved from: http://staging.unep.org/10YFP/Portals/50150/downloads/publications/ABC/ABC_ENGLISH.pdf

UNEP (United Nations Environment Programme) (2011). *Decoupling Natural Resource Use and Environmental Impacts from Economic Growth: A Report of the Working Group on Decoupling to the International Resource Panel.* Retrieved from http://www.unep.org/resourcepanel/decoupling/files/pdf/decoupling_report_english.pdf

The Sustainable Scale Project (n.d.). The IPAT equation. Retrieved from http://www.sustainablescale.org/ConceptualFramework/UnderstandingScale/MeasuringScale/TheIPATEquation.aspx on 1 July 2015.

The Week (2014, November 10) One in three jobs at risk from robots: Which jobs will die out? *The Week.* Retrieved from http://www.theweek.co.uk/technology/61262/one-in-three-jobs-at-risk-from-robots-which-roles-will-die-out

Trucost (2013). Natural capital at risk: The top 100 externalities of business. Retrieved from https://www.trucost.com/publication/natural-capital-risk-top-100-externalities-business

US Geological Survey (2013). *Mineral Commodity Summaries 2013.* Retrieved from https://minerals.usgs.gov/minerals/pubs/mcs/2013/mcs2013.pdf

Vroom, G., & McCann, B.T. (2009). Ownership structure, profit maximization and competitive behaviour. Working paper. IESE Business School. Retrieved from http://mba.americaeconomia.com/sites/mba.americaeconomia.com/files/paper_IESE.pdf

Waldman, M. (2003). Durable goods theory for real world markets. *Journal of Economic Perspectives,* 17(1): 131-154.

WCED (World Commission on Environment and Development) (1987). *Our Common Future.* Oxford, UK: Oxford University Press.

Webster, K. (2015). *The Circular Economy: A Wealth of Flows.* Cowes, UK: Ellen MacArthur Foundation Publishing.

Weybrecht, G. (2013). *The Sustainable MBA: The Manager's Guide to Green Business* (2nd ed.). New York: John Wiley & Sons.

Wilson, A., & Boehland, J. (2008). Small is beautiful: US house size, resource use, and the environment. *Journal of Industrial Ecology,* 9(1–2): 277-287.

Woolf, N. (2016, June 27). Airbnb and house-sharing firms reduced New York housing stock by 10%: study. *The Guardian.* Retrieved from https://www.theguardian.com/us-news/2016/jun/27/airbnb-new-york-city-housing-stock-reduction-study

World Economic Forum (2011). The consumption dilemma, Leverage points for accelerating sustainable growth. Retrieved from http://www3.weforum.org/docs/WEF_ConsumptionDilemma_SustainableGrowth_Report_2011.pdf

Zellweger, T.M., & Astrachan, J.H. (2008). On the emotional value of owning a firm. *Family Business Review,* 21(4): 347-363.

Glossary

Anthropocene: A term coined by P. Crutzen; refers to a new geological era, in which human action guides environmental change. The Anthropocene is a product of industrial production and consumption.

Appropriate scale: See *Optimal scale*

Artefact: Anything human-made. Used interchangeably with *object, product, item.*

Beneficiary-owner: A company owner who is also the direct beneficiary of the company's product or service. Beneficiary-owners can be customers or a particular geographic community.

Business model: The channel through which revenue is generated, which comes from specific business activities.

Concentrated operations: Business operations that are designed to reap economies of scale, and are therefore usually large, the location of which is often unimportant for customer-facing business activities but may have some logistical or commercial advantages for supply chains.

Crowded Planet: A term used to describe the Planet, in light of unprecedented population numbers and the resource use that comes from current lifestyles (in the Global North).

Debound: The capacity to amplify resource use reduction.

Decoupling: The process of reducing the environmental resources needed for each unit of economic activity, increasing the efficiency with which natural resources are used to generate economic value.

Degrowth: The planned, deliberate process by which we can transition from an economy in ecological overshoot to one that operates within its host planetary environment. One example academic definition is the "equitable downscaling of production and consumption that increases human wellbeing and enhances ecological conditions at the local and global level" (Schneider *et al.*, 2010).

Diseconomies of scale: The scale at which further increases in size present disadvantages rather than advantages. More specifically, the scale at which the environmental benefits of scale that usually come through better resource efficiency are lost, and scale instead presents a threat to resource use reduction.

Dispersed operations: Business operations positioned to facilitate business activities that support resource use reduction, often close to customers. These operations are appropriately scaled, usually smaller than concentrated operations.

Durability: One of the properties of long-lived objects, achieved through technical design interventions.

Ecological impact: See *Planetary impact.*

Economies of scale: The phenomenon by which increases in production volume are associated with a decline in the unit cost of production, because the fixed costs of production are spread more widely across units. In addition to cost benefits, economies of scale are also likely to yield resource efficiencies.

Economy of distance: A widespread, but not universal, feature of the legacy economy. Distance takes multiple forms: it is the distance between sites of production and sites of consumption, the distance between companies and their suppliers, customers or markets, and owners.

Economy of proximity: A widespread, but not universal, feature of the economy-in-Planet. Proximity takes multiple forms: it is the proximity between sites of production and sites of consumption, the proximity between companies and their suppliers, customers or markets and owners.

Economy-in-Planet: A term used to describe the sustainable global economy, with two key features: first, a sustainable rate of inflow of resources into the economic system from the planetary system, determined through scientific and ethical consensus; second, slow, circular flows of resources within the economic system.

Efficiency: Used as shorthand for resource efficiency: that is to say, the process of using minimal resources per unit of production. Tends to increase resource use overall.

Efficient product: A product that requires minimal resource use for its creation and operation, achieved through three key features: efficient products are resource-sparing, nature-inspired and user-centred.

External shareholders: Company equity holders that are neither workers nor beneficiaries, whose interest in firm ownership is exclusively financial; usually thought of as the archetypal business owners of the legacy economy, even if ownership in the legacy economy takes multiple forms.

Externality-created profit: A type of profit usually generated by companies in the legacy economy, by minimising costs through negative externality generation.

Externality: A company's environmental and social impacts that affect parties other than the business itself or its customers. While externalities can sometimes be "positive", they are usually "negative".

Fast linear economy: The central characteristic of resource flows in the legacy economy, from the planetary system, through use in the economy, before expulsion back into the planetary system as waste and pollution.

Financial profit: The type of profit generated for owners whose motivation for firm ownership is exclusively financial; the type of profit usually considered paradigmatic in the legacy economy. Tends toward maximisation, driving negative externality generation and growth.

Frugal innovation: Innovation in all facets of a company—products, activities, business models, ownership structure, legal form, financing—that contributes to absolute resource use, resource use stabilisation and the building of resilience.

Frugal product: A product that is both efficient and sufficient.

Frugal value: The type of value created by pioneering companies through frugal innovation.

Growth-created profit: A type of profit usually generated by companies in the legacy economy, through company growth.

Investor-owner: A company owner whose interest in the company is primarily financial. In the legacy economy, these owners are known as external shareholders and present significant problems for sustainability; in the economy-in-Planet, there may be benefits to this type of ownership under specific circumstances only.

Legacy economy: A term used to describe the current, unsustainable economy, the unsustainability of which is rooted in resource inflows from the planetary to the economic system determined through market mechanisms; and fast, linear resource flows of resources within the economy, before expulsion back into the planetary system as waste and pollution. The legacy economy is a product of the industrial era, relies on industrial machines and fossil fuel energy; consumption and production are unsustainable.

Legacy product: An object in the legacy economy, which often relies on industrial machines and fossil fuels for its creation and operations.

Lifecycle approach: An approach to product design, in which the environmental and social impacts of products from manufacture, through use and disposal, are taken into account at design stage.

Longevity: One of the key features, along with shareability, of sufficient products; longevity contributes to absolute resource use reduction by reducing the need for artefacts over time.

Machine intensity: The share of machines in the transformation process (as opposed to the share of workers). The greater the machine intensity of a transformation process, the smaller its worker intensity. During the industrial era, transformation processes are usually of high machine intensity.

Machine: Refers to all the equipment, ranging from laptops, to vehicles, factories and tools, which help workers produce customer-ready goods and services; also known as technology.

Nature-inspired: A property of efficient products. A product is nature-inspired when its impacts on planetary sinks and regulation are minimal.

Optimal scale: The scale at which the resources used in a company for its value creation, both in its operations and business activities, is minimised.

Path independency: The opposite of path dependency: that is to say a lock-in to certain technologies chosen in the past, despite the more recent availability of better, more environmentally efficient alternatives; an important feature to design into long-lived products to counter the risk of path dependency posed by durability.

Peer-to-peer economy: The type of economy supported by platform companies, which purport to support direct consumer-to-consumer exchange (rather than producer-to-consumer exchange).

Pioneering company: A company that responds to the challenges posed by the Crowded Planet through frugal value creation.

Planetary boundaries: The planetary boundaries, conceptualised by J. Rockström, identify the upper permissible limits of environmental degradation brought about by human activity to retain the ecological conditions necessary to support human life. Three of the nine planetary boundaries (the phosphorus cycle, stratospheric ozone depletion, ocean acidification, global freshwater use, change in land use, atmospheric aerosol loading and chemical pollution, biodiversity loss, climate change and nitrogen loading) have already been breached.

Planetary impact: The impact of resource use on environmental conditions, including on sinks and regulation.

Platform companies: Companies that provide a digital platform for peer-to-peer exchange, supporting prosumption.

Product-access company: A company the activities of which contribute to resource use reduction through boosting product shareability, making products available to multiple customers through rental, leasing, service provision or through peer-to-peer exchange. Product-access companies play an important role in the economy-in-Planet. Pioneering companies are often product-access companies.

Product lifecycle: The "life" or journey of a product from inception into final disposal, including design, materials sourcing, manufacture, distribution, use, materials recovery and eventual disposal.

Product Service System: An academic approach that conceptualises product as providers of particular services, which could support business activities and models whereby these services are sold in lieu of the product itself. The classic example may be the sale of carpet services—providing insulation, warmth, comfort, a particular feel—rather than the carpet itself.

Product steward: A company engaged in product stewardship activities; pioneering companies are often product stewards.

Product stewardship: Refers to all activities that contribute to resource use reduction by boosting product longevity, including maintenance, retrieval, remanufacture and redistribution; could also include the management of secondary markets for user-owned objects, or leasing models for user-accessed ones. Pioneering companies are often engaged in product stewardship and are known as product stewards.

Prosumption: A term coined by A. Toffler, which refers to the act through which people traditionally thought of as "consumers" also engage in the act of production.

Re-activities: The types of activities taken on by product stewards to extend product lifetimes, including refurbishment, remanufacture.

Regulation (planetary): The capacity of the Planet to maintain certain conditions, through its capacity to absorb waste, the great natural cycles. The central problem of climate change is one of deregulation.

Resource efficiency: See *Efficiency*.

Resource sufficiency: See *Sufficiency*.

Resource-intense lifestyles: The lifestyles that prevail in the legacy economy (in the Global North), which come from a process of unsustainable production and consumption, often created by profit-maximising firms.

Resource-light lifestyles: The lifestyles that prevail in the economy-in-Planet, which come from a process of sustainable production and consumption, to which profit-seeking firms contribute. Pioneering companies contribute to the creation of these types of lifestyles.

Resource-sparing: A property of efficient products. A product is resource-sparing when it uses the least amount of resources possible in order to perform its job.

Resources (planetary): Earth's stocks, "things", which provide the material basis for our economy. F. Krausmann identifies four categories of resources: biomass, construction materials, fossil fuels, ores and industrial minerals.

Shareability: One of the key features, along with longevity, of sufficient products; contributes to absolute resource use reduction by reducing the need for artefacts now.

Sinks (planetary): Earth's capacity to effectively absorb the waste that comes from human economic activity; exceeding the Earth's sink capacity results in irremediable pollution and planetary deregulation.

Slow circular economy: The central characteristic of resource flows in the economy-in-Planet, once resources have entered the economic system.

Substitution: The suggestion that scarce, impactful resources could be replaced by bountiful, less impactful alternatives to support continued economic growth; only possible to a certain extent.

Sufficiency: Used as shorthand for resource sufficiency: that is to say, the process of contributing to resource use reduction overall, or absolute resource use reduction.

Sufficient product: A product that contributes to overall or absolute resource use reduction through two key features: longevity and shareability.

Sustainability: The state or ongoing conditions in which sustainable development has been achieved.

Sustainable consumption and production: Using the UN's definition, sustainable consumption and production (SCP) is "the use of services and related products, which respond to basic needs and bring a better quality of life while minimizing the use of natural resources and toxic materials as well as the emissions of waste and pollutants over the life cycle of the service or product so as not to jeopardize the needs of future generations" (UNEP, 2010).

Sustainable development: Using the 1987 Brundltand Report definition, sustainable development is development that "seeks to meet the needs and aspirations of the present without compromising the ability to meet those of the future" (WCED, 1987).

Sustainable economy: An economy congruent with sustainability, which provides us with the goods and services that we need for lives of decent material comfort, without undermining the ability of future generations to meet their own material needs.

Transformers: In operations, refers to machines and workers, who together transform production inputs into customer-ready goods and services. During the industrial era, the transforming capacity of machines and workers was revolutionised through fossil fuel energy.

Unsustainability: The state or ongoing conditions in which sustainable development has not been achieved

User-accessed product: An item for which access alone allows the product to perform its function. An increase in the number and types of user-accessed items at the expense of user-owned items would reduce the number of objects in the world, without losing the benefits that come from products.

User-centredness: A property of efficient products. A product is user-centred when it optimises the human activity required in its job performance.

User-owned product: An item for which object ownership is integral for the object to perform its function. Whether a product is user-accessed or user-owned is in part culturally determined.

Worker intensity: The share of workers in the transformation process (as opposed to the share of machines). The greater the worker intensity of a transformation process, the smaller its machine intensity. The operations of the pioneering company often have high worker intensity.

Worker-owner: A company owner who also works for the company. Worker-owners can be entrepreneurs, managers, small business owners or employees.

Worker-centredness: A feature of business operations that take into account the nature of work required in transformation, in order to create "good" jobs. The exact quality taken on by worker-centredness depends on the types of machines required in the transformation process. At its most basic, worker-centredness is about creating occupations that are safe, pay a secure wage, enough to meet living expenses, while respecting labour rights; at its best, it is about creating occupations also offer fulfilment by allowing the application and development of skills and autonomous working. The pioneering company prioritises worker-centredness and makes it core to its value proposition.

Worthwhile profit: The type of profit generated for owners whose motivation for firm ownership is not exclusively financial, but rather includes other goals such as lifestyle, enjoyment of running a business or service to a community. This type of profit is widespread in the legacy economy, but not usually recognised, and is the type of profit generated in the economy-in-Planet. It does not necessarily tend toward maximisation.

About the author

Carina Millstone is a sustainability professional and campaigner. She has held a variety of advisory, programmatic and advocacy roles in the UK and the US, working with public, private and non-profit organisations on behalf of Environmental Resources Management, the New Economy Coalition, and Changing Markets. She has been a Visiting Research Fellow at the Global Development and Environment Institute at Tufts University and is a Research Fellow of the Schumacher Institute. She founded The Orchard Project and currently serves as the Executive Director of Feedback Global.